Managing Secondary Classrooms

Principles and Strategies for Effective Management and Instruction

Patricia A. Williams

Sam Houston State University

Robert D. Alley

Wichita State University

Kenneth T. Henson

Eastern Kentucky University

Allyn and Bacon

Boston ■ London ■ Toronto ■ Sydney ■ Tokyo ■ Singapore

Vice President and Editor-in-Chief, Social Sciences and Education: *Sean W. Wakely*
Series Editorial Assistant: *Jessica Barnard*
Director of Education Programs: *Ellen Mann Dolberg*
Marketing Manager: *Brad Parkins*
Production Editor: *Christopher H. Rawlings*
Editorial-Production Service: *Omegatype Typography, Inc.*
Composition and Prepress Buyer: *Linda Cox*
Manufacturing Buyer: *Megan Cochran*
Cover Administrator: *Jennifer Hart*
Electronic Composition: *Omegatype Typography, Inc.*

Copyright © 1999 by Allyn & Bacon
A Pearson Education Company
160 Gould Street
Needham Heights, MA 02494

Internet: www.abacon.com

Library of Congress-in-Publication Data
Williams, Patricia
      Managing secondary classrooms : principles and strategies for
effective management and instruction / Patricia A. Williams, Robert
D. Alley, Kenneth T. Henson.
          p.   cm.
      Includes bibliographical references and index.
      ISBN 0-205-26725-4 (alk. paper)
      1. Classroom management—United States.   2. Education, Secondary—
United States.   3. High school students—United States—Discipline.
4. Teacher-student relationships—United States.   5. Effective
teaching—United States.   I. Alley, Robert D.   II. Henson, Kenneth
T.   III. Title.
LB3013.W53   1999
373.1102'4–dc21   98-33966
                                                                               CIP

Printed in the United States of America

10   9   8   7   6   5   4   3   2   1   04   03   02   01   00   99

CONTENTS

PART TWO   Preventive Management   35

3   Before School Begins   37

Practical tips for beginning the school year to circumvent potential discipline problems will be given.

4   Communication Strategies   57

Teaching is communication. By enhancing communication skills, secondary teachers can work more effectively with students, parents, administrators, and faculty.

10   Youths in Crises: Solving Social Problems   168

With gangs and cults moving into secondary schools, these may well be dangerous times. This chapter will provide reasons why students join deviant groups and offer classroom strategies so that all can work together effectively. Techniques and strategies to help teachers deal with crises such as weapons in the classroom will also be provided.

PART FOUR   Special Populations   193

11   Students with Special Needs   195

With the emphasis on inclusion of special needs students, teachers must be prepared to manage all students. Specific techniques such as behavior modification strategies will be examined.

12 Cultural Differences   206

This chapter will help secondary teachers understand and address cultural concerns, especially as these relate to management.

PART FIVE   A Problem-Solving Model and the Development of a Philosophy   223

13 A Model for Solving Discipline Problems   225

Teachers need to evaluate their performance and solve problems through a systematic action plan. This chapter will offer strategies to help secondary teachers become problem solvers and create a personal classroom management plan based on their philosophies.

PREFACE

> *"Children are now tyrants. . . . They contradict their parents, chatter before company, gobble up dainties at the table, cross their legs, and tyrannize their teachers."*
>
> —Socrates (469–399 B.C.)

According to *The Phi Delta Kappa/Gallup Poll* on attitudes toward schools, the public has consistently believed that classroom discipline is one of the most pressing problems facing schools and teachers. It is no wonder, therefore, that new teachers are apprehensive about classroom discipline even though they look forward to beginning their teaching careers. Obviously, we, the authors of this book, agree that classroom management is a major concern for teachers. After all, why else would we put so much effort into writing this book? But we take a positive, proactive stance toward classroom management. Yes, we agree that teachers should be concerned about their management skills as they begin their careers. *But we also believe that they can have the skills necessary to manage their classrooms successfully.* That is our goal. (Throughout the book, we will use the pronoun *you* because we want to address *you* as a teacher and *your* needs.)

As you work with the ideas we present here, we believe you will gradually feel quite confident about your classroom management skills. We have attempted to share the vast body of classroom management information so that you can be prepared to manage your own classroom. To that end, we have included several features that you'll not find in other texts. Furthermore, you will find numerous activities throughout the book to help you plan your classroom environment, work effectively with secondary school students, and be a successful teacher.

In Part One we have reviewed social and emotional contexts that will dramatically influence your ability to work effectively with secondary students. We have also included an overview of the most crucial legal issues confronting you as you manage your classroom in today's complex social environment. Following your review of social, emotional, and legal contexts, we ask you to focus on the many steps you can take to prevent management problems. Even before you begin your first year of teaching, there are many actions you can take to prepare for your initial experience. Communication skills, managing instruction, and working with parents are but three specific topics discussed in depth in Part Two. Understanding the behavior of secondary students and applying appropriate consequences for both positive and negative student behavior are the focus of Part Three. We also recognize that today's youth are often in crisis situations. Drug use, suicide attempts, teen pregnancy, and other personal crises experienced by secondary students are discussed. In Part Three, we devote a chapter to the influence of cults and gangs on secondary students. We're confident you'll agree, after studying that chapter, that we have provided you with strategies to help you work more effectively with youth who are confronted with pressures to join or be active in cults or gangs.

Addressing the needs of special students and understanding diverse cultural and ethnic backgrounds, while maintaining an effective relationship with all your students, is the central theme of Part Four. Then, in the final section, we ask you to formulate a personal management philosophy and develop a classroom management plan.

Acknowledgments

As we worked on *Managing Secondary Classrooms: Principles and Strategies for Effective Management and Instruction,* we relied on many individuals to support, encourage, and aid us. We deeply appreciate the long telephone conversations and consistently helpful advice from Nancy Forsyth and Sean Wakely, our editors. We also thank the reviewers who provided specific, meaningful suggestions about the book. We wanted to know what other faculty members who teach classroom management believed about our efforts, and their comments were forthright and positive: Marlene Anthony, North Georgia College; Melba Spooner, University of North Carolina at Charlotte; Harry M. Teitelbaum, University of Portland; Luis Valerio, University of Southern Colorado.

In addition, we wish to thank several contributors who added sections to the text. Elden Barrett, Professor of Education at Baylor University, spent numerous hours working on this book and specifically helped write two of the chapters. He is to be commended for his outstanding contributions and sage advice. We also appreciate the efforts of Pat Kieffer, secretary in the Department of Curriculum and Instruction at Wichita State University, who prepared the room layout graphics in Chapter 3, and Marsha Harman, Assistant Professor of Education at Sam Houston State University, who allowed us to use the crisis scenarios that she created in Chapter 10.

We thank all of our colleagues at Sam Houston State University, Wichita State University, and Eastern Kentucky University for their continual support. Without the encouragement of our administrators, such as Patricia's department chair, John Huber, we would have finished the text during the next century. Christie McWilliams, Patricia's graduate assistant, deserves a special thank you for her tremendous contributions. Bob's fall semester sabbatical gave him time to write and revise sections of the text. And we are indebted to Carolyn Spurlock, Ken's typist, and the education faculty at Eastern Kentucky University, who have consistently supported Ken both in his role as dean and writer.

To our families, who understood when we had too little time for recreation, ate junk food dinners on the run, and did not always complete the list of errands, we are eternally grateful. Shirley Alley (Bob's wife), Sharon Henson (Ken's wife), and Frances Williams (Patricia's mother), you are our strength.

And we thank those thousands of former undergraduate and graduate students who inspired and taught us over the years. We have truly learned more from our students than they have learned from us. They provided ideas to incorporate in this book, and we hope that our words will aid our new colleagues, the beginning teachers, in becoming excellent classroom managers.

PART ONE

Contexts and Legal Issues

For many years, we have known that student behavior is strongly shaped by social contexts. Adolescents and teenagers are especially susceptible to the influence of their classroom environments. Chapter 1 examines both social and educational contexts that affect behavior. During this decade, our society has become increasingly litigious. To avoid being sued, teachers need not be legal experts, but they must have some understanding of the laws that shape and limit their behavior. Chapter 2 discusses some landmark legal cases and their implications for teachers.

1 Social and Educational Contexts

Providing opportunities for social development is one of our schools' most important functions.

OBJECTIVES

1. Describe how student behavior in classrooms has been changing over the last few decades.
2. Contrast traditional classroom management strategies with contemporary approaches.
3. Define *learning community* and explain how this concept can be applied to classroom management.

Close your eyes and recapture the experiences you had during your high school years. Visit your old high school one more time. Step up the front steps of your old high school building and open the door. Is it heavy? Does it make any sounds? Step inside. Is there a foyer? A trophy case? Photos of former graduates? Now walk slowly down the hallway toward your locker. Do you remember any odors from any of the rooms? Maybe the biology or chemistry lab or the lunchroom?

What about the classroom environments? Are there any specific feelings that you can still associate with any of the teachers? Humor? Sullenness? Fear? Did you and your friends call teachers "pet" names? (During her first year of teaching, one of the authors' high school students called her Miss Willy B. Later, she discovered that Willy B. was a gorilla.)

What about your former classmates? Any smart mouths who tested the teacher's ability to remain in charge? Can you remember specific remarks from former classmates?

What classes did you like least? What were these classes like? What classes did you enjoy most? Why?

Effective classroom managers create positive relationships. As you progress through this book, use each day to discover ways to create an inviting atmosphere in your classroom where each student will feel important.

Overview

Teaching is a great profession for individuals who enjoy learning and helping others. Every day puts the teacher in an environment in which young minds are confronting new information. What could be more exciting? All young people proceed through developmental stages that, at times, leave them feeling lost, confused, and awkward, not knowing whether to act like children or adults. Englander (1999) says that learners will work for over thirty psychological motives such as curiosity, affiliation, achievement, power, and activity. Finding the right combinations to arouse these motivations is exciting. For former Nebraska teacher of the year Duane Obermier it's the opportunity to develop relationships with hundreds of students, including students who fail. The challenge is never to give up on a student. Teaching provides the opportunity to help people at times in their lives when they need it most. What could be more gratifying? After an extensive review of the research, Carter and Doyle (1996), concluded, "On the balance, most teachers find their careers satisfying" (p. 133).

We congratulate you on selecting what we believe to be among the greatest professions of all. Like all other professions, teaching is a challenge. One of the greatest and perhaps most daunting responsibilities teachers face is managing student behavior. As other educators have noted, "New teachers worry that they may not be adequately prepared to meet the needs of students from diverse backgrounds" (Wilson, Ireton, & Wood, 1997, p. 396). During the twenty-nine years that it has been administered, the Gallup Poll of Public's Attitudes Toward the Public Schools has reported that poor classroom discipline brought on by drugs and violence has been one of the greatest public concerns. Teachers have the responsibility for the behavior in their classrooms. As Savage (1999) explains, "Teachers should not think that they have no rights, nor should misbehaving students interfere with their right to teach and the right of others to learn" (p. 204). Hanny (1994) agrees, "Those who want to learn have a right not to be disrupted by others" (p. 252).

But, you may ask, haven't teachers always had the task of disciplining their students? So how has their responsibility changed? Table 1.1 shows how much the problems teachers face have changed over the years.

TABLE 1.1   The Top Problems Perceived in Schools in 1940 and 1982

1940	1982
1. Talking	1. Rape
2. Chewing gum	2. Robbery
3. Making noise	3. Assault
4. Running in the halls	4. Burglary
5. Getting out of turn in line	5. Arson
6. Wearing improper clothing	6. Bombings
7. Not putting paper in wastebaskets	7. Murder
	8. Suicide
	9. Absenteeism
	10. Vandalism
	11. Extortion
	12. Drug abuse
	13. Alcohol abuse
	14. Gang warfare
	15. Pregnancy
	16. Abortion
	17. Venereal disease

Source: Reprinted from *Harper's Magazine,* March 1985, and the Presidential Biblical Scoreboard with permission from the Biblical News Service, Costa Mesa, CA. Taken from W. J. Johnston, *Education on Trial* (San Francisco: ICS Press, 1985), p. 20. Used by permission.

As seen in Table 1.1, the types of problems that teachers face have taken a gradual and sustaining turn for the worse. The major causes for deterioration of behavior in the classrooms can be attributed to changes in society. As Oana (1993) explains, "The problem is, today's schools, no matter how much they change, cannot cope with all the social ills its clients bring to their doors each day" (p. 5). Let's examine some of those societal changes.

A Changing Society

In his novel *A Tale of Two Cities,* Charles Dickens wrote:

> It was the best of times, it was the worst of times, it was the age of wisdom, it was the age of foolishness, it was the epoch of belief, it was the epoch of incredulity, it was the season of Light, it was the season of Darkness, it was the spring of hope, it was the winter of despair, we had everything before us, we had nothing before us, . . .

Although written in another time and place, Dickens captures the paradoxical qualities in America as the twentieth century closes. Indeed, in many ways this is the best time to live. Unfortunately, this is also the most challenging time for teachers to survive. Some of the darkness and despair teachers face today are: (1) the fall of the family, (2) increased poverty, (3) latchkey children, and (4) increased drug abuse. Let's examine each of these causes of concern to teachers.

The Fall of the Family

Which country put the first man on the moon? Which country has produced the most Nobel Prize winners? Which country has sustained the highest standard of living ever known? It is indeed ironic that a nation that has become so advanced could be experiencing the biggest problems. For example, the 1950s family with the mother waiting at the door to greet the children as they returned from school, serving them milk and cookies while preparing a proper evening meal and waiting for the father to return home from work each day has become a fantasy to most school-age youngsters. In 1989, the Massachusetts Mutual Life Insurance Company (Seligmann, 1989) surveyed 1,200 randomly selected adults, asking them what *family* means to them. The survey provided a list of definitions for *family* and asked the respondents to select the one that best describes their concept of family. Fewer than one in four (22 percent) chose the traditional definition, "a group of people related by blood, marriage, or adoption."

Poverty

For a nation of wealth, far too many of our children live in poverty. As Armstrong, Henson, and Savage (1997) have noted, almost half of the nation's white children (45.4 percent), over four-fifths of all African American children (81.8 percent) and 43.8 percent of all Hispanic children live in poverty; furthermore, these percentages have been increasing over the past twenty-five years (p. 213). In homes of extreme poverty, parents are not likely to have the education or time to provide proper support for their children's education. As Erb (1997) said, "Emotionally-barren homes, unsafe neighborhoods, and the deprivation of property can leave some children scarred long before they enter a middle school" (p. 2). Children who live in poor neighborhoods are likely to have their well-being challenged at school as well as at home.

Latchkey Students

Over 50 percent of today's students come from one-parent families, or families with both parents working. The absence of parents from the home creates special obstacles for poor children. Middle school teachers often experience the results of this problem. The previously discussed deterioration of the family and poverty have forced many single parents to leave home to work full-time. In fact, a growing number of parents are holding down two and even three jobs. Unable to afford adequate supervision, they are compelled to leave their children at home alone while they work. Without parental supervision, these youngsters are labeled *latchkey children.* Latchkey children are defined as "those who are at home alone with no adults or parents present" (Henson & Eller, 1999, p. 15). How extensive is this problem? Some 70 percent of working-age women are now employed and the number is growing (Hodgkinson, 1989). This creates 5 million latchkey children in the United States today.

The lifestyle pattern for females has changed rather dramatically and become more balanced over the past half century as shown in Table 1.2.

No longer do young females plan to devote their lives exclusively to being wives and mothers. Now and in the future, it appears that not all women will choose to get married and have children, and most who dream of marriage and family also want a career. Notice, too, that the shift described in Table 1.2 involves a physical location shift from inside to outside the house and at work for those who have children.

TABLE 1.2   Lifestyle Patterns for Females

1950s	1990s
• get married • have children • be a housewife	• get a job • get married or stay single • perhaps have children • continue a career

Taken from K. T. Henson and B. F. Eller, *Educational Psychology for Effective Teachers* (Belmont, CA: Wadsworth, 1999).

Drugs

Drug abuse is another problem that has become more prevalent as a result of leaving children alone. For the first fifteen years that the Gallup Poll of the Public Attitudes Toward the Schools was administered, discipline was perceived as the number-one problem. Then in the mid-1980s discipline slipped to second place, replaced by drug abuse.

The chances that you will teach students who abuse drugs and alcohol on a regular basis are astronomically high. By the mid-1980s, approximately 80 percent of high school students had smoked marijuana and two-thirds of American children had used an illicit drug other than marijuana and alcohol before they graduated from high school (Johnson, 1986). Half of all high school students were regular drinkers and a third of them drank heavily at least once a week (Horton, 1985). Perhaps most disturbing of all, teen drinkers accounted for almost half of all the fatal automobile accidents in the United States (Sherouse, 1985). Yet, programs that were instigated to help eliminate these problems have not been totally successful. For instance, although the Drug Abuse Resistance Education program (DARE), an

ACTIVITY **1.1**

What Changes Have You Witnessed?

Examine Table 1.2. Now review the societal changes that have occurred in recent years and see whether you can find one or more changes in society that have caused young women to focus more on work. List the changes in the appropriate columns below.

Changes in Society   **Changes in Goals**

_____   _____

_____   _____

_____   _____

As you think about these changes, answer the following questions.

- What is your focus?
- What are your goals? Are they different from your parents' goals? Grandparents' goals?
- Are roles of men and women less defined today?

anti-drug, anti-alcohol curriculum, is promoted in schools, it may be "only marginally successful in steering youth from drug abuse" (Mason, 1998, p. 8A). Gay, a social scientist and researcher, concluded from his study of one large metropolitan district that "there is very little compelling evidence to suggest that the primary goal of the DARE program is being reached at a statistically significant level" (Mason, 1998, p. 8A).

Where to from Here?

By now perhaps you are wondering how teachers handle discipline in their classrooms. How have teachers in the past addressed this responsibility and how do contemporary teachers do it? How do these methods differ? Can teachers really prepare for managing classroom behavior, and if so, does it work? These issues will be addressed next.

How Teachers Plan to Manage Their Classrooms

Before developing a strategy for managing your classroom, it seems prudent to consider how experienced teachers have organized their classrooms through the years. Unfortunately, the news isn't good. Traditionally, teachers have done a poor job planning to manage their classrooms. In fact, rather than approaching their classroom management scientifically, teachers have elected to emulate other teachers around them.

What's wrong with that? After all, shouldn't a teacher use strategies that work? Certainly, teachers want to use approaches that work, but the flaw in the method of selecting strategies that you see other teachers using is that the process is inadequate. You don't necessarily know why a strategy works and, therefore, when you try it under different circumstances, it may or may not work. If it doesn't work, you probably won't know how to make the proper adjustments. Martin (1997) explains: "Traditionally, educators have learned to manage classrooms from each other where the focus is on practice rather than theory. When classroom management is taught and learned in this manner, we run the risk of making the same mistakes without realizing why" (p. 6).

ACTIVITY **1.2**

Which Needs Do You Put First, Society's or Individuals'?

Some teachers choose not to use theory to design their management program because they believe in meeting the needs of society at large, not individuals' needs.

1. How would you respond to a teacher who makes this claim?
2. Must a teacher choose between meeting society's needs and meeting individual students' needs?
3. Should students have the right to question why we have certain rules in our classes?
4. Are student or teacher rights more important?

Designing a Management Program to Meet Students' Behavioral and Learning Needs

A major shift in approaches to managing classroom behavior has been in the goals teachers have had for their classroom management programs. Traditionally, teachers have sought to control students so as to prevent major disruptions and student challenges to teachers. Many contemporary educators say that this goal is inadequate because it does not reflect concern for meeting students' needs, and that the schools' major purposes should be at least twofold by meeting both intellectual and social development needs. Erb (1997) explains: "While the public and legislatures may be mandating evaluation only in academic areas, success then can only come if the young adolescents we teach are socially and emotionally healthy as well" (p. 2). The claim here is that perhaps it is impossible to have a desirable classroom climate without meeting students' academic, social, and emotional needs. One way to engage students intellectually and help them raise their self-esteem is through creating a learning community.

Using the Curriculum to Shape Student Behavior

One factor that increases classroom misbehavior is the failure of teachers to design appropriate and interesting curriculum. For example, eighteenth-century philosopher, Jean-Jacques Rousseau, urged that school activities be designed to meet students' needs (Armstrong, Henson, & Savage, 1997). The level of impact that the curriculum has on student behavior is stressed by the National Middle School Association (1995) in its report titled *This We Believe.* This report says that the curriculum, which refers to every planned aspect of a school's program, is the primary vehicle for achieving the goals and objectives of a school (Thompson & Gregg, 1997, p. 28).

Given that the curriculum is an effective tool to control student behavior, you may ask: "How do teachers plan to manage their classrooms? What types of curricula work best? How do effective teachers approach curriculum planning? What qualities can I incorporate into my curriculum to minimize behavioral problems in my classroom?"

A Collaborative Approach to Planning

In response to the question of how teachers should plan, the best advice is to work with other teachers. Getting involved with others in planning has several advantages: (1) improved teacher attitudes, (2) improved communication, (3) higher morale, and (4) increased self-empowerment (Clark, Clark, & Irvin, 1997). With so many advantages, it would seem likely that most teachers would prefer to get involved with others in planning and teaching; however, the research shows that teachers are reluctant to collaborate. Even when teachers team teach, during both the planning phase and delivery of instruction, each teacher tends to focus on the specific discipline without much intervention. Thompson and Gregg (1997) say, "Even middle schools that organize their teachers on interdisciplinary teams still organize the curriculum in a way that separates the disciplines" (pp. 29–30). They commented, "In fact, most interdisciplinary teams operate as multi-disciplinary teams with each teacher or team responsible for his or her content" (p. 30).

Students are more likely to understand rules they helped make than rules that are handed to them (Latham, 1998; Schimmel, 1997). Collaborative planning should involve the students. Remember the study that reported that involvement leads to self-empowerment (Clark, Clark, & Irvin, 1997). Students, too, need to be empowered. Good discipline is self-discipline, and self-discipline requires self-confidence. In other words, before students can take control of their behavior, they must believe that they have the power to control their lives. Vars (1997) addresses this concept in terms of locus of control.

> People with an external locus of control see their lives as controlled by other people or by "luck." They are unlikely to exert much effort on their own behalf. . . . On the other hand, people of internal locus of control see themselves as having at least some influence over other events. . . . Hence, it is important to invite students to work with their teacher to make critical decisions at all stages of the learning enterprise, especially goal setting, establishing evaluation criteria, demonstrating learning, self-evaluation, peer evaluation, and reporting. (p. 45)

Ironically, although student input is an essential part of a student-centered classroom management plan, teachers are reluctant to involve students because of what others may think (Martin, 1997).

Developing a Learning Community

A concept that became highly popular recently is that of the school as a learning community. A community is a collection of people with a common goal. The term *learning community* means an environment where all members are partners in creating understanding. One underlying premise that supports the idea of learning communities is the belief that we understand better the knowledge that we discover ourselves as opposed to secondhand knowledge gained from teachers or textbooks. Therefore, a learning community is a collection of school personnel, including teachers and students, who share a specific, common goal—learning. As early as 1916, John Dewey (1916) explained the benefits of a learning community: "If, however, they (a collection of people) were all cognizant of a common end and all interested in it so that they regulated their specific activity in view of it, then they would form a community" (p. 5). Following are several characteristics that all learning communities should possess.

- Teacher development must be an ongoing process as all teachers research the institutional goals that they agree are important.
- Students must be involved with generating knowledge.
- The climate must be relatively free of fear from the urgency to complete assignments by given deadlines.
- Teachers must make research a part of their self-images.
- Successful learning community building requires the support of the school administrators.
- Community building must be a collaborative process in which all of the members discuss the long-term goals.

These elements transform a collection of disconnected and independent individuals into a unified team committed to the same group goals. Keller (1995) explains, "When these elements are combined to form a community, its members strengthen their images of themselves and their colleagues and are more trusting and a supportive environment is formed" (p. 12).

Correctly planned, a learning community can serve as a proactive means of diminishing discipline problems in the classroom. Manning and Saddlemire (1996) say, "Learners sometimes feel 'lost' or anonymous in secondary schools, especially those with large student bodies" (p. 43). They state, "The late 1990s and the turn of the century will be excellent times to initiate the process" (p. 47). Although it is conceivable that a middle school or high school department can form a community, the best size for a community is the whole school. Eisner (1994) notes:

> By and large, the "natural" unit in schooling is the school. The school both physically and psychologically defines the environment: a school district is too large and a classroom is an integrated part of the physical structure of the school. The school stands out as an entity; it is something that secures allegiance and provides students with an identity. (pp. 376–377)

How Is a Learning Environment Developed?

Students should be involved in developing a learning environment. Remember that the community must have a common goal, one that all members believe is important. Glasser (1992) explains, "No matter how well the teacher manages them, if students do not find quality in what they are asked to do in their classes, they will not work hard enough to learn the material" (p. 690). But you may think, "As a beginning teacher, I can't rearrange the total faculty of the school." Although you may not be able to influence the entire faculty, you can influence those teachers with whom you work most closely and directly. The opportunity to talk about your professional work is especially important because in the past teachers have had limited opportunities to share their work experiences with their peers (McElroy, 1990; Santa, 1990). Discussions with colleagues provide the opportunity to reflect on and analyze your teaching and classroom management practices.

Paramount in developing a learning community is forming a mission and then translating it into goals. Clear goals give energy, which is directed in positive ways toward learning. The goals should (1) clearly reflect a change from current conditions, (2) be perceived as difficult but achievable, (3) be clear and concrete, and (4) be short term yet connected to long-term directions of the learning community (Leithwood, Menzies, & Jantzi, 1994).

A learning community's mission and goals must reflect certain views. Knowledge must be viewed as temporary. Members should hold the constructivist view of learning, which is the belief that we learn by doing, and to learn we must discover knowledge as opposed to

---

ACTIVITY **1.3**

Sense of Community

1. What communities are you involved in at school? At work? At home? Religious affiliations? Organizations?
2. What are the missions and goals of the various groups? Why did you join?
3. Are some communities more important to you than others? If so, why?
4. What communities are available to secondary students in your area?

gathering information by reading or listening to others. By now, you are probably thinking that developing a learning community takes time. That's right, it does. Manning and Saddlemire (1996) explain, "Communities and a sense of community, however, will not occur overnight and will not be an easy task" (p. 47). The learning community works because it brings a sense of common purpose and because it organizes the environment so that each member's time is spent engaged in the attainment of its goals.

Action Research

Action research is conducted by teachers to solve problems such as: What types of commands or requests get the best results? How much does teacher proximity affect behavior? Does assigning students to sit in the front row help diminish their inappropriate behavior? Is behavior better or worse when the teacher uses lectures? Games? Small group assignments? Handouts? Inquiry learning? Do daily quizzes influence behavior?

The International Reading Association (1989) has explained the nature of action research:

> Any time you try an experiment with one group in the classroom and set up another group as a control for comparison, you have the foundation for research. When you decide a method worked or didn't work as judged from the results, you have done some classroom research.
>
> Classroom action research may be as formal or informal as the teacher chooses. It may be done alone in the privacy of the classroom or teachers may prefer to collaborate with a university educator or other members of their faculty or district staff. (p. 216)

Teachers gain advantages from being involved in action research. They become better problem solvers (Bennett, 1993) and better teachers (Stevens, Slanton, & Bunny, 1992). But perhaps more importantly, involvement with action research changes teachers' perceptions. Earlier in this chapter, the importance of mission to developing a learning community was stressed. Marriott (1990) reported that after being involved with action research, "The drudgery of complacency has been replaced with a sense of mission. I have experienced more professional growth then than at any other time in my career" (p. 2).

Another area of growth brought on by involvement with action research is the development of an attitude that supports change (Neilsen, 1990) and causes teachers to want to stay current (Sardo-Brown, 1992). Chattin-McNichols and Loeffler (1989) said, "Learning how to do research in my own classroom has started me growing again" (p. 25). Remember that the essence of constructivism—the center of developing a learning community—is the belief that the only way to truly learn is by creating one's own knowledge. Boyer (1990) and Brownlie (1990) have attested to this belief. Boyer (1990) said, "As teachers become researchers they become learners" (p. 57).

Perhaps the greatest advantage that involvement in research offers is its ability to make teachers reflective, analytical, and critical of their own teaching (Cardelle-Elawar, 1993). Literature on reflective practice indicates that continued professional growth occurs through reflection (Valli, 1997). These traits lead to continuous improvement of teachers and their teaching. Rogers, Noblit, and Ferrell (1990) explain,

> Action research is a vehicle to put teachers in charge of their craft and its improvement. Yet there is considerable variation in what people see action research accomplishing for teachers. These variations range from mundane technical improvement in classrooms to transforming a teacher's identity. (p. 179)

ACTIVITY **1.4**

Where's the Action?

1. Write two questions that you would like answered through action research. For example: Do rewards, such as candy and gum, work with secondary students? Do students behave better in classes where they design the rules, or is it better for the teacher to design them? (For an actual action research project to answer the rule question, see Kennedy and Williams, 1993.)
2. Follow the steps outlined in this chapter to complete your research and write the results of your findings.

Beginning teachers and experienced teachers can benefit at both the schoolwide and classroom levels from becoming involved with action research. By involving students, you can also bring some of these positive changes to them. When students become seriously engaged with learning, there is little desire or need to be disruptive.

Your Role in the Community

Like the larger community that surrounds it, the school is composed of many physical characteristics such as space, objects, and people. Like the outside community, the most important ingredient is people, for it is the people who give meaning to the community and, indeed, the people make it into either a safe haven or a dangerous place. As a teacher, you will have the power to shape your learning community into a climate of safety and support, or you will have a classroom in which students experience fear, rejection, and abuse.

When John Steinbeck addressed the Kansas State Teachers Association, he described his former biology teacher as an artist whose medium is the human mind and spirit. Steinbeck concluded that he was the unsigned manuscript of that teacher: "What deathless power lies in the hands of such a person." He also said that his three best teachers had one thing in common: They loved what they were doing.

ACTIVITY **1.5**

Your Favorite Teacher

Of all your former and current teachers, can you recall your favorite? List several qualities that make this teacher special.

- _____
- _____
- _____
- _____

ACTIVITY **1.6**

Hale-Bopp: Using Current Events

You don't have to go far in this world to find miracles. Remember the comet Hale-Bopp? Teachers of all subjects had a teaching tool in this astronomical phenomenon that was priceless. Can you imagine the excitement that a clever teacher could generate through an assignment that required students to watch Hale-Bopp for thirty minutes and then write all the physical observations and feelings this comet inspired? Or what about giving students opportunities to form small groups and write their own assignments?

Good teachers bring to the school each day a love for their work and a passion for their subject. Metzger (1996) a veteran teacher of twenty-five years, said, "Strong teachers convey to their students a passion for a particular discipline, theory, or idea. But the teachers go beyond their own enthusiasm for the subject; they convince their students that learning has intrinsic value" (p. 347).

Beginning teachers often ask how they can develop a strong passion for their subject. We have a few suggestions. First, continue to study and master your discipline. Never be satisfied with your level of mastery. We believe that a near perfect correlation exists between an educator's level of mastery and love for the subject. Second, let your students know that although your subject is extremely important, individuals are even more valuable.

Our first piece of advice is easy to follow. By the time students receive a college degree, most have developed a desire to continue learning. Mark Twain told of his going away to college and how little his father knew at the time. After graduating, he returned home to visit his father and was amazed at how much the old man had learned in the past four years. When we remain in school long enough, most of us are surprised to discover how little we know. At this point, we are ready to begin learning.

Our second piece of advice is not so easy to follow. How can you let your students feel your passion for your subject? We agree with Metzger (1996) who says you should always be honest with your students. "Don't claim the material you teach is important if it isn't" (p. 347). Dispose of any topics that are frivolous.

Third, help your students find applications for your subject. When planning lessons, part of your classroom management plan should be assigning activities that let students see the significance of the topic. Stay current with the news. Capitalize on outstanding world events. The daily news is an inexhaustible source of information. More importantly, it is an avenue for making class content authentic and interesting.

Never underestimate the power our emotions can have on learning. Just weeks before his death, Abraham Maslow (1973) wrote:

> As I go back in my own life, I find my greatest education experiences, the ones I value most in retrospect, were highly personal, highly subjective, very poignant combinations of the emotional and the cognitive. Some insight was accompanied by all sorts of autonomic nervous system fireworks that felt very good at the time and which left as a residue the insight that has remained with me forever. (p. 159)

Therefore, when planning your lessons always incorporate joy or excitement into them and, whenever possible, some hands-on activities that let students "feel" the importance of the lesson.

Finally, help your students see the larger picture. We saved this advice for last because we realize that it is probably the most difficult to follow, especially for beginning teachers. This one you must grow into because it comes with discovering great truths.

Some of the great truths are found in literature. Hemingway used an old fisherman to teach us that it's best to learn how to accept some forces in life, and Lewis Carroll used a Cheshire cat to tell us that if we don't know where we're going, then it doesn't matter what path we take, along with a hundred other great lessons in life. Ironically, the great truths don't lend themselves as well to being taught as they do to being learned. Don't overlook the fine arts as sources from which students can discover great truths. Through paintings, we may discover truths about ourselves. The great artists have also taught us that as artists who teach, we must discover the artist within us. We can learn about acting from watching Robin Williams, about golfing from watching Tiger Woods, and about painting from visiting museums, but we can't become great actors, golfers, painters, or teachers until we master our subject and discover the artist within us.

Through using the arts, you can help students discover their own great truths. John Steinbeck said that great teachers don't tell, they catalyze a burning desire to know. We believe that great teachers don't give great answers; they ask great questions and help their students discover the answers. Great teachers create a learning community in which students work together to discover truths in a nonthreatening atmosphere that encourages experimentation and even failure. The only way teachers can create and sustain a rich learning community is to work hard, take risks, make mistakes, and continue learning.

Summary

Teaching is a great profession only if you possess effective classroom management skills. As a teacher, you will have the responsibility for managing students' behavior, and your success as a teacher will not exceed your classroom management skills.

Through the last half century, society has changed. In some ways, such as technologically and scientifically, it has improved beyond the dreams of earlier generations; however, in other ways it has steadily deteriorated. Increasing poverty and drug abuse, along with the diminishing family unit, have become major obstacles to today's youths. Teachers must find ways to help their students overcome these obstacles.

Today the challenges that threaten teachers are often too great and too many to face alone. Through cooperating with your colleagues and through involving students in planning, you can help design school-guided curricula to beat those odds that society brings to the schools daily. One effective approach is the development of a learning community, a community in which teachers and students work together to create understanding and meet clear goals that are important to all.

Action research is an essential tool in developing and sustaining a learning community. It is a method of staying current and helping today's youths master the level of knowledge required for twenty-first-century living. It is the essence of classroom management for effective teaching and learning.

REFERENCES

Armstrong, D. G., Henson, K. T., & Savage, T. V. (1997). *Teaching today: An introduction to teaching* (5th ed.). New York: Macmillan.

Bennett, C. K. (1993). Teacher-researchers: All dressed up and no place to go. *Educational Leadership, 51*(2), 69–70.

Boyer, E. (1990). *Scholarship reconsidered: Priorities of the professorate.* Princeton, NJ: Carnegie Foundation for the Advancement of Teaching.

Brownlie, F. (1990). The door is open. Won't you come in? In M. W. Olson (ed.), *Opening the door to educational research* (pp. 21–31). Newark, DE: International Reading Association.

Cardelle-Elawar, M. (1993). The teacher as researcher in the classroom. *Action in Teacher Education, 15*(1), 49–57.

Carter, K., & Doyle, W. (1996). Personal narrative and life in learning to teach. In J. S. Sikula, T. S. Buttery, and E. Guyton (eds.), *The Association of Teacher Educators handbook on teacher education,* (2nd ed.). New York: Macmillan.

Chattin-McNichols, J., & Loeffler, M. H. (1989). Teachers as researchers: The first cycle of the teachers' research network. *Young Children, 44*(5), 20–27.

Clark, S. N., Clark, D. C., & Irvin, J. I. (1997). Collaborative decision making. *Middle School Journal, 28*(5), 54–56.

Dewey, J. (1916). *Democracy and education.* New York: Macmillan.

Dickens, C. *A tale of two cities.* Introduction by D. G. Pitt. New York: Airmont Publishing Co., 1963.

Eisner, E. (1994). *The educational imagination* (3rd ed.). New York: Macmillan.

Englander, M. E. (1999). A view from the field. In K. T. Henson and B. F. Eller (eds.). *Educational psychology for effective teaching.* Belmont, CA: Wadsworth.

Erb, T. (1997). Student-friendly classrooms in a not very child-friendly world. *Middle School Journal, 28* (5), 2.

Glasser, W. (1992). The quality school curriculum. *Phi Delta Kappan, 73*(9), 690–694.

Hanny, R. J. (1994). Don't let them take you to the barn. *The Clearing House, 67*(5), 252–253.

Henson, K. T., & Eller, B. F. (1999). *Educational psychology for effective teaching.* Belmont, CA: Wadsworth.

Hodgkinson, H. L. (1989). *The same client: The demographics of education and service delivery systems.* Washington, DC: The Institute for Educational Leadership.

Horton, L. (1985). *Adolescent alcohol abuse.* Bloomington, IN: Phi Delta Kappa.

International Reading Association. (1989). Classroom action research: The teacher as researcher. *Journal of Reading, 33*(3), 216–218.

Johnson, L. (1986). *Drug use among American high school students, college students, and other young adults.* Washington, DC: National Institute on Drug Abuse.

Keller, B. M. (1995). Accelerated schools: Hands-on learning in a unified community. *Educational Leadership, 52*(5), 10–13.

Kennedy, M., & Williams, P. (1993). Does it matter who makes the rules? *Kappa Delta Pi Record, 29,* 43–45.

Latham, A. S. (1998). Rules and learning. *Educational Leadership, 56*(1), 104–105.

Leithwood, K., Menzies, T., & Jantzi, D. (1994). Earning teachers' commitment to curriculum reform. *Peabody Journal of Education, 69*(4), 38–61.

Manning, M. L., & Saddlemire, R. (1996). Developing a sense of community in secondary schools. *NASSP Bulletin, 80*(584), 41–48.

Marriott, V. (1990). *Transition.* Unpublished paper. Mount Saint Vincent University, Nova Scotia, Canada.

Martin, N. K. (1997). Connecting instruction and management in a student-centered classroom. *Middle School Journal, 28*(5), 3–9.

Maslow, A. (1973). What is a Taoistic teacher? In L. J. Rubin (ed.), *Facts and feelings in the classroom.* New York: Walker.

Mason, J. (1998, August 27). Study questions DARE program. *The Houston Chronicle,* pp. 1A, 8A.

McElroy, L. (1990). Becoming real: An ethic at heart of action research. *Theory into Practice, 29*(3), 209–213.

Metzger, M. (1996). Maintaining a life. *Phi Delta Kappan, 77*(5), 346–351.

Neilsen, L. (1990). Research comes home. *The Reading Teacher, 44*(3), 248–250.

Oana, R. G. (1993). *Changes in teacher education: Reform, review, reorganization.* A Professional Development Leave Report. Bowling Green, OH: Bowling Green State University.

Rogers, D. L., Noblit, G. E., & Ferrell, P. (1990). Action research as an agent for developing teachers' communicative competence. *Theory into Practice, 29*(3), 179–184.

Santa, C. M. (1990). Teaching as research. In M. W. Olson (ed.). *Opening the door to classroom research* (pp. 64–76). Newark, DE: International Reading Association.

Sardo-Brown, D. (1992). Elementary teachers' perceptions of action research. *Action in Teacher Education, 14*(2), 55–59.

Savage, T. V. (1999). *Developing self-control through classroom management and discipline* (2nd ed.). Boston: Allyn & Bacon.

Schimmel, D. (1997). Traditional rule-making and the subversion of citizenship education. *Social Education, 61*(2), 70–74.

Seligmann, J. (1989). Variations on a theme. *Newsweek, 22*(2), 38–46.

Shalaway, L. (1990). Tap into teacher research. *Instructor, 100*(1), 34–38.

Sherouse, D. (1985). *Adolescent drug and alcohol abuse handbook.* Springfield, IL: Charles C. Thomas.

Stefkivich, F. A., & O'Brien, G. M. (1997). Students' Fourth Amendment rights and school safety: An urban perspective. *Education and Urban Society, 29*(2), 149–161.

Stevens, K. B., Slanton, D. B., & Bunny, S. (1992). A collaborative research effort between public school and university faculty members. *Teacher Education and Special Education, 15*(1), 1–8.

Thompson, S., & Gregg, L. (1997). Reculturing middle schools for meaningful change. *Middle School Journal, 28*(5), 27–31.

Valli, L. (ed.). (1997). *Reflective teacher education: Cases and critiques.* Albany: State University of New York Press.

Vars, G. F. (1997). Student concerns and standards too. *Middle School Journal, 28*(4), 44–49.

Wilson, B., Ireton, E., & Wood, J. A. (1997). Beginning teacher fears. *Education, 117*(3), 396–400.

2 Legal Issues in Managing Student Behavior

Concern for legal issues that affect education exists at all levels, including local school boards as they make decisions and set policies.

OBJECTIVES

1. Identify the sources of law.
2. Explain student teachers', teachers', students', and parents' legal rights and responsibilities.
3. Analyze the legal ramifications of U.S. Supreme Court decisions.
4. Explain where to locate answers to legal questions. Analyze student/faculty handbooks.
5. Examine the legal precedents for such matters as corporal punishment and sexual harassment.
6. Analyze the key concepts of judicious discipline.

Overview

Two high school females have been dating the same senior, and all three are in your history classroom. Before class begins, you overhear the females exchanging insulting remarks. As the class progresses, one passes the other a note. Then the other immediately jumps up and a physical fight ensues. How do you handle such an outbreak? Are you legally responsible if anyone gets hurt? Should you leave to get help? Send a student to the office? Tell the students to stop immediately? Step in between the two and demand that they behave? As a professional educator, you must respond. However, you are not required to put yourself in physical danger to stop such an incident. Telling students to stop immediately and sending another student to the assistant principal's office for help is usually what is done. In some classes today, telephones and intercoms are installed for quicker help in a dilemma. You might also have a tape recorder available to document what was said and done by all parties. Even though someone may be hurt in the mayhem, you are not liable because you acted as a reasonably prudent person would. However, you must take into consideration such points as the students' ages and maturity level. For instance, you may not be acting reasonably if you allow two five-year-olds in your kindergarten class to fight until help arrives or if you knowingly let two students who are emotionally disturbed chide each other.

ACTIVITY **2.1**
What Are Our Freedoms?

1. What are the basic freedoms? Can you name them without looking at the following list?
   a. Freedom of speech
   b. Freedom of religion
   c. Freedom of the press
   d. Freedom of peaceful assembly
   e. Freedom to petition
   f. Freedom from unreasonable search and seizure
   g. Individuals cannot be denied life, liberty, or property without due process.

2. Write the following freedoms on the board.
   Speech   Religion   Press   Assembly   Petition   Due Process

3. Give each member of the class a sticky Post-it note. Ask the individuals to put the note under the freedom that they would give up if they were required to lose one.

4. Count the number of notes under each category and discuss why particular categories had more notes under them. Are some freedoms more important than others?

5. Conduct a discussion concerning what each of these freedoms means in school.

6. Collect newspaper articles for the next month that relate to these freedoms, for example, "Mother Declares Due Process Rights Denied," "Religious Groups Rally for School Prayer," or "Students Blast New Dress Code Policy."

7. Have the university students complete this assignment with their secondary students.

8. Plan additional lessons for the secondary classroom concerning legal issues. An excellent activity book is McEwan's *Practicing Judicious Discipline: An Educator's Guide to a Democratic Classroom.*

We completed a similar sticky note activity during the Texas Association for Curriculum Development Conference held on November 4, 1995. Yvonne Greenwood, the speaker, discussed "Freedom of the Press and First Amendment Rights."

School Law

This chapter is not designed to answer questions regarding every legal aspect of situations you may encounter. No book, much less a chapter, can tell you how to handle every situation. However, we can provide you with some basic steps to guide you in locating sources, such as the U.S. Supreme Court decisions, which have influenced our nation's schools. In his 1998 presentation, "The Relevance of School Law to Teacher Education Programs," Gullatt commented that from 1953 to 1959, the U.S. Supreme Court ruled on thirty-six decisions affecting education. From 1959 to 1996, over two hundred decisions dealt with educational issues. And, he added, the NCATE accreditation Standard I.D.1 recommends that undergraduate ". . . candidates shall complete a well-planned sequence of courses . . . in which they acquire and learn to apply knowledge about . . . school law and educational policy" (NCATE Standards, I.D.1). Furthermore, states such as Texas are emphasizing the need to know the law. The 1998 State Board for Educator Certification's Code of Ethics and Standard Practices for Texas Educators, Principle IV, Ethical Conduct Toward Students, states that "the educator . . . shall seek to resolve problems including discipline according to law and school board policy" (Code of Ethics and Standard Practices for Texas Educators brochure). Yet, only two states, Washington and Nevada, mandate specific courses in school law for initial certification (Gullatt, 1998).

Sources of Law

To understand how the legal system operates, teachers need to be aware of the different sources of law. Although most of us are familiar with the U.S. Supreme Court's landmark decisions, or have at least heard of cases that have made national headlines, we may not know much about statutory, administrative, or case law (Kemerer, 1996, p. 77). The Supreme Court bases rulings on constitutional issues, including our basic freedoms.

Along with Court decisions, legislators pass both state and federal statutes that influence education. For instance, the Family Rights and Privacy Act of 1972 (Buckley Amendment)

A C T I V I T Y **2.2**

What Happened in . . . ?

Explain the following U.S. Supreme Court decisions concerning these cases. How do the rulings affect you and your classes?

Ingraham v. Wright (1977)
Baker v. Owens (1975)
Goss v. Lopez (1975)
Honig v. Doe (1988)
Franklin v. Gwinnett County Public Schools (1992)
New Jersey v. T.L.O. (1985)
Hazelwood Independent School District v. Kuhlmeier (1988)
Bethel School District No. 403 v. Fraser (1986)

ACTIVITY **2.3**

Comparison Chart

a. Compare two different high school faculty or student handbooks. Note the similarities and differences.
b. Find any court decision or legal citings within the handbook.
c. Make a chart depicting the school's rules and the rulings influencing them. (See the following sample charts.)
d. Write a three-page reaction paper describing how you feel about judges and legislators influencing your rights and responsibilities in the classroom.
e. Explain why you believe that these handbooks are fashioned accordingly.
f. Decide whether teacher or student rights are more important. Or are they equal?

To locate court citings and state laws in your area, your professor may ask you to locate actual court case documents in your university's library or find books related to school law. See reference citations at the end of this chapter. In addition, you may need to locate your state's laws dealing with educational issues. Surfing the Internet also will aid you in your research, especially if you are seeking information regarding the implementation of federal laws and regulations. Happy hunting!

Sommers High School
Student Code of Conduct

Corporal Punishment School district administrators may use corporal punishment.	*Ingraham v. Wright*
An individual may be held liable for using excessive force in disciplining students.	*Texas School Law Bulletin,* T.E.C. 22.051
Search and Seizure Personal belongings may be searched if there is reasonable suspicion that a student is carrying contraband.	*New Jersey v. T.L.O.*
Expulsion A student may be expelled for assaulting a teacher or other individual while on school property or at a school-sponsored activity.	*Texas School Law Bulletin,* T.E.C. 37.007

Wheeler High School
Student Code of Conduct

Sexual Harassment Anyone who suspects that a student is being harassed must follow the school policy and contact _____.	*Franklin v. Gwinnett* *County School District*
Corporal Punishment When using corporal punishment, you must take into account such factors as age and physical limitations of the student.	*Baker v. Owens*
Uniforms The school board may require all students to wear uniforms.	*Texas School Law Bulletin,* T.E.C., 11.162

ensures confidentiality concerning student records. This federal law restricts the reading of certain information to students, their parents, and other parties who need to know. A third source, administrative law, covers all the rules and regulations that help implement the federal and state statutes. They are written to eliminate ambiguity and provide the details about the implementation process. In fact, sometimes these laws are much longer than the actual statute. For example, the Individuals with Disabilities Education Act (IDEA), which was amended in summer 1997, details how school districts can comply with the law.

Case law refers to the decisions reached through both federal and state courts. At the federal level, the lowest court is the district court. If the defendant appeals the findings, the case may be heard in one of the twelve appellate federal courts and eventually reach the Supreme Court.

As you read student and faculty handbooks, you will find that the regulations are typically developed from court rulings and laws passed as a result of major court findings. Now we will discuss the Supreme Court decisions and other legal documents concerning the cases.

Corporal Punishment

Although many school districts have outlawed the use of corporal punishment, others consider it a viable option. In twenty-nine states, the law has made corporal punishment illegal in public schools. However, some states have maintained its use. What part has the Supreme Court played in this issue? In 1977, the Supreme Court ruled that corporal punishment is not cruel and unusual punishment. Therefore, it does not violate Eighth Amendment rights. State legislators can outlaw corporal punishment, and school boards may prohibit its use in their districts. Yet, school districts, not parents, make the decision. If a student is paddled in a district in which corporal punishment is permitted, the parents may protest, but they will not win any corporal punishment lawsuits unless they prove that excessive force was used.

Although we, as educators, are not advocating or encouraging the use of corporal punishment in our nation's schools, we believe that teachers and administrators should be aware of the laws and court cases. What procedures do lawyers recommend? Strahan, a professor and lawyer for numerous school district personnel, advocated several procedures for districts that decide to use this method.

- Have a clear policy in the student code of conduct or handbook that delineates the forms of punishment and consequences used. Students need to be informed at the beginning of the year that specific behavior may warrant corporal punishment (*Baker v. Owens,* 1975).
- Use corporal punishment as a last resort. Teachers should use behavior contracts, conferencing, d-hall, parent notification, and other means first.
- Contact the parents before the punishment is administered. As Strahan (1987) noted, "most parents do not like to be surprised." Even though it is not against the law to use swats without parental permission, he felt that it improves public relations by calling first.
- Ask a teacher, administrator, or other professional to witness the paddling. That individual can testify in court concerning the demeanor of both parties, the number of swats given, and the instrument used. Some school boards (pardon the pun) have approved the use of only certain types of paddles.

In the *Ingraham* case, a student was given more than twenty swats with a 2' × 4' × ½" paddle. The injury was so severe that the student was absent for eleven days and required medical attention. Even though the U.S. Supreme Court ruled that corporal punishment was a viable option, the judges noted that individuals using excessive force could be held liable. And states, such as Texas, have specifically added statutes to reiterate that point (*Texas School Law Bulletin,* T.E.C., 22.051). In fact, part of the law reads that someone can be held liable for using "excessive force in the discipline of students or negligence resulting in bodily injury to students."

What is excessive? Did the seventeen-year-old male student who was swatted sixty-six times for bringing a bottle of brandied cherries to school receive too many swats? Yes, even in 1894 that was considered excessive. The pupil had given cherries to his classmates. While the teacher administered the swats, the boy counted until he reached sixty-three. According to the court documents, the teacher intended to continue the punishment until the boy stopped counting or the teacher became exhausted. The judge commented that the law "declares that the punishment inflicted shall be moderate," and that the punishment "cannot exceed the limit fixed by statute, which is that the correction must be moderate." The teacher was fined ten dollars for his actions (*Whitley v. State,* 1894).

In applying moderate restraint today, the courts consider such factors as the age, size, maturity level, and sex of the offender. Plus, physical limitations, including whether or not the student has a disability, even though it may not be readily apparent, must be given consideration (*Baker v. Owens,* 1975). For example, a student who has a heart condition should be an unlikely candidate for swats.

Before using a paddle, teachers need to consider several points.

- Ensure that the paddler and paddled individual are the same sex. Strahan provided a clear example to show why this advice is important. He mentioned that students often jump when being given swats. If a male teacher accidentally touched a female student's breasts in trying to keep her still, the student might state that he fondled her. In Texas, there is a law regarding sexual knowledge of a minor that carries a two- to ten-year prison term. This law refers to "fondling of any outside sexual genitalia" (Strahan, 1987).
- Administer the punishment outside the view of other students. According to the former court rulings, a student has a right to his or her good name and reputation. By humiliating a student, especially in the presence of others, the paddler may not be protecting that right. Some school personnel have decided to use a specific place, such as the assistant principal's office, and as one teacher called himself, a "designated hitter," rather than allowing all employees to give swats.

Several groups, including the American Medical Association, American Psychological Association, the National Coalition to Abolish Corporal Punishment in Schools, Parents and Teachers Against Violence in Education, and People Opposed to Paddling of Students (POPS), have advocated the abolition of any means of causing physical pain as punishment (*PTAVE Newsletter,* n.d.). Jimmy Dunne, the founder of POPS, is seen in the June 22, 1987, *Newsweek* issue wearing a shirt that states, "Paddling is child abuse." He is frequently a guest on talk shows and in education classes where he argues that "paddling encourages students to 'grow up believing violence is the way to resolve things' " (*Newsweek,* p. 61). Several groups produce newsletters, gather statistics about paddling, and provide help to the families in court cases.

A C T I V I T Y **2.4**

Whole Class Debate

1. Ask the students in your class to decide whether corporal punishment should be used in schools.
2. Have the students select sides and stand in a line facing their opposing counterparts.
   Example: ☺ ☺ ☺ ☺ ☺ ☺ ☺ ☺ ☺ ☺ (those for corporal punishment)
   ☹ ☹ ☹ ☹ ☹ ☹ ☹ ☹ ☹ ☹ (those against corporal punishment)
3. Allow a student on one team to make a point. Then allow a member on the other team to make a counterargument. For example, "I believe that corporal punishment works because it worked on me at school. I never was in trouble after I was swatted for being tardy ten times to shop class."

   A counterargument is: "We had a swat club in my high school. You could only join after receiving at least twenty whacks from Coach. We tried to see how many swats we could get, so I don't think that it helped."

   These examples are typical comments from beginning teachers. Every semester, this argument seems to be used.
4. After debating for twenty minutes, ask the team members if anyone would like to change sides. What arguments were most convincing? Is paddling child abuse? Should all paddling, including parental swats, be made illegal as it has been in countries such as Sweden? In 1928, the Swedish Education Act was amended to forbid corporal punishment in secondary schools (Durrant, 1996). Did anyone mention court cases or research? How many members of the class have been paddled? Should there be an age limit to paddling? As Dobson recommends (Wolfgang, 1995), should paddling only be used until the child reaches adolescence (p. 279)? Are other methods more effective? If so, which ones?
5. Write an exit slip for today's class. During two minutes of freewriting, complete the following statement: I believe that corporal punishment . . .

 # EXIT SLIP

I BELIEVE THAT CORPORAL PUNISHMENT . . .

Codes of Conduct

Many student codes of conduct or handbooks delineate other appropriate techniques. For instance, the Conroe Independent School District's *1996–97 Student Code of Conduct* lists four types of violations and numerous consequences among their discipline management techniques. Types of violations involve those resulting in general misconduct, removal by a teacher, removal to an alternative education program, and expulsion. In the *1996–97 Student Code of Conduct* (Like-Denio, 1996 presentation), consequences include the following:

- oral correction
- seating changes in the classroom
- temporary confiscation of items that disrupt the educational process
- after school, noon, recess, and Saturday detention
- withdrawing or restricting bus privileges
- withdrawal of privileges, such as participation in extracurricular activities and eligibility for seeking and holding honorary offices (p. 1)

Therefore, transportation and student activities may be curtailed. In fact, some schools throughout the country have recently installed video cameras on buses. Actions are then documented, and bus drivers are now being trained in discipline management techniques and ways to handle situations legally.

AEP, Suspension, or Expulsion

In most instances, the teacher will not be the person deciding whether a student should be sent to the alternative educational placement (AEP), suspended, or expelled. In secondary schools, usually an administrator, such as an assistant principal or vice principal, has that duty. Again, the student handbook often details the consequences for certain infractions, and in some cases, lists certain levels. For instance, a level-one infraction may be for talking at an inappropriate time in class, whereas a level-four infraction may be for cursing another student in the cafeteria. We caution school district officials against using too many rules, levels, and consequences because teachers are so busy being enforcers that they have little time to *teach!* According to Black (1994), "In one Michigan high school . . . teachers spend the first week of school drilling students on school rules. These Michigan students are expected to know— without exception—some two hundred regulations and the consequences for breaking them" (p. 44). When do the students or teachers have time to prepare their lessons?

For teachers, our advice is to read the handbooks carefully and know what is expected. Again, there are typically state laws that address infractions and dictate AEP, suspension, and expulsion regulations. In Texas, the expulsion law states that a student "*shall* be expelled" for such offenses as possessing a firearm, club, illegal knife, or weapon on school property or while attending a school-related activity. In addition, a student who commits aggravated assault, arson, murder, indecency with a child, or aggravated kidnapping must be expelled (*Texas School Law Bulletin,* T.E.C. 37.007).

For teachers, handling major discipline problems usually involves documenting what occurred and discussing the situation during the due process hearing. Everyone is guaranteed rights through both the Fifth and Fourteenth Amendments to the U.S. Constitution. These

ACTIVITY **2.5**

An Objectivity Lesson—Documentation

Read the following scenario and write your documentation concerning the situation. Then exchange papers with a classmate and have that person pretend to be the assistant principal at Ball Middle School. Determine whether your documentation was objective. Did you include the necessary details? Were you accurate? Were you fair? What was your first step?

Scenario

On January 20, during your sixth-period physical education class at Ball Middle School, two seventh grade boys, Joey and John, begin chiding and shoving each other. The class is supposed to be completing an aerobics unit, and Joey has been pointing and laughing at John all period. He starts calling him "Mr. Macho," and soon the entire class is laughing. You tell them to "quiet down," but the giggling, although lower, still continues. Then the shoving begins. You think Joey pushed John first, but you are not sure because you were not looking directly at them. The shoving match soon escalates, more name calling erupts, and John pulls an Xacto knife from his pocket. He tells Joey "to come and get it." When Joey lunges forward, John sticks the knife in his side. As blood splatters on the gym floor, Joey falls to the floor and all eyes turn toward you. You know that both boys have been in rival gangs, but the rumors around school have been that they quit the gangs last year.

Complete the documentation sheet. Hopefully, you helped Joey first by having another student go to the nurse's office while you attempted to help him. Did you call the assistant principal on the gym phone? What did you say to the other students? To John? What do you do if John leaves the gym? Do you contact other teachers? Do you call the parents?

Referral Form

Date of Incident _____ Time _____ Teacher's Name _____

Student(s) Name(s) _____

Grade Level(s) _____

Where Incident Occurred _____

Situation _____

_____

_____

_____

_____

_____

How You Handled the Situation _____

_____

_____

_____

_____

_____

Teacher's Signature _____ Today's Date _____

include both substantive (the law is fair) and procedural (the proper procedures are followed) due process. In another landmark ruling, the Supreme Court found that "the total exclusion from the educational process for more than a trivial period . . . is a serious event. . . . Neither the property interest in educational benefits temporarily denied nor the liberty interest in repu-tation, which is also implicated, is so insubstantial that suspensions may constitutionally be imposed by any procedure the school chooses, no matter how arbitrary" (*Goss v. Lopez,* 1975).

Therefore, teachers are highly likely to be involved in due process hearings during their careers. Typically, these informal hearings occur in an assistant principal's office. Stu-dents know the types of infractions that require suspension because they are outlined in the handbooks. During the hearing, the administrator, the students, teacher, and often parents are told what allegedly occurred. Students are given the opportunity to tell their version of the story, call witnesses to support them, and follow the appeals process. The Court requires that "the student be given oral and written notice of the charges against him and, if he denies them, an explanation of the evidence that authorities have and an opportunity to present his side of the story" (*Goss v. Lopez,* 1975). In circumstances where the offender may be a threat to the safety of others, the student may be suspended before the due process hearing. How-ever, the individual must be given a hearing within three days.

Special Education

In recent years, special education issues have received more attention and more litigation than ever before (Phi Delta Kappa Meeting, Special Education Panel, January 22, 1998). In disci-plining a student who has a disability, the teacher or administrator must be sure that the dis-ability did not cause the behavior problem. In the Indiana federal district court, the judges "held that a school district may not expel a special education student whose misbehavior is caused by the disability, but may expel the student if the misbehavior is not caused by the disability" (Osborne, 1996, p. 161). In our opinion, it would be difficult for someone not trained in psy-chology or psychiatry to prove that a seriously emotionally disturbed youth pushed the desk over simply to irritate the teacher, and that the action was not precipitated by the disability.

Stringent guidelines exist in removing a student with a disability from the least restric-tive but most appropriate placement. According to the Individuals with Disabilities Education Act (IDEA, PL 101-476), students must be afforded a free, appropriate, public education. Ac-cording to the definition in IDEA, students with disabilities include the following classifica-tions: physical disability, mental retardation, emotional disturbance, learning disability, speech impairment, autism, multiple disabilities, traumatic brain injury, auditory impairment, visual impairment, and other health impairments (Bradley, 1997; Harper, 1996). A committee, typically composed of the parents, a special education teacher, a diagnostician, a counselor, other teachers, sometimes another administrator, and the student, meets to determine the best placement for the student.

During the meeting, they discuss the individualized education program (IEP) to best serve the student's needs. Both academic and behavioral needs, especially for students who are mentally retarded or emotionally disturbed, are stipulated in the plan. Several behavior modification strategies often used include time-out, contracts, and positive rewards for appropriate actions. In fact, some students are monitored and rewarded for every ten minutes that they stay on task. After receiving a certain number of reinforcers, such as ten tokens, they may trade them for a reward or get a positive note to take home to their parents. These methods mentioned in the IEP must be adhered to even if a teacher disagrees with them. Rather than disregarding the plan, the teacher needs to request another IEP committee meeting to voice concerns and rework the program.

With the movement toward more inclusion, students who were unfortunately ostracized from the regular classrooms now have a right to participate with their peers. Therefore, virtually all teachers today work with students with disabilities. In situations where a student becomes disruptive in class, the school district personnel may remove the student for no more than ten days without reconvening the committee and having that group decide if a change of placement is appropriate. If either party, school officials or parents/guardians, disagrees with the committee decision, they can begin the appeals process, which usually includes conducting an impartial due process hearing.

In the landmark case *Honig v. Doe,* the high Court "held that IDEA's status quo provision prevented the exclusion of students with disabilities for disruptive behavior" (Osborne, 1996, p. 161). Two students, John Doe and Jack Smith, were suspended from school pending expulsion for improper behavior. Whereas "John had attempted to choke another student, leaving abrasions on the victim's neck, Jack had made lewd comments and on previous occasions had stolen, extorted money, and made sexual comments to female classmates. It was undisputed that these behaviors were related to the students' handicapping conditions" (Kemerer & Hairston, 1990, p. 178). The Court concluded that the "stay put" provision is not subject to exclusions for dangerous students. If the parents do not agree with the suspension and appeal the matter, the school officials must seek the court's approval before removing the student from school for longer than ten days (Kemerer & Hairston, 1990, p. 179).

Sexual Harassment

In another area of litigation, sexual harassment cases have increased dramatically in recent years. Districts have written and distributed specific guidelines for both students and employees to follow if harassment is suspected. In Livingston Independent School District, all students receive a separate handbook on sexual harassment, and Conroe Independent School District has written a detailed policy. According to the Conroe district, sexual harassment of one student by another "includes unwanted and unwelcome verbal or physical conduct of a sexual nature, whether by word, gesture, or any other sexual conduct, including requests for sexual favors" (Like-Denio, Presentation, 1996, Conroe FNCJ Exhibit-A). California law allows "expulsion of students for sexual harassment from fourth grade up" (Gomez, 1995, p. 11). Therefore, teachers need to be acutely aware of their responsibilities in this area.

According to McGee (1995), a former professor of school law, the intent of the harasser does not matter. The test for harassment is from the viewpoint of a reasonable and/or actual victim. In handouts for law class, he mentioned five categories:

- threatening—a direct or implied threat usually accompanies the proposition, for example, reward for cooperation
- physical—unwanted touching, such as fondling, patting, pinching
- verbal—comments about someone's appearance, inappropriate jokes
- nonverbal—flirting, staring at certain body parts, prolonged eye contact
- environmental—suggestive pictures, cartoons, calendars displayed

Two major laws, Title VII of the Civil Rights Act of 1964 and Title IX of the Education Amendments of 1972, prohibit discrimination on the basis of sex. State statutes and school board policies have reiterated that harassment will not be tolerated. A teacher who suspects that harassment is occurring is obligated to follow the school policy and report it to the proper authorities. In the 1992 *Jane Doe v. Taylor Independent School District* case, the Fifth Circuit Court of Appeals held that district personnel have a constitutional duty to intervene if they have knowledge about alleged sexual abuse. This particular case involved a high school freshman and a coach. When Jane Doe's best friend told the administrators about the affair, they decided not to take action. Then Jane Doe's mother discovered love notes, a Valentine's card, and photos with intimate inscriptions from the coach in her daughter's room. At first the coach denied the allegations but finally confessed, resigned from school, and pled guilty to sexual assault charges. The court held that the administrators could be sued individually because they acted with deliberate indifference to the rights of students (Wright, 1996, p. 129).

Similar findings were made in the 1992 Supreme Court ruling in *Franklin v. Gwinnett County Public Schools.* Not only had the teacher engaged in sexual conversations with the female student, but also he had sexual intercourse with her while on school grounds. The Supreme Court held that a student could collect monetary damages for acts of intentional discrimination. Because school administrators had allegedly downplayed the situation and discouraged the student from pursuing the complaint, they had acted improperly.

ACTIVITY **2.6**

What's Sexual Harassment?

Role-play the following scenarios and decide whether you believe that the situation would warrant contacting the proper authorities about alleged sexual harassment.

1. Your "best" student in your tenth grade English class has just had an argument with her boyfriend. They have been dating for four months. She confides in you that he is "pushing her to go all the way." She doesn't want anyone else to know that she told you.
2. You find your "favorite" student, Jim, in the hallway before class begins. Dana, your "least favorite" student, starts complaining that Jim has been popping her bra straps. You don't know if she's telling you the truth or simply trying to cause trouble once again. Do you send Jim to the office?
3. An overweight student in your seventh grade physical science class walks in crying. When you ask her what happened, she tells you that two boys in your class have been making mooing sounds. How do you handle this situation?
4. You find three of the most popular cheerleaders in school looking at a *Playgirl* magazine and commenting to one of the boys, "you only wish you looked that good." They quickly hide it when you approach, but you know it's there. Do you confiscate the material and give it back at the end of the day? Turn the magazine into the office? Pretend that you didn't know what was happening? Faint?

Are any of the foregoing scenarios sexual harassment? If so, which ones?

Search and Seizure

In most situations, teachers will not actually be responsible for searching a student's possessions. However, teachers still need to know the court rulings regarding this matter. In the case *New Jersey v. T.L.O.,* a female student was reported to the principal for smoking in the restroom. When the girl's pocketbook was searched, the principal found cigarettes, rolling papers, and a small bag of marijuana. The student was then turned over to the police. She argued that the principal conducted an illegal search because he was not looking for many of the aforementioned items. The Court sided with the district because the search was conducted on school premises, the administrator believed that the student had violated school rules, and the search was not unduly intrusive in considering the age and sex of the defendant and the nature of the offense (Kemerer & Hairston, 1990, p. 219).

With the major concern over drug traffic in our nation's schools, many districts have relied on canines to patrol parking lots, lockers, dressing rooms, and other school sites. This type of investigation has been upheld in the courts. For instance, in the 1982 *Horton v. Goose Creek Independent School District* case, the court of appeals decided that the use of sniffer

ACTIVITY **2.7**

What Do You Think?

1. Answer these questions. Are schools becoming too much like prisons? Do metal detectors and canine patrols make students feel safer or more afraid? Should video cameras be installed on school buses? Is big brother/big sister watching too much?
2. Brainstorm in groups and make a list of ways you will help the schools in your community be safer places. How can you make your students feel safe in your classroom?
3. Act on your suggestions. Have each student select one way to make a difference. Make a bulletin board with the class action plan (see the following chart). Check the plan periodically to discover if everyone is following through on the goals.

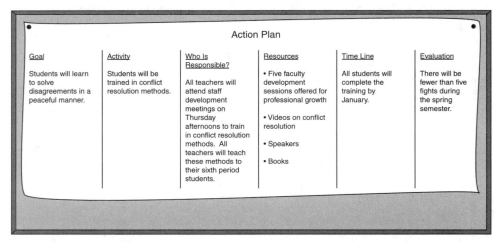

Action Plan

Goal	Activity	Who Is Responsible?	Resources	Time Line	Evaluation
Students will learn to solve disagreements in a peaceful manner.	Students will be trained in conflict resolution methods.	All teachers will attend staff development meetings on Thursday afternoons to train in conflict resolution methods. All teachers will teach these methods to their sixth period students.	• Five faculty development sessions offered for professional growth • Videos on conflict resolution • Speakers • Books	All students will complete the training by January.	There will be fewer than five fights during the spring semester.

dogs in this context is not a search. Other forms of checking for contraband include using metal detectors at school entrances and installing video cameras on school buses and in hallways. Some experts, such as Ron Garrison, a violence prevention specialist, believe that these techniques do not really stop students who want to bring weapons or illegal materials to school. Students have found ways to smuggle contraband in and defy the system.

Censorship

Two other U.S. Supreme Court cases dealt with our fundamental rights and school-related activities. In the *Hazelwood Independent School District v. Kuhlmeier* (1988) decision, the Court ruled in favor of the school. The justices noted that because the school newspaper was part of the journalism class curriculum, it could be censored. The students had decided to write about such topics as divorces occurring in families and teen pregnancy. When the administrators discovered the subject matter, they thought it was inappropriate. The students argued that they had the right to print what they deemed of interest to the student body. With this ruling, other school-sponsored activities, including school theatrical productions and yearbooks, are likely to be scrutinized in some districts (Kemerer & Hairston, 1990, p. 131).

A second censorship issue, freedom of speech, involved the 1985 *Bethel School District No. 403 v. Fraser* case. Fraser, an honor student and debate team member, made a speech in the assembly about his friend who was running for student body officer. During the school-sponsored meeting, he made several sexual innuendoes that evoked laughter and gesturing by attendees. The administrator then suspended Fraser for three days, even though the student argued that he had the right of free speech. In their ruling, the Supreme Court judges noted that indecent comments are not protected in the Constitution.

Judicious Discipline

Forrest Gathercoal, a professor at Oregon State University and a lawyer, designed the judicious discipline model. He believes that classrooms should reflect a democratic rather than authoritarian society. To make this occur, he recommends teaching students about their constitutional rights, including the freedoms discussed earlier. For example, one activity he suggests is to have secondary students make a free speech bulletin board such as the one in Figure 2.1. They are to write any message, unless it's profane, on the board. To show students

ACTIVITY **2.8**

You Be the Judge

1. Pretend that you are one of the U.S. Supreme Court judges hearing either one of the censorship cases mentioned.
2. Write an opinion in which you agree or disagree with the majority.
3. Exchange papers and discuss the issues. Did most of the class agree with the rulings? Why? Why not?

FIGURE 2.1   Free Speech Bulletin Board

Christie McWilliams, a middle school journalism teacher, designed this bulletin board. Used by permission.

that the teacher respects them, he advocates that students be given receipts if a teacher confiscates any of their property. By completing these activities, he argues that they are truly practicing their fundamental rights while in today's classrooms.

Gathercoal (1993) particularly denounces the way teachers often grade. For instance, he thinks that participation grades are discriminatory. According to him, teachers actually control who speaks in the classroom by whom they call on. Gathercoal also notes that we probably would not want the person packing our parachute to have received good grades based on a friendly attitude or being on time. Why then do we base grades on such trivia? He also finds fault with the idea that students cannot participate if they did not bring their supplies to class. In his opinion, this practice is inconsistent with the right to an equal educational opportunity. And he notes that returning graded papers from highest score to lowest probably violates the Buckley Amendment, the students' right to confidentiality.

Instead of only discussing their fundamental rights, Gathercoal believes that students should participate in a democracy while in the classroom. To accomplish this feat, he believes that students should form the classroom expectations based on both individual and compelling state interests. These include four areas.

- *Property Loss or Damage.* Return the gym equipment when class is over.
- *Legitimate Educational Purpose.* Bring your supplies and books each day.
- *Threat to Health and Safety.* Pull the fire alarm only in an emergency.
- *Serious Disruption of the Educational Process.* Keep gang activity off school premises.

In balancing the rights of the majority with the freedoms of the individual, Gathercoal seeks ways to empower the students and give them responsibilities. When an academic or behavior problem exists, teachers need to ask themselves, "What needs to be learned from this situation?" Then ask the students to tell what they have decided to do. In other words, hold them accountable for their actions (Gathercoal, 1993). What do you think? Will this management style work for you?

Summary

In developing this chapter, we first considered reasons teachers need to know educational law and how the legal system is organized. We then focused on constitutional issues relating to corporal punishment, due process rights, special education, sexual harassment, search and seizure, and censorship. Finally, we examined Gathercoal's judicious discipline model and described how it offers students fundamental freedoms in the classroom.

REFERENCES

Baker, J., Shapiro, D., Wingert, P., & Joseph, N. (1987, June 22). Paddling: Still a sore point. *Newsweek, 61.*

Black, S. (1994, April). Throw away the hickory stick. *The Executive Educator, 16* (4), 44–47.

Bradley, D., King-Sears, M., & Tessier-Switlick, D. (1997). *Teaching students in inclusive settings: From theory to practice.* Boston: Allyn & Bacon.

Durrant, J. (1996). *Family violence against children: A challenge for society.* New York: Walter de Gruyter Co.

Gathercoal, F. (1993). *Judicious discipline* (3rd ed.). San Francisco: Caddo Gap Press.

Gomez, F. (1995, June). *Principal laws on sexual harassment.* Paper presented at the Academic Affairs Council meeting, Sam Houston State University, Huntsville, TX.

Greenwood, Y. (1995, November). *Freedom of the press and the First Amendment.* Paper presented at the Texas Association for Supervision and Curriculum Development Conference, Forth Worth, TX.

Gullatt, D. (1998, February). *The relevance of school law to teacher education programs.* Paper presented at the 78th Annual Association of Teacher Educators Conference, Dallas, TX.

Harper, M. (1996). Special education in Texas. In C. Funkhouser (ed.), *Education in Texas: Policies, practices, and perspectives* (pp. 331–338). Upper Saddle River, NJ: Prentice-Hall.

Kemerer, F. (1996). An overview of education law and Texas schools. In C. Funkhouser (ed.), *Education in Texas: Policies, practices, and perspectives* (pp. 77–84). Upper Saddle River, NJ: Prentice-Hall.

Kemerer, F., & Hairston, J. (1990). *The educator's guide to Texas school law* (2nd ed.). Austin: University of Texas Press.

Like-Denio, D. (1997, January). *Legal issues in education.* Handouts presented to the class, Responsibilities of a Professional Educator, Sam Houston State University, Huntsville, TX.

Lynch, S., moderator (1998, January). Panel of Special Education Speakers *Changes in IDEA.* Presentation at the Sam Houston State University Chapter Phi Delta Kappa Meeting, Conroe, TX.

McEwan, B. (ed.). (1994). *Practicing judicious discipline: An educator's guide to a democratic classroom.* San Francisco: Caddo Gap Press.

McGee, J. (1995). *Sexual harassment.* Handouts presented to the Educational Leadership class, School Law, Sam Houston State University, Huntsville, TX.

Osborne, A., Jr. (1996). *Legal issues in special education.* Boston: Allyn & Bacon.

Parents and Teachers Against Violence in Education. (n.d.). *Understanding corporal punishment of schoolchildren.* [Brochure]. Danville, CA: Author.

State Board for Educator Certification. (1998). *Code of ethics and standard practices for Texas educators.* [Brochure]. Austin, TX.

Strahan, R. (1997, October). *Legal issues: What teachers need to know about the law.* Presentation made at the Consortium of State Organizations for Texas Teachers Education Conference, Houston, TX.

Strahan, R. (1987, June). *Disciplining students.* Paper presented at the Annual School Administrators Conference, Sam Houston State University, Huntsville, TX.

Texas School Law Bulletin. (1996). 74th Texas Legislature, Regular Session (1995) Austin, TX: Texas Education Agency.

Williams, P. (1996). The law and corporal punishment. In C. Funkhouser (ed.), *Education in Texas: Policies, practices, and perspectives* (pp. 119–123). Upper Saddle River, NJ: Prentice-Hall.

Williams, P., & Harman, M. (1998, February). *Juveniles in crisis: Voices of the perpetrators.* Paper presented at the 78th Annual Meeting of the Association of Teacher Educators, Dallas, TX.

Wolfgang, C. (1995). *Solving discipline problems: Methods and models for today's teachers* (3rd ed.). Boston: Allyn & Bacon.

Wright, J. (1996). Sexual harassment and sexual abuse of students. In C. Funkhouser (ed.), *Education in Texas: Policies, practices, and perspectives* (pp. 125–130). Upper Saddle River, NJ: Prentice-Hall.

LEGAL CITATIONS

Baker v. Owen, 96 S. Ct. 210 (1975).

Bethel School District No. 403 v. Fraser, 106 S. Ct. 3159 (1986).

Franklin v. Gwinnett County Public Schools, 112 S. Ct. 1028 (1992).

Goss v. Lopez, 95 S. Ct. 729 (1975).

Hazelwood School District v. Kuhlmeier, 108 S. Ct. 562 (1988).

Honig v. Doe, 108 S. Ct. 592 (1988).

Horton v. Goose Creek I.S.D., 693 F.2d 524 (5th Cir. 1982).

Ingraham v. Wright, 97 S. Ct. 1401 (1977).

Jane Doe v. Taylor Independent School District, 975 F.2d 137 (1992).

New Jersey v. T.L.O., 105 S. Ct. 733 (1985).

Whitley v. State, 33 Tex. Crim. 172, 25 S.W. 1072 (1894).

PART TWO

Preventive Management

Preventing classroom management problems should be the goal of every teacher. Those teachers who have good classroom management skills have more time for instruction and a much better chance of having a classroom in which high levels of learning take place. Successful teachers engage in a number of practices to prevent management problems. They carefully plan; they vary their instructional strategies; they seek to enhance student motivation; they make parents their partners; and they work toward a sense of belonging on the part of their students. Planning during the months preceding the school year will be discussed in Part Two as will the necessity for teachers to give careful attention to the first days of the school year. Other chapters in this section address communication strategies and planning for effective instruction. Working successfully with parents is also discussed in the final chapter of this section.

CHAPTER

3

Before School Begins

Before school begins, teachers share ideas and plan for the new year.

OBJECTIVES

1. Sketch the arrangement of your classroom including the student desks, your primary teaching spot, computers, available storage space, the teacher's desk, file cabinets, the pencil sharpener, and the open space(s) of the room, along with the doorway.
2. Develop a floor plan for your classroom that provides a clear line of sight between your teaching station and each student desk.
3. Identify the teaching materials and equipment that you will use in your classroom.

Overview

Every year in late August or early September teachers find themselves with one of two complex sets of feelings. Following are two scenarios that represent the extremes of those feelings. Imagine there are two groups of teachers gathered at opposite ends of the faculty lounge. Both groups are engaged in intense conversation.

SCENARIO 3.1

This group of teachers is complaining about having to go back to work and looking for any-thing to do other than preparing for the school year. If you overhear them, they'll be going over their class rosters and mumbling about how difficult the coming year will be because of the students who will be in their classes. They expect the upcoming school year to be miser-able. In fact, this group doesn't seem to have a sense that their efforts will positively influ-ence their students. They are also comparing notes about specific students—by their general tone the listener would think that all students cause problems, have few skills, and lack the motivation to do better.

SCENARIO 3.2

The teachers at the other end of the room are eagerly preparing teaching materials and gen-erally making plans for the start of a new school year. They too are discussing students who will be in their classes, but their discussion is positive and affirming. These teachers are excited and enthusiastic. It is obvious that they enjoy working with students. These teachers are confident that they can handle anything that emerges.

Let's assume that you've been thinking about the start of the school year. If you lean toward the first group in your attitudes, you can expect that the group is right; you probably will have a miserable year. Furthermore, your students are likely to sense your reluctance to teach them, and they may react negatively to your attitude. The danger is that your negative attitude toward teaching will create attitudinal problems among your students, which can then result in management problems as the school year progresses.

On the other hand, if you're among the group in Scenario 2, you've probably developed some excellent materials for your classes. Plus, you are developing a management plan that will affirm your positive attitude and help you establish successful learning communities. You are doubtlessly excited about the upcoming days and meeting the new students you'll be privileged to work with this year. This excitement and anticipation will be contagious and your students are likely to catch your excitement.

What are the differences in the two preceding scenarios? Into which group do you fit? Into which group do you want to fit? The choice is yours; it is your decision as to whether you have a productive year or a year that causes you to constantly question the wisdom of choos-ing teaching as a career. What is the difference? Read on!

What planning process is necessary for developing a quality learning environment? You will find a number of suggestions about (a) appropriate arrangement of room furnishings; (b) the availability and storage of teaching materials, textbooks, and supplemental materials such as scientific equipment for the sciences, maps for the social studies, anthologies for En-glish classes, computers, and other technology; and (c) the supplies, paper, pencils, and other materials for your classroom. Finally, specific suggestions will be made for those of you who will not have a specifically assigned room and will be sharing your classroom(s) with other teachers.

The Planning Process

Planning for the school year begins long before the first day of school. Ideally, in the summer (at least a month or more before school), you will begin making extensive plans. Schell and Burden (1992) point out that beginning teachers are particularly at a disadvantage because they are expected to begin their very first day of teaching with the same abilities in classroom management as their more experienced colleagues. Whether you are a beginning teacher on the first day of school or you bring several years of teaching experience, as Shell and Burden mention, you will be expected to (a) be thoroughly familiar with your classroom and the general school environment, (b) have a fully functional classroom management system organized for the first day, (c) be ready to implement a fair and efficient system for student assessment and grading, (d) have both long-range and short-range instructional plans that meet your district's curriculum standards, and (e) acknowledge the differences in your students' abilities, interests, preferred learning styles, and backgrounds.

Experienced teachers generally find their planning time reduced somewhat, particularly if they engaged in extensive planning prior to their first year of teaching. Obviously, there is a lesson here for beginning teachers: Time spent preparing for the first day of class will be immensely helpful that year and save planning time in subsequent years.

Planning for Teaching

Extensive research about the teacher planning process began to appear in educational literature in the 1980s (Anderson, 1989; Bellon, Bellon, & Blank, 1992; Evertson & Emmer, 1982; Schell & Burden, 1992). It has been said, "Teacher planning is the thread that weaves the curriculum, or the what of teaching, with the instruction, the how of teaching" (Freiburg & Driscoll, 1992, p. 22). Although this book is not intended to substitute for detailed discussion of the planning process more often found in methods texts, several recommendations can be made.

In his seminal work, Tyler (1950) outlined a linear process for planning centered around four basic questions.

1. Where are the students now?
2. Where do you want to take them?
3. How are they going to get there?
4. How will you know whether they are making progress or have arrived?

Anderson (1989), summarized the research on planning and identified the following principles, which we encourage you to consider carefully.

■ *Teachers should engage in planning.* According to Freiburg and Driscoll (1992), "Teaching is not a haphazard process" (p. 22). Just as you need a road map to assist you in

ACTIVITY **3.1**

Making a Plan: Are You Ready?

Think about the planning you expect to do for your classes. Brainstorm in groups of three to identify several functions (purposes) that planning for instruction encompasses. How many and which ones directly relate to the effective management of a classroom? Add to the list as you read and study this chapter.

getting to your destination during an auto trip, you need a teaching plan to help you get to your destination (accomplish your instructional goals) within the classroom. People without a teaching plan are much more likely to get lost as they move from point to point in the classroom just as travelers without a map are more likely to take the wrong route. Both long-range plans and daily lesson plans are recommended.

■ *Teachers should put their plans in writing.* Most authorities on planning suggest that you keep written documents from year to year because you will be more likely to remember what worked well and what didn't as you begin your subsequent years. Several lesson formats are available, and you might ask several experienced teachers about the way they keep their plans.

■ *Teachers should develop plans that work for them.* Although it is definitely recommended that your lesson plans be in writing, there is no specific, recommended way to do them. Many planning formats exist, and no one way is correct to the exclusion of others. Some plans are as simple as a list of topics to include in the day's lesson; only experienced teachers should have plans this brief, however. Beginning teachers' plans should be much more detailed. Tuckman (1995) suggests that lesson plans should include (a) objectives, (b) motivational strategies, (c) a content outline, (d) a specification of teaching methodologies including classroom activities, (d) a list of needed materials and media, (e) summaries and reviews, and (f) assignments or homework. Other planning formats include a list of goals, an outline of the content to include, an indication of the way in which the content will be taught, and an indication of the way(s) in which the outcomes will be assessed. Your school or district may mandate a particular planning process. If not, we suggest that you select a format that you like and use it. Remember that we said there is no one correct way to plan, whether for a unit or a daily lesson. The important point is to plan!

For beginning teachers, one of the most frightening events that can happen is to suddenly discover that there are twenty minutes of class time left and no material. Thirty or more pairs of eyes staring expectantly at you is unnerving. Therefore, to avoid this dilemma, plan each lesson for at least one-third more activities than you think you can accomplish. If you have more material than you can teach on any given day, you simply have a head start on tomorrow's plans.

■ *Teachers should both plan the content and determine what instructional strategies to use.* Too many secondary teachers limit their planning time to studying and outlining content exclusively, without thinking about how best to teach the material. Because they are typically

ACTIVITY **3.2**

Reflection Questions

What went well today (this week, etc.)?
How do I know that? (What evidence do I have?)
What did not go well today?
How do I know that? (What evidence do I have?)
What will I change for tomorrow (next week, next year, etc.)?

thoroughly steeped in their disciplines, they can easily become absorbed by the content and forget to consider what they want to prepare their students to do—the purpose of the lesson. As you plan, give attention to both the *what* and the *how* of teaching.

■ *Periodically, teachers should stop and ask themselves: "How is it going? How am I doing?"* Reflection about their actions is a powerful tool for all teachers, regardless of their level of experience. DiGiulio (1995), arguing for more teacher reflection, suggests: "Systematic reflection is essential to improving effectiveness and meeting challenges in today's classrooms" (p. ix). Although continuous reflection throughout the school year is advisable for most teachers, DiGiulio suggests that teachers give special attention to evaluating their teaching at four critical times in the school year:

■ the end of the first day
■ the end of the first week
■ the last week of the fall semester
■ the end of the school year

Engaging in self-reflection at these particular points will enable you to examine your teaching practices and determine whether they are working. We urge you to especially keep three questions in mind when you plan: "Are the goals that I've established for my classes logical and reasonable? Am I doing all that I can to ensure that my students meet the learning goals established for my classes? What methods can I use that will help my students learn and retain the most?"

Planning for the Start of School

Schell and Burden (1992) questioned hundreds of teachers about their preparation for the start of school and concluded that advanced planning involves three dimensions: (a) getting acquainted with your teaching environment, (b) establishing a positive classroom environment, and (c) planning for instruction.

Your Teaching/Classroom Environment

Two elements of the classroom environment, the physical and the psychological, can be manipulated by teachers to increase learning and improve behavior (Anderson as cited in Cruickshank, Bainer, & Metcalf, 1995). The physical environment exists independently of the people who inhabit the classroom, whereas the psychological environment only exists in the minds of those who inhabit the classroom. The psychological environment, sometimes referred to as the social or emotional climate, includes the emotional tone of the classroom and the comfort level the students feel with the teacher, the learning tasks, and each other as a social group. Specific, observable teacher behaviors and management skills affect both the physical and the psychological environments (Cruickshank et al.).

Planning the Physical Environment of the Classroom

Preparing your classroom carefully so that it is arranged as you'd like it when school starts is an important step. If possible, several weeks before school starts find out which room you'll be assigned for the upcoming year. Then become acquainted with your teaching environment

---

ACTIVITY **3.3**

Designing Your Floor Plan

Prepare a scaled floor plan of your classroom by using graphing paper and the architectural symbols found in Figure 3.1 or a computer program. Experiment with varying room arrangements until you find one appropriate to your assigned room. As you read further, be prepared to change your floor plan. When school starts, use this activity to guide arrangement of your classroom furnishings.

---

by surveying key points. First, are there enough desks and chairs for the size of the class you expect to have? If not, contact your school administrator. Nothing will disrupt the first day of school more than finding yourself with a class of thirty-five students and a room with only thirty desks. At times, you will not know exactly how many students will be in class, but you can usually find fairly accurate estimates.

After you've made sure you have enough desks and chairs, check out the other physical facilities. Are there chalkboards, a screen, bulletin boards, a teacher's desk, a file cabinet, other storage space, or computer equipment? If some of these furnishings are missing, ask your building administrator or department chair for help. For example, are there file cabinets somewhere else? Can they be moved to your room? Will you have an office? Where can you store materials that you're not going to use during the first few days of school?

On the other hand, is there excess furniture in the room? Too many furnishings clutter up the room and inhibit the students' and teacher's movement. Excess furnishings also diminish your freedom to use the room as you wish to use it; this will become especially evident as you plan the arrangement of the student desks, teacher's desk, tables, files, and storage cabinets. You may need to contact the designated administrator or custodial staff member to request that items be removed and complete the necessary work order forms.

Wall	———	Electrical Outlets		Carpet	
Window		Sink		Hanging Cabinets	
Door		Switches	S	Desks, Tables, Computer Workstations	
Counter/ Floor Cabinets		Radiators		Chairs	

FIGURE 3.1   Drawing a Floor Plan: Useful Architectural Symbols

When you know the room and its attributes well and have settled on the furnishings, drafting a room floor plan is something we'd suggest. As you plan your basic room layout, keep the following points in mind.

Arranging the Furnishings of Your Room

Once you know which furnishings your room will contain, you can begin arranging the room to facilitate your teaching. Think about the following.

Are the student desks in your room moveable, or are they fastened to the floor? Is your room equipped with tables and chairs or computer workstations rather than individual student desks? Check out these variables early in your planning process; they will determine the flexibility you'll have in arranging the student desks, tables, and workstations.

Will you arrange the furniture in rows or group it in some other way? Will you put the teacher's desk at the front or rear of the room, or perhaps in a back corner? Don't automatically assume that your desk should be at the front. Think about the implications of the desk's location. What message are you sending to students? What are the implications of putting your desk at the front of the room? At the back? In a back corner? If your desk isn't at the front, is there a table or some shelving close by where you can place your immediate teaching materials? You'll want to have some materials readily available as you teach; plan for that.

A good place to start your room arrangement plans is with the student desks and your primary instruction spot. Adams and Biddle (1970) used videotapes to establish the dominant communication pattern in classrooms. Their research shows that there is an "action zone" or center of activity in most classrooms. They discovered that the teacher most often was the leader of the class, who assumed a teaching position near the front and center of the room. The action zone includes most of the front row of students and those directly in front of the teacher in a wedge-shaped pattern, ever narrowing to the back of the room, as shown in Figure 3.2. Students seated in the action zone are physically closer to the teacher; consequently, they interact more with the teacher than other students. According to Adams and Biddle, students in the action zone participate more in class, work more persistently, and hold more positive attitudes toward the class. Those students seated outside the zone and farther from the teacher attain lower levels of achievement and hold less positive attitudes toward learning. Others (Dykman & Reis, 1979; Walberg, 1969) found that students who choose to sit outside the action zone tend to have lower self-esteem, to doubt their academic ability, and to feel threatened by the classroom environment or the teacher. Students seated along the periphery of the classroom are less engaged with the teacher and the instructional tasks at hand and are more easily distracted. This, in turn, leads to failure, which reinforces their self-doubt and low self-esteem.

Do you like to use a lectern when you teach? After reading about the classroom action zone, determine the implications of placing a lectern at the front center of the room. Where will you designate your teaching spot? Will you have more than one teaching spot—perhaps one in the front of the room and another at the side of the room where you'll often write on the chalkboard? Perhaps you'll need a location where you can use the keyboard for your PowerPoint presentations. Teachers' desks are often at the front and center of the room in secondary classrooms, but that need not be so! One thing is certain, the line of sight between each student's desk and your instruction spot(s) should be unobstructed. Each student should be able to see you, your demonstration materials as you use them, and the chalkboard or screen where you'll write key points. Only with unobstructed lines of sight between student desks and your teaching area can you observe students and move to assist them if they are

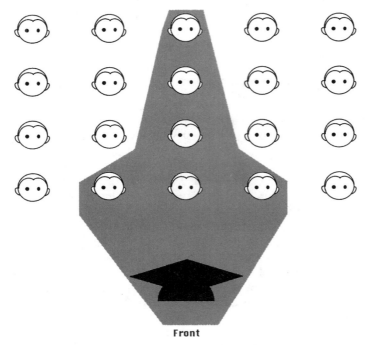

Front

FIGURE 3.2   The Action Zone

Source: Adapted from Adams, R. S., and Biddle, B. J. (1970). *Realities of teaching: Explorations with video tape.* New York: Holt, Rinehart and Winston. Reprinted by permission of Holt, Rinehart and Winston.

having problems. Unobstructed lines of sight also facilitate monitoring students' actions so that you can prevent inappropriate behavior.

Movement about the Room

Can you move freely around the room as you've planned it? Monitoring seatwork is an important function for the effective teacher, and you'll want a room arrangement that facilitates rather than impedes your movement. Ideally, you want adequate open space so that you can move to a student's desk, assist with whatever problem has arisen, and at the same time watch all students in the class as they continue their work. Remember to leave adequate space between groupings or rows of desks so that students can have free access to their desks without unnecessary physical contact with others. Bumping or shoving each other while moving from the doorway to their desks is common in secondary classrooms. To minimize the physical contact between students, be certain that the students can walk from the doorway to their desks without physically touching one another.

You should also be keenly aware of special accomodations that students may need, such as wider aisles for crutches, walkers, and wheelchairs. By planning your room arrangement ahead of time and adjusting it according to special needs, you are showing students that we are all part of this classroom.

ACTIVITY **3.4**

Have You Considered?

How would you arrange the classroom to accommodate students with the following disabilities?

1. A student who is blind and uses a cane.
2. A student who has cerebral palsy and is confined to a wheelchair.
3. A student who has a hearing impairment and reads lips.

Have you made plans for handling fire drills? Group work? Copying material from the board?

Special Considerations of Space

Keeping certain space free of furnishings is a good idea. For example, a pencil sharpener will probably be located somewhere in your room. Place the furnishings in such a way as to keep enough open space so that students have unobstructed access to high-traffic areas, such as the sharpener, trash can, and announcement board. When you survey your room, examine it closely for any furnishings to which you'll want your students to have easy access. If you have your desk at the front, for example, can you comfortably move from behind the desk into areas reserved for student seats? If not, rearrange the room to accommodate unrestricted movement among the teacher's desk, students' desks, and other key furnishings, including the lab equipment table, countertops, and book shelves.

Using the Perimeter of the Room

Leave space between the walls of the room and student desks, if possible, so that you can move freely around the perimeter. Moving along the perimeter is especially important because from those areas you can observe all the students. Likewise, you'll want the students' eyes on you during presentations. Leaving space between the walls and the student desks also enables you to reach the chalkboard, maps, sinks, or storage areas at the side.

Location of Student Desks

Many different room arrangements will be possible depending upon certain key factors related to your classroom, such as (a) the size and shape of the room, (b) the number and type of desks and chairs in the room, (c) the amount and type of other teaching equipment, and (d) your personal preferences. Musgrave (1975) illustrated and discussed a number of possible room arrangements. In his discussion he listed the advantages and limitations of each room arrangement. Common room arrangements that teachers have found particularly useful are shown in Figures 3.3 through 3.7. Following each illustration, we have summarized the advantages and the limitations of that particular room arrangement. Various room arrangements, each with its own strengths and weaknesses, can be found in the literature (Cruickshank, Bainer, & Metcalf, 1995; Emmer, Evertson, Clements, & Worsham, 1997; Musgrave, 1975; Weinstein, 1996).

Vertical Rows (Figure 3.3)

Advantages
- Centers attention on the teacher.
- Facilitates housekeeping (your custodian will like it).
- Facilities whole-class presentations.
- Enhances individualized recitation activities.
- Facilitates monitoring of the class (you can move about the room).
- Aids the teacher in monitoring exams.
- Encourages independent seatwork.

Limitations
- Centers attention on the teacher.
- Gives students unequal seating status (the action zone is clearly operable).
- Inhibits class discussion and interaction among students.
- Results in poor eye contact with students outside the action zone.

Horizontal Rows (Figure 3.4)

Advantages
- Uses tables and chairs as furnishings often.
- Promotes independent seatwork.

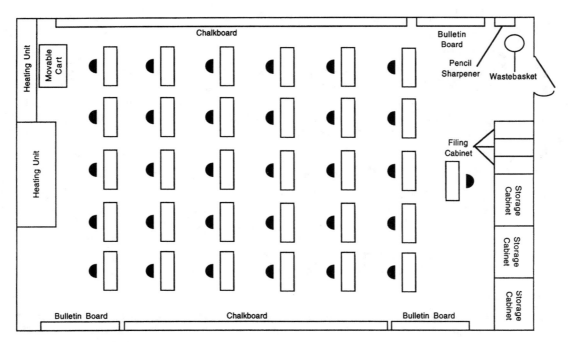

FIGURE 3.3   Vertical Rows

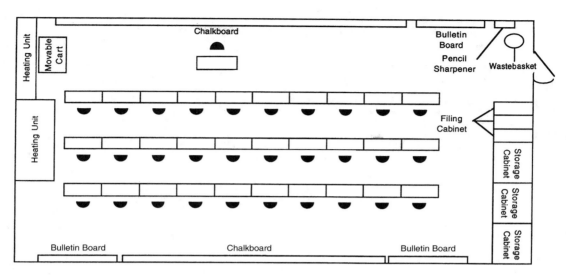

FIGURE 3.4   Horizontal Rows

- Permits students to work in pairs.
- Facilitates housekeeping.
- Allows teacher to walk up to each student from either front or rear.
- Aids teacher demonstrations.
- Facilitates monitoring of individual work.

Limitations
- Discourages student and group interaction.
- Focuses on the teacher.
- Impedes monitoring of exams.
- Promotes a lecture or discussion style in which all students receive the same instruction.

Square (Figure 3.5)

Advantages
- Permits independent study.
- Permits interaction among individual students.
- Promotes discussion among all students.
- Provides a stage as the center area.
- Enhances teacher and student demonstrations.
- Allows small groups to demonstrate to entire class.

Limitations
- Limits whole-group presentations.
- Discourages the use of films, overhead, and computer-based presentations.
- Causes special problems for the custodian.
- Affects teacher control mechanisms.

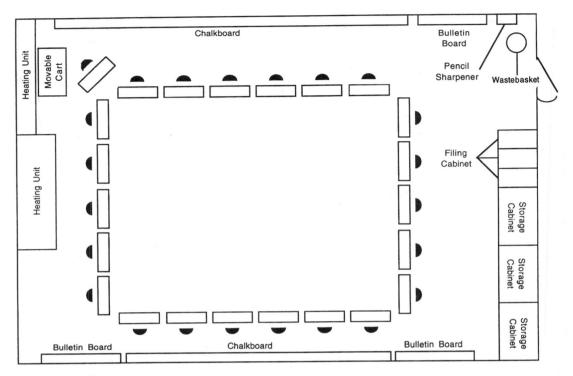

FIGURE 3.5   Square

Circle (Figure 3.6)

Advantages and Limitations
■ Quite similar to the square; the same advantages and limitations apply.

Facing Groups of Four (Figure 3.7)

Advantages
■ Accommodates either tables and chairs or individual student desks.
■ Encourages student interaction.
■ Allows sharing of equipment and supplies.
■ Enhances any type of group work such as cooperative learning.
■ Promotes student-centered teaching approaches.

Limitations
■ Discourages teacher presentations, lectures, and other types of whole-class teaching.
■ Promotes cliques.
■ Leads to unwanted student interactions (too much talking) at times.
■ Impedes monitoring of exams.

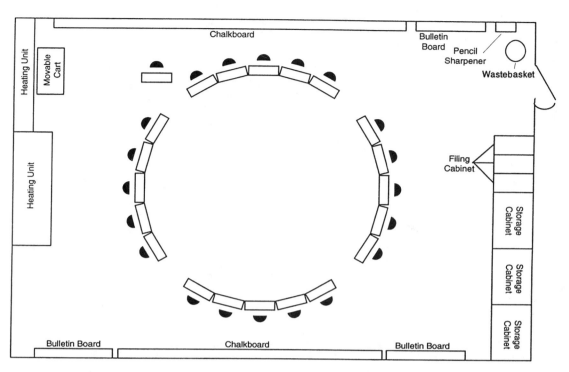

FIGURE 3.6   Circle

Again, we call your attention to the fact that the preceding illustrations of room arrangements are a representative sample of well over a dozen possible arrangements that you might consider for your classroom. Consider others if these do not meet your needs.

Changing Room Arrangements

No single seating arrangement is ideal for all classes, learning situations, or individuals (Cruickshank, Bainer, & Metcalf, 1995). For specific teaching purposes, many teachers rearrange their classrooms. For example, when teachers wish students to engage in discussion, they often rearrange the seating into small groups of four or five students each. Or they may choose to rearrange the entire class into a circle to encourage total class discussion of some key point. Musgrave (1975) suggests using a "home base formation" that serves as the semipermanent room arrangement. This formation should be suitable for many different types of instructional purposes and should be easily movable to alternative arrangements as desired. Borich (1992) specifically suggests the traditional vertical rows as the home base formation because it conveys a businesslike appearance, is easily monitored, and can be reorganized quickly to small groups, circles, or other alternative arrangements. Weinstein and Mignano (1992) suggest the traditional rows especially for beginning teachers until they feel confident in their management skills.

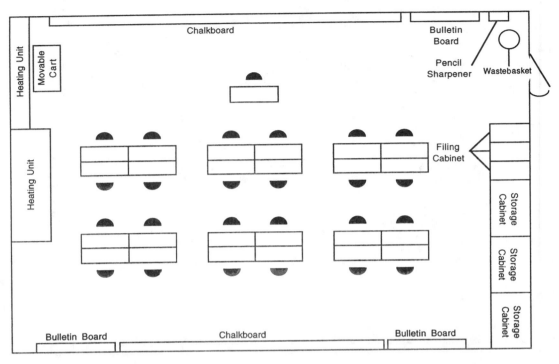

FIGURE 3.7   Facing Groups of Four

Teaching Materials

An equally important aspect of your before-school planning is a thorough acquaintance with the teaching materials to which you'll have access. If you are an experienced teacher returning to the same school, you'll already know the answers to the following. If you are new in this school or if this is your first year of teaching, you'll want to give attention to the following points.

Textbooks.   As you make your initial visit to your school, contact your principal or department head and secure a copy of the text materials you'll be expected to use. You'll want important questions answered. Does the school furnish textbooks for students on a loan/sign-out process of some type, or will the students be expected to buy their textbooks? If the school is furnishing them, will there be enough so that you can assume each student will have a copy to use for the semester or year? Or will there be only enough textbooks to provide a classroom set, which must be loaned out at the beginning of class and returned at the end of each day's class? Plan for whatever situation you discover.

One of the authors of this book learned a valuable early lesson in textbook management. When she was a beginning teacher, her entire eleventh grade teaching team checked out the books to students. When the books were supposed to be returned at the end of the year, several copies were missing. The eleventh grade team was expected to pay for the books. A quick search of lockers ensued because the students had not been held responsible for the books and simply didn't care if they were returned.

Supplemental Materials.   If you are new to this school or a beginning teacher, you'll want to inquire about the available supplemental materials. Supplemental texts and dictionaries are possibilities. Some schools have classroom sets of supplemental textbooks; others do not. Some departmental budgets provide funds for faculty to select additional material; others do not. You'll need to know the options available.

Teachers' Editions.   Most publishing houses produce teachers' editions for their textbooks. You'll want to secure one for each of your textbooks because it usually includes useful suggested classroom activities, a test bank, or suggestions for authentic assessment. Still others will offer supplemental materials such as CD-ROMs, videos, and sets of transparencies, which accompany and augment the contents of the published text. Knowing your options will enable you to plan more effectively for the upcoming school year.

Bulletin Boards.   Sometimes secondary teachers overlook the value of bulletin boards as teaching devices, thinking of them as an elementary teacher's tool. However, bulletin boards can be used to post classroom rules, to make announcements, to increase interest in the current topic, or to simply make the room more colorful and inviting to your students. Certainly, you'll want to survey the bulletin board space your classroom will have and, if you have not yet begun teaching, begin to collect materials that can be used. Having students create these bulletin boards saves you time and gives students an opportunity to shine. Peers are noticing their work, not just the teachers.

Grade Book, Attendance Rosters, Paper Work.   Secondary teachers must keep track of absent and tardy students. Many schools will require you to take attendance and to report to the office both absent and tardy students on special forms each class period. You'll need to know what is expected of you and how to report absences and tardiness. Be sure you have a supply of the correct forms before school begins (see Figure 3.8).

Another responsibility, closely related to the attendance process, is the recording of grades in some type of semipermanent format, such as either a printed grade book or computer program. Therefore, you'll want a copy of a grade book or a computer-based grading program. Often attendance is recorded in the same book or computer program that you'll use to keep track of grades. Be sure to check with your department chair, principal, or mentor about your options and the school's expectations regarding grades and attendance.

Specialized Equipment.   Some teaching fields commonly use specialized equipment. For example, a science classroom will likely have sinks, gas burners, and glassware for various purposes. Likewise, a language class may have tape and video recorders in the room, or a mathematics class may have computers available for student and/or faculty use. And, of course, vocationally oriented fields such as technology education, family and consumer sciences, or computer studies have extensive specialized equipment. Often this equipment is located in the laboratory, but not always. Sometimes specially equipped classrooms must be shared with other classes and other teachers. Such specialized equipment is then likely to be kept in some common storage space such as a departmental office or the storeroom. Again, you'll want to know just what equipment you'll have either assigned to your room on a permanent basis or that you'll share with other teachers. In the latter case, you'll want to know the procedures for checking out such equipment. For instance, do you need to request the video player two or three days in advance? Do you need to reserve the computer lab? Do you get the equipment or does someone deliver it to your classroom?

FIGURE 3.8   Sample Form for Reporting Absences

TEACHER'S REPORT OF ABSENCES
12th GRADE

Teacher's name _____

Date _____ Period _____

Names of pupils absent: _____

_____

_____

_____

_____

_____

_____

_____

_____

_____

Teacher's signature

Use other side if additional space is needed.

014176

Specialized Materials.   Most teaching fields have specialized teaching materials as well as equipment. These ancillary materials may be visual or audio in nature. For example, a German language teacher may use audio tapes to accompany the text, or a science textbook may have a CD-ROM that shows a heart beating, or a social studies teacher may use a set of pull-down maps to emphasize the region being studied. Every year new computer programs supplement the basic materials of the classroom. These specialized teaching materials may also need to be shared among several teachers. In that case, knowing the location of the material as well as the checkout procedures is imperative.

Most teachers use supplements to the basic classroom text. These materials may be a set of photocopied materials taken from supplemental sources unrelated to the textbook, ancillary materials that accompany the text, or self-generated teacher materials. Ask for a teacher's guide if you don't have one. Then be sure to check for useful teaching suggestions.

Because of rising costs of paper and copying, many school administrators limit the amount furnished to teachers. Then too, as a matter of policy in some schools, copying can only be done centrally by a designated person, and the teacher is expected to turn in materials to that person well in advance, usually twenty-four to forty-eight hours before the materials are needed. In addition, teachers need to be aware of what is copyrighted, and therefore cannot be duplicated. For instance, in most cases, it is illegal for teachers to reproduce class sets of chapters in books instead of having the school district purchase them. In addition, they are usually not allowed to duplicate workbook pages rather than giving each student the entire book. Lawsuits between schools and publishers concerning copyright infringement have increased dramatically over the last ten years.

Using self-generated materials presents a different challenge. Whereas some schools have classified personnel to assist teachers with the typing, others don't. Teachers may be expected to develop and type their own teaching materials. Knowing the specifics of (a) the amount and type of help you'll have for producing teaching materials, (b) the amount and type of publisher-furnished teaching materials available and whether you'll have to share them with colleagues, (c) the amount of copying you can do, and (d) the time lines to be followed in getting such materials produced will be necessary as you prepare for the upcoming school year.

Computers and Other Technology.   Classroom computers are increasingly available for student and teacher use. Sometimes there are banks of computers located in classrooms; in other cases a single computer may be available. Obviously, taking a tour of your classroom will give you definitive information about the computer resources that you'll have access to in your teaching situation. If multiple computers are available, you will also want to determine the nature, scope, and extent of the software. Furthermore, you'll want to know whether you will share both the hardware and software with other teachers and other classes. Finally, if you have only one computer, you may want to station it in the room or departmental office to limit student access. Whatever computer equipment you have, some student-oriented rules or procedures regarding its use are in order.

You may also have Internet access. If you do, special rules and procedures for your students are in order. Like any other classroom rules, computer and Internet usage rules should be fair, clear, and fully understood by the students. You may want to hold class discussion to elicit student input before developing class expectations.

ACTIVITY **3.5**

Computer Whiz: The Rules of the Game

Create a list of three to five *positively* stated rules for students who are using technology in the classroom. Then, decide what the logical consequences will be for breaking these rules. Think of answers to these questions as you develop your rules.

1. May a student come to class before or after school to use the computer?
2. Will each student need a separate disk? Where will these be stored? Do you need a checkout procedure?
3. What are the consequences for violating the computer rules?
4. Will you have other technology, such as scanners and video recorders, in the room?
5. Must all out-of-class assignments be typed on a computer? Do all of your students have access to computers?
6. When and under what conditions may students browse the Internet?
7. Should students have any input in determining the technology rules?

Sharing Your Classroom with Another Teacher

Often teachers, especially beginning teachers, find themselves sharing classrooms with other teachers, or "floating" as it is often called. If you find yourself floating between classrooms, certain steps ease the burden. Each teacher's situation will be different, but you'll want to consider several points.

Work with the teachers with whom you share a room so that you can have (a) an overhead readily available; (b) a section of the chalkboard to post assignments, due dates, and other important announcements; (c) a storage area for materials; and (d) a portion of the bulletin board to post announcements specifically for your class or supplemental materials to aid oral instruction.

Sharing the Overhead

If you are a floating teacher, the overhead will be particularly helpful to enable you to prepare visual materials in advance. Assignments, for example, can be typed on a transparency, carried from room to room, and shared with students. That way you won't be forced to limit your assignment making to oral instructions. Plus, you can list key concepts on the transparency rather than wasting valuable class time rewriting them each day on the chalkboard.

Sharing the Chalkboard

A section of the chalkboard may be designated as your class's area. Often it is desirable to have visual materials, such as long-term assignments, key concepts, or vocabulary words, posted for several days or weeks. When this is the case, a chalkboard or bulletin board can be especially helpful because the overhead can then be devoted to visual materials that are needed for a shorter duration. Some teachers also post a monthly calendar so that assignment due dates and other class notes are prominently displayed.

Sharing the Storage Space

Floating teachers often have materials that are needed for one class but not for another. Having a portion of the classroom's storage space, both closet and file, allocated for your use can be very helpful. To have such storage space designated, you'll need to work closely with other teachers who share the room.

Sharing the Bulletin Boards

Teachers often supplement their oral instruction with visual displays. Obviously, sharing a room and floating each hour places an added burden on you. If you can negotiate a share of the available bulletin board space, you can supplement your instruction in that particular classroom.

Experienced teachers know that floating adds to the workload. But they also know that if they can negotiate the four classroom features just noted (i.e., use of the overhead, chalkboards, bulletin boards, and storage space), they will have solved some of their problems.

ACTIVITY **3.6**

Checklist of Things to Do before School Starts

_____ 1. Is the classroom ready for school to start?

   _____ Do you have enough student desks?

   _____ Where will you locate your teacher's desk?

   _____ Do you have your teaching station(s) identified?

   _____ Can you see all students from your teaching station?

   _____ Can you move freely about the room?

   _____ Can students get to their seats with minimal physical contact?

_____ 2. What equipment do you have in your room? Is all the equipment in operating condition?

_____ 3. Is the equipment located in appropriate places?

_____ 4. Are the high-traffic areas (e.g., around the pencil sharpener) easily accessed?

_____ 5. Are the textbooks ready for distribution? Do you have the necessary forms?

_____ 6. Do you have any supplemental teaching materials? Are they ready for use?

_____ 7. Do you have adequate storage for materials?

_____ 8. Do you have copies of the teachers' editions of your textbooks?

_____ 9. Do you have a grade book or a computer-based grading program?

_____ 10. Will you have class rosters before school starts?

_____ 11. Have you decorated your room? Bulletin boards? Walls?

_____ 12. Have you planned for pets or plants in your room?

_____ 13. Other?

_____

_____

_____

_____

_____

Some Cautions for Beginning Teachers

As you plan for the upcoming year, you'll be thinking of the type of environment you want to establish in your classroom. It is appropriate to do so, but as you do, keep this caution in mind. Don't try to become a buddy to your students. More than one teacher has become a buddy only to discover that students then do not recognize that teacher's abilities. This is not to say that you don't want to be a friendly, outgoing person; you do! But being a personable individual is not the same as being a buddy. Remind yourself that you are a teacher; that is your role.

In our years of observing student teachers, we have seen individuals who step over the imaginary line and want to be best friends with their students, or at least a particular group of students. For instance, they may allow students to call them by their first name, visit them at home frequently, or call them to chat about their personal lives. Then these student teachers wonder why they are having behavior problems in class and feel that students do not respect them. Would you want your best friend to be your teacher? As you think about your first year, visualize how you will interact with students. Plan how you will introduce yourself in your classes, get aquainted with students through school-sponsored events, and serve as a role model.

Summary

The planning that you do before school starts will pay handsome dividends. If you start planning a month or more before that first bell, using the tips we've provided in this chapter, you will feel much more in control of your classroom situation, and your students will also have a better sense of your expectations. You will also find that you are helping students learn at their potential, and your teaching will be much more pleasurable.

R E F E R E N C E S

Adams, R. S., & Biddle, B. J. (1970). *Realities of teaching: Explorations with video tape.* New York: Holt, Rinehart and Winston.

Anderson, L. W. (1989). *The effective teacher.* New York: Random House.

Bellon, J. J., Bellon, E. C., & Blank, M. A. (1992). *Teaching from a research base.* New York: Merrill.

Borich, G. D. (1992). *Effective teaching methods* (2nd ed.). New York: Merrill.

Cruickshank, D. R., Bainer, D., & Metcalf, K. (1995). *The act of teaching.* New York: McGraw-Hill.

DiGiulio, R. (1995). *Positive classroom management.* Thousand Oaks, CA: Corwin Press.

Dykman, B., & Reis, H. (1979). Personality correlates of classroom seating position. *Journal of Educational Psychology, 71*(3), 346–354.

Emmer, E. T., Evertson, C. M., Clements, B. S., & Worsham, M. E. (1997). *Classroom management for secondary teachers.* Boston: Allyn & Bacon.

Evertson, C. M., & Emmer, E. T. (1982). Effective management at the beginning of the school year in junior high classes. *Journal of Educational Psychology, 74,* 485–498.

Freiberg, H. J., & Driscoll, A. (1992). *Universal teaching strategies.* Boston: Allyn & Bacon.

Musgrave, G. R. (1975). *Individualized instruction.* Boston: Allyn & Bacon.

Schell, L. M., & Burden, P. (1992). *Countdown to the first day of school.* Washington, DC: National Education Association of the United States.

Tuckman, B. W. (1995). The competent teacher. In A. C. Ornstein (ed.), *Teaching: Theory into practice* (pp. 57–75). Boston: Allyn & Bacon.

Tyler, R. W. (1950). *Basic principles of curriculum and instruction.* Chicago: University of Chicago Press.

Walberg, H. (1969). Physical and psychological distance in the classroom. *School Review, 77*(1), 64–70.

Weinstein, C. S. (1996). *Secondary classroom management.* New York: McGraw-Hill.

Weinstein, C. S., & Mignano, A. J., Jr. (1992). *Elementary classroom management: Lessons from research and practice.* New York: McGraw-Hill.

CHAPTER

4 Communication Strategies

A teacher expresses enthusiasm through both nonverbal and verbal communication.

OBJECTIVES

1. List attributes that students like in a teacher.
2. Describe six ways to communicate with students besides talking to them.
3. Explain the significance of the nonverbal message in behavior management.
4. Analyze a communication exchange between a teacher and student to determine whether the teacher's portion of the exchange gives evidence of verbal and nonverbal congruence.
5. Name three characteristics of effective praise.
6. Describe how paraphrasing enhances your listening skills.
7. Use the PPL strategy in your teaching and evaluate its effectiveness.

Can teaching be described as communicating? Although they are not totally synonymous, communication skills are essential to good teaching. As a teacher, you will find yourself communicating with four specific groups on a regular basis: students, parents, school administrators,

ACTIVITY **4.1**

Classroom Climate

Arrange to visit a secondary classroom if you haven't been assigned to visit one by your instructor. Focus on the "climate" of that classroom and the school. What is the feeling tone of the classroom you visited? What are the physical characteristics of the room? For example, observe the bulletin boards, seating arrangements, plants, colors, and student work displayed. What effect does the classroom climate have on students and teachers? How does climate influence classroom management? What message has the teacher sent the students through the room arrangement?

and colleagues. Each of these groups is important in a different way. We will suggest key ideas to help you communicate effectively.

Communicating with Students

For decades researchers have been querying students about teacher behaviors that they like and dislike. The data are amazingly consistent. Students like teachers who possess the attributes listed in Figure 4.1 (Hindle, 1994; Weaver, Wenzlaff, & Cotrell, 1993). In addition, students prefer teachers to be well organized, knowledgeable about their subject, open-minded, and compassionate. Of course, teachers are human, and not all possess all the preceding attributes in equal measure. However, knowing these preferred attributes provides teachers with a set of guidelines to which they can aspire. We especially recommend that you use the preferred teacher attributes as a checklist and consider your own skills. How do you measure up? What steps could you take to strengthen your teaching skills and behaviors related to those attributes? Where do you need further work?

FIGURE 4.1   Attributes Students Prefer in Their Teachers

Students like teachers who

- Are passionate about their work and interests.
- Use a vibrant, animated approach to teaching.
- Are enthusiastic about teaching and inspire kids to work harder.
- Are optimistic that all kids can learn and routinely create multiple opportunities for student success.
- "Pitch the ball where kids can hit it" so that kids can be successful.
- Offer up-to-date, relevant materials beyond the textbook.
- Respect students as human beings and are interested in students' lives outside the classroom.
- Have clear ground rules and expectations that are "tough but fair."
- Are approachable and make the classroom safe and supportive.

Modes of Communication

As you work with your students, you'll quickly realize that there are multiple communication avenues (modes) available to you. Examples include arrangement of furniture in the classroom, location of your teacher's desk, materials on the bulletin boards, use of color to decorate, lighting, and plants or other unique furnishings. As an example, a math teacher in Harlem furnished her classroom with couches, lamps, and comfortable chairs so that it looked like a living room. What would her classroom arrangement communicate to her students?

Still other communication modes include your physical presence, your movement about the room, your voice, your use of time, the words you speak, and the words you write on the chalkboard, overhead, or on handouts.

Of these various modes of communication, the most prevalent form in the secondary classroom is clearly the spoken word. Studies show that secondary teachers talk about 70 percent of the time. Because verbal communication is so prevalent, teachers should carefully consider use of the spoken word as a mode of classroom communication. Several communication pitfalls and appropriate communication strategies for teachers will be described.

Explicit versus Implicit Language

Think about the teacher who says to her students: "Open your book to page 25." Explicitly, the students are being told to turn to a specific page. Implicitly, however, the teacher probably expects the students to do much more. The teacher may be announcing today's topic. Or the statement may be made to admonish a small group of inattentive students to pay closer attention. Finally, the command may be a signal that the class is about to move from one activity to a new one.

As the students open their books to the appropriate page, they too are communicating both explicit and implicit messages. Explicitly, they are complying with the teacher's request. Implicitly, they are communicating a readiness to begin the lesson, a willingness to follow the teacher's directives, and an acceptance of the teacher's authority to direct whatever event will follow. The teacher and students send each other hundreds of messages each day; these messages help establish the class norms for activity and acceptable classroom behavior.

Messages that the teacher believes to be explicit often are not, however. Puro and Bloome (1987) provide an interesting example of a message that the teacher thought was explicit but that was interpreted quite differently by one student. In the example they provide, students were asked to write their names on a lined sheet of paper five times for a class activity. One student, Charles, carefully printed the letter *C* five times in a vertical column. He then placed another column of the letter *h* five times to the right of the *C* column. He then printed the letter *a* five times, and so forth, until he had his name written five times on the paper.

The teacher was, of course, then confronted with a dilemma. Should she accept Charles's list of five names? Should she clarify her request? Whatever her response to the situation, it becomes a message back to Charles. If she accepts his paper, she is suggesting to him that the product (the names on the paper five times) is more important than the process by which he wrote his name. The teacher must ask herself, "Is this the message I wanted to send to my students?" Only she can answer the question.

ACTIVITY **4.2**

Collecting Data Regarding Your Classroom Interactions (Classroom Talk)

Collecting data regarding the nature of the verbal interactions (talk) in your classroom is a useful activity. You will be able to get a much clearer picture of the interactions taking place in your classroom—including your own talk. The following is a combined observation and coding activity. It is a modified and shorter version of the ten-point scale for measuring classroom interaction developed by Flanders (1960).

Categories
O = silence or confusion
I = inappropriate student talk
C = constructive student talk
T = teacher tells students (lectures, instructs, etc.)
R = rejecting behavior of teacher (sarcasm, criticism, negative comments)
A = accepting behavior of teacher (positive verbal language such as praise, encouraging remarks)
Q = questioning strategies—two categories
    Q1 = narrow question eliciting a short answer
    Q2 = broad questions eliciting longer responses

Recommended Data Gathering Procedures
1. Prepare a table for observation and tabulate as illustrated.

Category of Talk	Tally of Frequency	Total
O		
I		
C		
T		
R		
A		
Q1		
Q2		
		Total

2. Enter a code every four seconds for a minimum of twenty minutes. You may want to enter an observation for more than one category. If there is a definite change of category during the four-second interval, mark both categories. However, there will be few of these. *Caution:* You must practice before you can become proficient in recording the fifteen observations per minute. Also, do not try to record during inappropriate activities (e.g., small groups, cooperative learning activities, etc.)
3. Add the marks for each category to arrive at the total for the observation period.

4. Calculate the percentage of:
   a. Teacher talk: T + R + A + Q1 + Q2 = Total
   b. Student talk: I + C = Total
   c. Direct influence: T + R = Total
   d. Indirect influence: A + Q1 + Q2 = Total
5. Calculate the ratio of Q1 to Q2.
6. Calculate the I/D ratio (indirect to direct): (A + Q1 + Q2)/(T + R)

There is no right or wrong way to teach. However, the higher the I/D ratio, the better, especially in the early stages of a class when you are planning, discussing, and explaining new materials.

Analysis
After calculating the I/D ratio, decide who dominated the verbal interaction. What does the ratio of Q1 to Q2 questions indicate to you? Explain how verbal interaction relates to classroom management.

Secondary teachers often ask students whether they have questions about the material just discussed. What appears to be a simple, straightforward question can be asked in at least three distinct ways, each communicating a different message. First, the teacher may say, "What questions do you have about this material?" Implicit in the teacher's question is a message suggesting the teacher expects students to have questions. The teacher may, however, phrase her question in a different manner such as, "Do you have any questions?" In this instance the implicit message is that the teacher is noncommittal regarding the desirability of questions. The message suggests that although questions are acceptable, they aren't necessarily expected. Quite likely such a noncommittal phrasing will result in fewer clarifying questions than the first example. Finally, to make an obvious point, the teacher might ask, "You don't have any questions, do you?" That, of course, would signal to the students that the teacher doesn't welcome any follow-up questions.

Communicating your intent to students with as little ambiguity as possible should be your goal. Think carefully about the messages you send your students and use language that clearly conveys the message you want to transmit. If there is something specific you want to communicate, only an explicit message will ensure that the students understand your intentions.

ACTIVITY **4.3**

Types of Questions Asked

Make a tape recording of one of your typical classes. After class analyze the recording. Did you invite questions from your students? Did you turn off your students and send them implicit messages that you'd rather not have questions asked? Did you answer their questions? How many students asked questions?

Using Supportive or Extending Language

Secondary teachers often want their students to engage in thoughtful discussion regarding the subject being taught. Eliciting such discussion can be difficult. Such discussions do not always occur without teacher prompting. Supportive or extending language can be helpful. For example, suppose a social studies class is discussing the concept of separation of powers at the federal level. Let's assume that the teacher asks for the students to define the term. Several students may volunteer a response. Let's suppose that the teacher calls on Marvin, who gives a partial definition. By using supportive language, the teacher can raise the discussion to the next level with a more complete definition of the concept, separation of powers. The teacher might say something like: "Marvin has given us a good start on a definition of separation of powers. Jean, can you add other points that help define the concept?" From this point, the teacher might ask the class for practical implications of separation of powers. The supportive or extending language in this instance serves two distinct and important purposes. First, it acknowledges Marvin's contribution to the class's efforts and thereby encourages him to respond again at a future time. Marvin was not told that he was wrong, nor was he ridiculed for his less-than-perfect response. Second, the extending language moves the discussion forward to more fully explore the definition of separation of powers and to other follow-up points that the teacher wishes to include in the day's lesson. Supportive or extending language is a significant tool for teachers to use in communicating with students.

Using Polite Language

Teachers often give directives to students that are, in effect, implicit commands. The teacher asks the student to do something, expecting the student to comply without question. For example, a teacher might want the classroom door closed because of noise levels coming from the hall, but she is busy working directly with an individual student, and it is neither convenient nor appropriate to stop what she is doing. In such an instance, the teacher may say, "Jerry, would you please shut the door?" The teacher is not expecting Jerry to answer with a verbal response. She doesn't intend it as a question. She has given an implicit command to Jerry, who is seated near the door. He is expected to get up, close the door, and then return to his seat with minimal disruption. After Jerry has returned to his seat, the teacher then follows with a "thank you," and Jerry resumes his participation in the class activity.

Use of "please" and "thank you" when asking students to carry out routine acts seems simple. Unfortunately, however, many teachers fail to use such polite forms of language when making requests or giving directions. As a result, simple directives sound as though

ACTIVITY **4.4**

Use of Polite Forms of Language

Tape record one of your typical classes. After class, listen to the recording and tally the number of times you used "please" or "thank you" during class. Then go back and record the number of times you didn't use these polite expressions when such expressions might have been appropriate. How did you measure up?

the teacher is talking to a family pet rather than another human. Polite language is a very powerful tool and will produce wonders if used routinely. Teachers who use polite expressions signal the class that they respect the students and appreciate their help. Furthermore, such expressions help create a community of learners as we've suggested in Chapter 1, Social and Educational Contexts. Duane Obermier (1999), former Nebraska teacher of the year, gives some good advice to help beginning teachers earn the respect of future students.

> I firmly believe in treating students like fellow human beings who have feelings just like I do. They don't appreciate being embarrassed, or humiliated, or confronted with problems in front of their peers. But they do respond to kindness, encouragement, a friendly tease, and a smile. I try to teach manners in the classroom by being mannerly. "John, I never interrupt you when you are speaking. Please don't interrupt me." (p. 1)

Using Inclusive Language

A secondary teacher might well be heard declaring, "In my classroom I expect you to . . ." thereby declaring class ownership. Although laudable in that it indicates that the teacher assumes responsibility for the class, such language is counterproductive. It suggests that the class problems are the teacher's problems rather than mutual problems or problems that belong to the student. A preferable language style, when describing norms of the class, is to state, "In this class, we. . . ." Such inclusive language suggests that the teacher sees the students as partners rather than subordinates. The statement implies that both the teacher and students share common responsibilities. Furthermore, it implies that solutions will be found through joint decision making rather than in action taken by the teacher alone. Teachers who cultivate the habit of using inclusive language, such as "our class," "we," "us," will be sending a powerful message. Although the comment may be directed toward one student, it is implicitly a statement to all.

Use of Praise

Great job! Wonderful! Super! You're great! The role of praise in teaching is widely discussed by educational writers (Burden, 1995; Good & Brophy, 1994; Jones & Jones, 1995; McIntyre & O'Hair, 1996). Contrary to common belief, praise is not always a positive act in the classroom. It can lead to problems if used inappropriately. For example, effusive praise can be embarrassing to the student, whereas praise of only a few students can lead others to believe that their actions are unappreciated. Then, too, students who are praised too frequently may grow to depend on it—even to demand it. At other times, students may think that the teacher does not really understand them or is not listening because the praise does not match the perceived actions of the teacher.

Praise, Prompt, and Leave (PPL)

SCENARIO 4.1 ■ Students Who Demand Too Much

In his biology class, Harry has two students who consistently ask for help following his demonstrations in class. The students seem to always want his help even before they have attempted the lab assignments. Harry has just completed a class demonstration on photosynthesis and has assigned the students the task of developing a definition for the term *photosynthesis*. Sarah, one of the students, has asked him to assist her with the seatwork.

One popular approach to the use of praise was developed by Fred Jones (1987), a clinical psychologist. Jones's approach is particularly appropriate in situations in which the students are assigned seatwork to complete after seeing a demonstration. Jones's Praise, Prompt, and Leave (PPL) process is described next.

Praise.   Most teachers define praise as saying something positive about students, their work, or their contributions. In the preceding scenario, Harry, as he is monitoring the students' seatwork, might say to Sarah, "Good, Sarah, you've got the right idea." In the PPL approach the teacher must go one step further and tell Sarah why the work that she has done is appropriate. Jones's idea of praise is to focus on the completed seatwork, identify characteristics within it that are correct, call attention specifically to the parts that are appropriate, and then praise that portion of the student's work.

Many teachers, by habit, focus on what is wrong or missing rather than what is right. They want the students to get the whole picture. Jones suggests that teachers focus on the portion of the student's work that coincides with the end product (in this case, the definition of photosynthesis) and praise that work. Harry might say, "Good, Sarah, you have the right idea. So far in your response you've identified two attributes that underlie the definition of photosynthesis we learned today." To reiterate, if the definition had three components and the student identified only two parts, the teacher should ignore the one that the student missed and call attention to the two correct responses. After praise, which consists of review of both the task and appropriate responses, the teacher then gives the student a prompt for further direction.

Prompt.   A prompt is a clear and concise verbal statement that tells the student what to do next. Teachers frequently tend to help the student complete the assignment rather than focus on only the next step. However, skipping steps necessary to complete the task may lead to confusion in the student's mind and may eliminate the opportunity for students to finish the task independently. To be an effective prompter, the teacher must keep it short and simple and communicate the next steps clearly and concisely. Harry's goal should be to help Sarah determine what intermediate steps are necessary to fulfill the assignment. A comment such as "You might check the ideas on page three in your text" may follow the praise.

Leave.   Leaving, a difficult step for many teachers, requires that teachers move away from the student as soon as the prompt has been delivered so that the student can complete the task without assistance. Jones (1987) insists that the entire PPL process be delivered in a ten- to thirty-second contact between the teacher and student. Those teachers who find it impossible to leave often reteach the entire lesson rather than insist that students use the information to analyze, evaluate, and solve problems independently.

Often the teacher literally does the student's work. Jones describes the typical teacher–student interaction this way: "I got to help Sarah, and I feel good that I was able to give her the help she needed." Sarah, on the other hand, may still not understand the point of the assignment and may be left thinking, "I still can't do this assignment, even though the teacher helped me. I really must be slow" (p. 53). The PPL strategy requires that teachers break their mindsets and encourage students to do their own work—as opposed to the teacher doing it for them (McIntyre & O'Hair, 1996). We strongly suggest that you try the PPL approach the next time you assign monitored work. You may be surprised at how well the process works.

Summary of the PPL Formula

The teacher does the following:

- Tells the student exactly what was done right (praises).
- Tells the student exactly what is expected next (prompts).
- Turns and walks away rather than staying to see that the student carries out the instructions (leaves).

General Forms of Praise

Teachers use praise frequently to motivate students to work harder, enhance their self-esteem, and be supportive. Effective praise has three key characteristics (Jones & Jones, 1995; O'Leary & O'Leary, 1977):

1. *Contingency.* Praise should immediately follow desired (specific) behaviors rather than be a generalized comment such as "good."
2. *Specificity.* Praise should describe the desired (specific) behavior rather than generalized to all behavior.
3. *Credibility.* Praise should be appropriate for the situation and the individual to whom it is directed. Highly motivated students may find generalized praise insincere or even insulting.

Systematic and appropriate praise improves student behavior. It helps students know that their efforts and progress are recognized and appreciated. Guidelines for effective praise are listed in Figure 4.2 (Burden, 1995; Good & Brophy, 1994).

I-Messages versus You-Messages

Teachers often respond to inappropriate student behavior. When doing so, it is very tempting to identify the student who is responsible for the immediate problem and confront that individual. Gordon (1974), in his best-selling book, *T.E.T.: Teacher Effectiveness Training,* notes

---

ACTIVITY **4.5**

Giving Praise

Pair with a student sitting next to you and give the individual specific praise, for example, for paying attention in class, having the assignment completed, or helping you define a critical term in the day's lesson. Your partner can then do the same for you. Discuss your praise giving in terms of the three characteristics identified.

FIGURE 4.2   Guidelines for Effective Praise

Effective praise:

- Works best when it is delivered as a spontaneous reaction to student accomplishments rather than as a calculated attempt to manipulate students.
- Should be simple and direct, delivered in a normal voice—without gushing or theatrics.
- Should usually be made in straightforward declarative sentences ("That's interesting; I never knew that" or "That's well done!") instead of flowery exclamations ("Wonderful") or rhetorical questions ("Isn't that great?"). Flowery exclamations or rhetorical questions are effective only if used judiciously.
- Specifies the accomplishment being praised and recognizes any noteworthy effort, care, or persistence by the student ("Good, you stayed with it and now you've made the connection between the two terms").
- Uses a variety of phrases. Avoids overuse of phrases such as "good."
- Backs verbal praise with nonverbal behaviors such as a touch on the *back of the student's shoulder,* a smile, or a tone of voice that projects warmth and interest. Touching students should be used very cautiously in today's secondary classrooms. Do so only if you have a solid, ongoing relationship established with the student.
- Avoids ambiguous statements such as "You were really good today." Relate the praise to the specific actions of the student ("When you read that last passage, you made me feel like I was there").
- Is made privately to individuals in most instances. Public praise sometimes embarrasses secondary school students. At times, praise the entire class rather than a few individuals.

that teachers, in such situations, often resort to put-down messages that inevitably begin with "You. . . ." Such messages can be classified into six categories.

1. Judging, criticizing, disagreeing, blaming: "You're always picking on someone in this class."
2. Name-calling, stereotyping, ridiculing: "You're acting childish today."
3. Interpreting, analyzing, diagnosing: "You always seem to need attention."
4. Praising, agreeing, giving positive evaluations: "When you work hard, you're a good student."
5. Reassuring, sympathizing, supporting: "I know you got home late last night because of the game and didn't have time to do your homework."
6. Probing, questioning, interrogating: "How do you expect to pass this course when you're absent all the time?"

These six kinds of teacher messages, even the seemingly positive ones, are heavily loaded with negative judgments and are in effect put-downs. In each case the teacher has made a negative remark and has expressed it with a "you-message." Often the "you" is implied rather than explicitly stated. For example, the teacher might say to a student, on a very hot day, "I know it's hard [for you] to concentrate on a hot day like today." In such an instance, the student hears a quite different message. The student hears, "You're not concentrating like you should," which is a put-down.

Instead of resorting to the you-message, Gordon (1974) and Jones and Jones (1995) urge teachers to confront undesirable student behavior through the use of I-messages. By using I-messages, teachers take responsibility for their own inner discomfort and feelings. I-messages should be used only when the student behavior affects the teacher directly.

Learning to use I-messages isn't easy. To send an effective I-message, the teacher must send the message intentionally with a nonblaming, nonjudgmental description of what is unacceptable. Instead of saying to a student who is continually interrupting the teacher while she is giving directions, "Don't [you] interrupt when I'm giving directions," the teacher might use an I-message as follows: "When I'm interrupted while I'm giving directions, I have a difficult time making the directions clear and I become very frustrated."

Good I-messages have three components. First, they begin with "when." It is important to let students know the specific type of situation that bothers the teacher. Second, I-messages pinpoint the effect the student's action has. The teacher describes the effect of the student's action in a nonjudgmental way. In our preceding example the teacher pinpoints the effect by saying, "I have a difficult time making the directions clear." This is the effect of the student's action and the principal reason for the frustration. The third part of the I-message states the feelings generated within the teacher, because she is the one affected by the action. In the preceding example the comment, "I become very frustrated . . ." identifies the teacher's inner feelings and places the problem where it belongs.

I-messages are effective because they pinpoint the locus of the feelings—within the teacher. Gordon (1974) also argues that I-messages are an effective means of communication for three fundamental reasons. First, they have a high probability of promoting willingness in the student to change. The student isn't attacked or placed on the defensive. Second, I-messages contain minimal negative judgment concerning both the student and the student's actions. The I-message, as noted earlier, places the feelings where they really are—within the teacher. The problem is with the student, but the feelings are with the teacher. Finally, I-messages do not injure the teacher–student relationship because the student is not put down.

Teacher Effectiveness Training (TET) is, however, a problem-solving process. For it to be effective the teacher must be a good, active listener capable of encouraging students to think about their behavior and identify ways to change. Six steps are part of the problem-solving process. As a teacher you should help students:

1. Define the problem.
2. Generate possible solutions.
3. Evaluate the merits of the various solutions.
4. Decide which solution will work best.
5. Implement the solution selected.
6. Assess the success of the solution in solving the problem.

For most students the process will be new; few will have been asked to help define appropriate behavior. Teachers should not only practice problem-solving techniques but also should teach their students to use these steps.

Listening

Listening is the most important factor in developing a good rapport with students. The primary goal of good listening skills is to help students express their real concerns, needs, and wants. Only through listening can teachers establish the kind of dialogue needed for effective communication. Often the student may simply request information, clarification of directions, or permission to leave the room. In such instances it is appropriate to respond in a direct,

ACTIVITY **4.6**

What's Your Problem?

Think of a problem you are having. It may relate to your personal life (I want to lose ten pounds) or your school (I want all students to be seated when the tardy bell rings). Use Dewey's problem-solving steps, as outlined by Gordon, to write a contract.

A Contract with Myself

My goal is _____

_____

Possible solutions are _____

_____

The best solution for me is _____

_____

I will implement this solution _____

_____

I will evaluate my success on _____

(Date)

Signature _____

forthright manner. At other times, however, the student's message masks a concern that isn't being stated and, thus, cannot be simply answered by the teacher. Students may express their emotions, confusion about life, or frustrations about an assignment. Often these student messages are masked by general, angry outbursts such as: "I hate this class!" or "I hate you!" In these instances, discovering the real problem requires empathy and nonevaluative responses.

Paraphrasing, or active listening, as Gordon (1974) called it, is also a very useful technique with several benefits (Jones & Jones, 1995). Most importantly, students learn that their feelings are accepted. This, in turn, reduces the tension and anxiety that students experience when trying to mask their true feelings. Second, students feel more accepted. Third, students are much less likely to act out their frustrations through inappropriate or unproductive behavior. Finally, teachers who listen with a nonevaluative attitude provide students with an opportunity to examine or clarify confusing and frightening feelings.

As suggested in Figure 4.3, good listening skills require more than just listening to the student. It is the teacher's role to hear what the student is saying, accept the feelings expressed, and understand that the anger and its intensity are transitory and rarely reflect the actual problem. The teacher must want to help the student find an acceptable solution.

Teachers often react to the idea of active listening by arguing that they are not counselors or that the process takes too much time. To some degree these arguments are valid. Class time is precious, and conscientious teachers try not to waste it. However, active listening is a powerful tool. By following the suggestions in Figure 4.4, teachers can use paraphrasing to help students solve their own problems. Teachers who teach this skill often report

FIGURE 4.3 Listening Skills

In discussing effective cooperative learning, Johnson and Johnson (1991) suggest seven specific listening skills that they urge teachers to consider. Their suggestions apply to all teacher–student communication.

- Clarify and communicate your ideas and feelings; use I-messages when appropriate.
- Make sure your messages are complete and specific.
- Keep your verbal and nonverbal messages congruent.
- Ask for feedback from the students concerning the way in which your messages are being received. Are the students hearing what you thought you said?
- Paraphrase individual student's ideas accurately in a nonevaluative way; try to capture both the student's ideas and feelings.
- Describe your perception of the student's feelings.
- State your interpretation of the student's message; work with the student until there is agreement on the message's meaning.

FIGURE 4.4 Guidelines for Paraphrasing

- Restate the sender's (student) ideas and feelings in your own words rather than using the student's exact words.
- Preface your paraphrase with "You think . . . ," "You are saying . . . ," "You feel that . . . ," and so on.
- Avoid indicating your approval or disapproval.
- Make your nonverbal messages congruent with your verbal paraphrasing. Be attentive, interested, and open to the student's ideas and feelings. Show that you are concentrating on whatever the student is trying to communicate.
- State what you heard the student say as accurately as possible and describe the feelings and attitudes evident in the student's message.
- Do not add or subtract from the student's message.
- Try to understand what the student is feeling and what the message means.

Taken from D. W. Johnson and R. T. Johnson, *Learning Together and Alone* (Boston: Allyn and Bacon, 1991), p. 153.

that it actually saves class time because problems that students experience are more quickly solved. Active listening:

- Helps students resolve strong feelings, thus permitting them to get back to the academic learning processes more quickly.
- Lets students know that it is acceptable to have the emotion they are experiencing and that such feelings are not "bad."
- Facilitates the habit of approaching situations by "talking it through" and applying problem-solving strategies.
- Keeps the responsibility for analyzing and solving the problem with the student.
- Makes students more willing to listen to teachers just as it makes teachers more willing to listen to students.
- Promotes closer, more meaningful relationships between students and teacher.

As a result, students who feel they can turn to teachers when they have emotions or feelings that are interfering with learning will be more willing to attend to the knowledge, concepts, and attitudes that the teacher is trying to teach.

ACTIVITY **4.7**

Active Listening

Go home this evening and practice active listening skills with others in your household. While you're clearing the table, watching TV, or reading the newspaper, stop for a few minutes and ask how a family member's day went. Then, truly listen to the response and paraphrase what the individual said. What was your family member's reaction? Did the loved one act surprised? If so, is it because he or she didn't expect you to really listen? How did you feel about the response you received? Did your efforts seem to open up or close down the lines of communication between you and others at home?

Nonverbal Communication

Imagine a classroom in which students are sitting in rows. Furthermore, imagine that a student sitting in a back seat has just spoken to another student after the teacher asked him to refrain from talking. Imagine also that June, the teacher, has had enough. Frowning, she walks back to the talking student with a purposeful and decisive walk.

Even if June, in the preceding situation, says nothing to the student and continues a verbal dialogue with the class, frowning and walking down the aisle with a firm, purposeful demeanor communicates a clear message. The teacher is using nonverbal communication to reinforce a verbal demand that the student stop talking. The teacher's actions say to the student, "I really meant it when I asked you to stop talking." The walk (nonverbal message) is reinforcing and emphasizing the verbal message. As the example illustrates, nonverbal communication skills are a tool any teacher can use to communicate more effectively. Nonverbal communication includes facial expression, eye movement, gestures, proximics (body movement and positioning), and vocal tone. Aptly named the "silent language" by Hall (1973), nonverbal communication does not involve words to convey meaning.

But beware! Not all cultural groups use the same nonverbal cues to communicate, and it will be easy to misread nonverbal communication in a multicultural class. For example, in the Anglo culture of the United States a student's refusal to look into the eyes of a teacher when responding is a major breach of etiquette and insulting to the teacher, who is likely to interpret the student's action as defiance. In contrast, a Native American student would consider it insulting to look into the teacher's face when responding.

ACTIVITY **4.8**

Nonverbal Communication

Pair with a partner. Practice conveying a nonverbal message by first using only your vocal tone and your partner's name to express key emotions and ideas. Let your partner do the same using your name. Can you ask a question? Express anger? Fear? Other emotions? Then experiment with your facial expressions. Can you express some of those same emotions or ideas through your "teacher look"? How did you instinctively know the "teacher look"?

Congruence

Secondary teachers routinely encode messages into verbal meaning and carefully select words to transmit messages to students. At the same time they engage in a series of nonverbal actions—sometimes quite subtle, other times obvious—which either reinforce or deny the words being transmitted. Congruent messages are messages in which the nonverbal portion of the message reinforces the verbal portion. In the preceding example June's nonverbal message was congruent with her verbal reprimand and message. However, had she not frowned and walked purposefully to the rear of the room, the message would have been less clear. The student might wonder, "Did she really mean it when she told me to stop talking to my neighbor, or can I talk some more?" The student would have received a mixed message if June seemed to forget him and moved on to other teaching tasks without reinforcing her verbal message. When students receive messages in which the verbal and nonverbal messages are not congruent, they believe the nonverbal message to be the correct one.

Congruent nonverbal messages may be thought of as "following through" when the teacher attempts to halt misbehavior.

SCENARIO 4.2 ■ Promises, Promises, Promises

Two middle school teachers, Karen and Sylvia, were talking in the teachers' lounge about the problems they were having with student behavior. Sylvia confessed that she was concerned about one student, Mike, who was not paying attention to her and wouldn't work quietly on his in-class assignments. She lamented, "Even though I threaten to send him to the principal's office, Mike just continues to talk." Karen immediately responded, "I learned very early in my career never to threaten students. I always promise that something will happen. I don't threaten to send students to the office; I promise I'll do so unless the behavior changes."

Karen has made a very important point. It does little good to threaten punishment or consequences for undesirable behavior if there is no follow-through. Sylvia's failure to follow through with promised consequences is a message in itself. Verbally, she has said she'll send Mike to the principal's office. Nonverbally, she has said to Mike, "I said I'd send you to the principal's office, but I really didn't mean it." Mike and every other student in the class who overhears Sylvia's comment will believe her nonverbal message and continue to waste time rather than stop talking and do the in-class assignments.

Furthermore, in Sylvia's situation, experienced teachers know that they should never promise something that they cannot do. For example, if Sylvia's school has a policy that no students are to be sent to the office for disciplinary reasons, she couldn't carry through with her plan. If she doesn't or can't follow through, she is likely to find the student continuing to misbehave. In such a situation, neither threats nor promises are effective as behavior management techniques.

Communicating with Parents

Working effectively with parents demands specialized communication skills and is so important that we have devoted Chapter 7 to the subject. We hope you will give it your attention as it contains vital information.

FIGURE 4.5   Referral Slip

_____

date/time

_____ is referred to you for the following

(name of student)

reason: _____

_____

_____

(teacher)

Communicating with Administrators

Most secondary teachers report to one or more administrators. If you are in a large school, there will likely be a department chairperson or team leader, as well as one or more principals. If you are in a small school, there may be only one administrator, the principal. If you are new to the building or district where you teach, you need to determine the administrative structure. Knowing with whom you need to communicate is the first step in working effectively. As you communicate with your administrators, keep a few simple points in mind.

First, the administrators are there to help you be a more effective teacher. Before school starts, be sure to meet the administrative staff of your school. When behavior problems arise and you need administrative support, you will know to whom you can turn. Often the duties within a school are divided among the administrators, with one specific administrator assuming responsibility for the maintenance of discipline. Is that true in your school? Who is that person? How can you reach that individual in the event of an emergency?

Under what circumstances does your administrator expect you to request help? Are you expected to handle problems in your classroom without the principal's assistance? Must you send a discipline slip with a student if you send someone to the office? Often schools require the use of a referral slip. Does your school use something like the referral slip in Figure 4.5? If it does, be sure to secure some to have on hand when needed. When you use the referral slip, give a specific, objective account of the incident.

Communicating with Your Peers

Getting help from peers is essential for beginning teachers. Several types of assistance may be available including the loan of teaching materials, locating and/or securing classroom furniture or equipment such as an overhead projector or computer, advice on "tried and true" classroom management ideas, and clarification of the occasions when it is appropriate to send students to an administrator.

Many schools ask experienced faculty to serve as mentors. Will your school appoint a mentor for you? If you don't know, contact your department chairperson or principal and request that someone be appointed. Most often mentors are master teachers with several years of experience. They usually teach in the same field and have a classroom that is located in close proximity. Most are teacher-leaders who enjoy helping beginning teachers.

Mentoring programs are based on the premise that beginning teachers go through defined stages of growth to reach professional maturity (Berliner, 1988; Fuller, 1969; Fuller & Brown, 1975; Steffy & Wolfe, 1997). Not only do experienced mentors improve the teaching performance of their new colleagues, but also they increase the retention rate and enhance the personal and professional well-being of the beginning teacher (Alley, Potthoff, Furtwengler, Clark, Kline, & Wojogbeh, 1995; Fox & Singletary, 1986; Huling-Austin, 1989). In addition, mentors are likely to have accumulated teaching materials and to have knowledge of school materials and equipment to which you will have access. They will also be familiar with policies related to classroom management and able to give you advice on the best ways to handle problems. Furthermore, they will know and understand the school's administrators and their preferences for the way you relate to them regarding classroom behavior (Alley et al.; Bombaugh, 1995). For example, mentors can answer the questions we posed earlier. Are you expected to handle your own discipline problems? Can you expect help if you refer students with behavior problems to the principal's office? Does your school have some type of in-school suspension room? What expectations are there for you to contact parents? Every school will have different policies related to these many questions. These are some of the management-related issues you will confront. Your mentor will be familiar with the procedures used.

Summary

Few skills you'll use as a teacher are more important than your communication skills. You'll find ample opportunity to use both verbal and nonverbal skills as you teach. No formula for effective communication exists, but many suggestions for improved communication can be found in educational literature. Some of the more important skills include your ability to engage in congruent verbal and nonverbal communication, using explicit and implicit language, extending language, and polite language. The Praise, Prompt, and Leave and I-message models, also discussed in this chapter, can be especially useful for secondary teachers while monitoring students' work. Plus, listening skills are also essential for communicating effectively with students, parents, and others.

REFERENCES

Alley, R., Potthoff, D., Furtwengler, C. B., Clark, F., Kline, F., & Wojogbeh, D. (1995, Winter). Mentoring beginning teachers: Lessons learned [Monograph]. *Providing Support for Fellows, 2* (pp. 13–40). Washington, DC: Peace Corps Fellows Program.

Berliner, D. (1988). *The development of expertise in pedagogy.* Washington, DC: American Association of Colleges of Teacher Education.

Bombaugh, R. (1995). Coping and growing: Peace Corps fellows in the urban classroom. *Journal of Teacher Education, 46*(1), 35–44.

Burden, P. (1995). *Classroom management and discipline: Methods to facilitate cooperation and instruction.* White Plains, NY: Longman.

Flanders, N. A. (1960). *Interaction analysis in the classroom: A manual for observers.* Ann Arbor: University of Michigan.

Fox, S. M., & Singletary, T. J. (1986). Deductions about supportive induction. *Journal of Teacher Education, 37*(1), 12–15.

Fuller, F. (1969). Concerns of teachers: A developmental conceptualization. *American Educational Research Journal, 6,* 207–226.

Fuller, F., & Brown, O. (1975). Becoming a teacher. In K. Ryan (ed.), *Teacher education: The seventy-fourth year book of the National Society for the Study of Education, Part II* (pp. 25–52). Chicago: University of Chicago Press.

Good, T. L., & Brophy, J. E. (1994). *Looking in classrooms.* New York: Harper Collins.

Gordon, T. (1974). *T.E.T.: Teacher effectiveness training.* New York: Peter H. Wyden.

Hall, E. T. (1973). *The silent language.* Garden City, NY: Anchor Books.

Hindle, D. R. (1994). Coping proactively with middle years students. *Middle School Journal, 25*(3), 31–34.

Huling-Austin, L. (1989). Beginning teacher assistance programs: An overview. In L. Huling-Austin, S. J. Odell, P. Ishler, R. S. Kay, & R. A. Edelfelt (eds.), *Assisting the beginning teachers* (pp. 5–18). Reston, VA: Association of Teacher Educators.

Johnson, D. W., & Johnson, R. T. (1991). *Learning together and alone.* Boston: Allyn & Bacon.

Jones, F. H. (1987). *Positive classroom instruction.* New York: McGraw-Hill.

Jones, V. F., & Jones, L. S. (1995). *Comprehensive classroom management.* Boston: Allyn & Bacon.

McIntyre, D. J., & O'Hair, M. J. (1996). *The reflective roles of the classroom teacher.* Belmont, CA: Wadsworth.

Obermier, D. (1999). A teacher's class. In K. T. Henson and B. F. Eller (eds.), *Educational psychology for effective teaching.* Belmont, CA: Wadsworth.

O'Leary, D., & O'Leary, S. (eds.). (1977). *Classroom management: The successful use of behavior modification* (2nd ed.). New York: Pergamon Press.

Puro, P., & Bloome, D. (1987). Understanding classroom communication. *Theory into Practice, XXVI,* 26–31.

Steffy, B. F., & Wolfe, M. P. (1997). *The life cycle of the career teacher.* West Lafayette, IN: Kappa Delta Pi.

Weaver, R. L., Wenzlaff, S., & Cotrell, H. W. (1993). How do students see master teachers? *Education Digest, 59*(2), 12–15.

5 Starting the Year Right: The First Days

The first few days of a new class set the tone for the rest of the term.

OBJECTIVES

1. Develop a coherent plan for your first day/class.
2. Explain school expectations on the first day of the school year.
3. Devise a management plan for your first class day.
4. Write a plan for day two and those subsequent to it.

Overview

What do I do the first day of school? Will the students like me? Should I start off tough? To whom do I speak if I need help? Am I supposed to have the answers already? Such questions are in the minds of all teachers as the school year begins. This chapter will provide you with a number of concrete tips for starting the year, with special emphasis on your first few class days.

Your first day, even the first few minutes of the first day, will likely set the tone for your entire year (McIntyre & O'Hair, 1996). Next semester you'll either be glad you planned that first day, or you'll wish you had. Unfortunately, your previous training may not have prepared you. The first day of school and your first class occur only once. You get only one chance to do it right. Think of that first day as a unique event in the history of each of your classes. Can you positively respond to the foregoing chapter objectives? If so, you have probably given the first day the kind of attention that we are advocating. If not, you need to. Please note that we are assuming you've followed the steps suggested in Chapter 3 *before* the school year starts.

The Students

In his study of the first day of school, Brooks (1985a) noted that students typically have several fundamental questions. Those questions might be expressed something like this.

1. *Right Room*—Am I in the right room? Is this my class? Are you the teacher?
2. *The Teacher*—Who is this person/teacher? Is this teacher a real human being or Mr. Grouch? Ms. Terminator?
3. *The Self*—Will this teacher care about me and my problems?
4. *Seat Assignment*—Where am I supposed to sit? Can I sit wherever I like? Can I sit by my friends?
5. *Nature of the Course*—What will we be doing? Will it be interesting or will I be bored?
6. *Grading*—How will this teacher evaluate my work? What kind of grades does this teacher give? Will this teacher be fair?
7. *Rules*—What rules does this teacher expect me to follow? What are the consequences if I don't?

As you address the seven preceding points, your first few minutes of class could be much like the following. "Hi! I'm _____ , your eleventh grade history teacher. The bell has rung so please be seated. I'm excited about this year and want to let you know about our class, the topics we will be discussing, the assignments, and the school requirements. Plus, not only do I want to meet each of you, but also I want you to know about me. Therefore, our first activity will be a get-acquainted game. You might be wondering who this person is you've just met. Let me direct your attention to the 'WHO AM I?' bulletin board."

After explaining who you are, your interests, hobbies, family members, pets, and so forth, you can have your students introduce themselves to others in the class or play Student Bingo using handouts with squares related to their interests. See Figure 5.1 for a sample Student Bingo card.

Or you might ask each student to complete an "All About Me" handout (see Figure 5.2) or a "Petals of My Life" design to share with classmates (see Figure 5.3).

A C T I V I T Y **5.1**

Remembering Your First Day of School

Divide into small groups of four or five. Ask everyone to think about their most memorable first day of school. Brainstorm and write on flip chart paper what made the class dynamite or disastrous. What distinguished it from all the others? What does the discussion tell you about your first day of school as a teacher?

FIGURE 5.1 Sample Student Bingo Card

Locate someone in class who has done each of the following and write that individual's name in the square. Fill all the squares, but use each person's name only once. You will have ten minutes to fill as many squares as possible. Winners who complete all the squares within the allotted time will receive a prize.

Someone who has milked a cow	Someone who earned an A in biology	Someone who ate fast food this week	Someone who snores
Someone who writes poetry	Someone who cooks Italian food	Someone who enjoys baseball	Someone who sings
Someone who has four sisters	Someone who has won a trophy	Someone who works after class	Someone who likes cabbage
Someone who plays the piano	Someone who likes to snow ski	Someone who skateboards	Someone who has traveled overseas

FIGURE 5.2 Sample "All About Me" Handout

All About Me

Name _____

Please complete the following statements. Then put the sheets on the bulletin board or around the room.

1. My favorite _____ .
2. If only I had _____ .
3. College courses _____ .
4. Classroom management is _____ .
5. My dream would be to _____ .
6. I can't wait until _____ .
7. Students should _____ .
8. Most people would say that I am _____ .
9. I really think that I am _____ .
10. Our leaders should _____ .
11. My first class will _____ .
12. I think teachers should _____ .
13. Textbooks are _____ .
14. What matters most to me is _____ .
15. Life is _____ .
16. My family is _____ .
17. No one knows that _____ .
18. My best friend is _____ .
19. My favorite place is _____ .
20. What I want from this class is _____ .

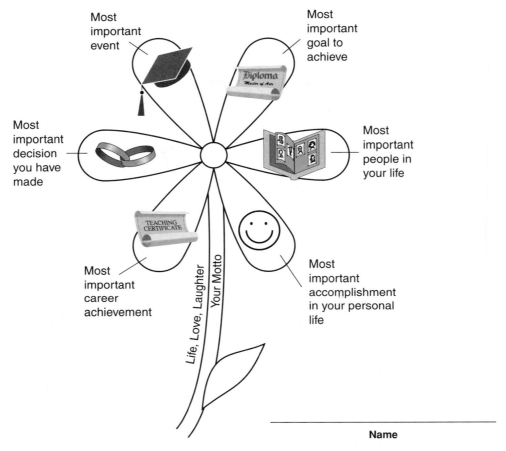

Most
important
event

Most
important
goal to
achieve

Most
important
decision
you have
made

Most
important
people in
your life

Most
important
career
achievement

Life, Love, Laughter   Your Motto

Most
important
accomplishment
in your personal
life

Name

FIGURE 5.3   Petals of My Life

By answering the fundamental questions identified by Brooks (1985b), you not only ease the students' minds, but also provide a structure to use during your first day of class. Emphasizing key management and procedural points that meet both student and teacher needs can be accomplished with careful planning. Resolving student uncertainties should be your highest priority for day one.

In the early 1980s Evertson and Emmer (1982a; 1982b) found that effective junior high teachers develop procedures and teach students how to act with regard to four general areas. Since then, others (Jones & Jones, 1995; Weinstein, 1996) have reaffirmed the Evertson and Emmer study. The four general areas identified are as follows:

1. Beginning the class
2. Whole-class activities
3. Academic accountability
4. Others, such as the end of the class, interruptions to the class, and fire drills

Assuming that you've prepared as suggested in Chapter 3, you are now ready to focus on the detailed planning necessary to ensure a successful first day. *Remember: Careful planning makes your vision about your class a reality.*

Planning for classes is very idiosyncratic; each experienced teacher has a preferred process. Some always put detailed plans in writing. Others operate with no written plans, seemingly "off the top of their heads." As a consequence, neophyte teachers are sometimes misled into believing that experienced teachers don't do any planning because they see little tangible evidence. Nothing, however, could be further from the truth; all teachers prepare for their classes. Excellent teachers spend considerable time getting ready—and usually have written plans that encompass both the content to be covered and the intended methodology. We suggest that you not only carefully prepare for your first class, but also put your plans in writing so that key elements will not be forgotten.

Your First Class

As implied earlier, there is no substitute for detailed planning—especially when preparing for your first day of school. Before you begin, you'll want to have some background information about your teaching situation from your school's administrators. Experienced teachers will doubtlessly have thought of these questions. Beginning teachers will find the following four questions particularly pertinent. All teachers, however, need answers to them.

How long will the class periods be on the first day? When you know the answer, you can plan your first day. In today's secondary schools, class periods may vary from about 40 minutes to as many as 120 minutes. Often, however, first-day classes are considerably shortened—sometimes to as few as 20 or 30 minutes. Nothing is more frustrating than planning for an hour class and finding you have only a half-hour to cover the key points that you had planned. On the other hand, you don't want to plan for a half-hour class only to find that the class will run 50 minutes. Trying to "fill" a 50-minute period when you planned for 30 minutes can make you look as though you hadn't planned at all. Avoid this dilemma.

Will an all-school assembly be held to discuss general school rules? Or will this discussion be your responsibility? Some administrators start the year with an all-school assembly to welcome the students and to remind them of the school's behavioral and procedural expectations. Other administrators will expect homeroom teachers to discuss the general school rules, leaving you to discuss only your own classroom rules and procedures that differ from or supplement the school's rules. Will you be responsible for a homeroom? The schedule your school uses for the first day will be critical to your planning effort.

A note of caution! Even if you don't agree with the school rules, plan to enforce them just like your own class rules (Weinstein, 1996). To do otherwise sends mixed messages to your students and leaves them wondering which rules you expect them to follow. Most contracts require teachers to abide by school policies. You may be very clear, in your mind, about which rules are your own and which are general school rules. That doesn't guarantee that your students are quite so clear. If rules are important, the teacher must clearly stress their importance. Avoid playing "guess what's in my rule book" games with your students; be clear and specific. Plus, you need to teach rules (Emmer, Evertson, Clements, & Worsham, 1997; Evertson & Emmer, 1982b) rather than reading a laundry list of do's and don'ts. When you teach math, you don't simply state that $2 + 2 = 4$ and then move to the next concept. You need to plan how you will teach your rules and procedures (expectations) and explain the reasons behind them.

One teacher's classroom procedures called for her students to push their chairs under the tables before leaving class. She explained the rule's purpose to her students this way. If she has six classes each day, and after each class period she spends five minutes straightening the classroom to get ready for the next class, she will spend thirty minutes of each day pushing chairs. A typical school year is approximately 180 days. If she teaches for twenty years, how much time will she spend pushing in chairs if students do not follow her rule? Calculate the time:

> 6 classes
> × 5 minutes
> 30 minutes per day
> × 180 days per year
> × 20 years
> TOO MUCH TIME!

Will you have all or only some of your students in class the first day? Many schools start with only the new students (perhaps the ninth graders) on the first day—believing that orienting them to the school demands special attention. In these schools, other students begin on the second day. What students will be there obviously influences what you teach. Will you have mixed grade classes, or will you teach only one grade? Having mixed grade classes, such as ninth and tenth graders, with only some of them expected to attend on the first day of classes, calls for special planning.

What will you emphasize on the first day and what will you hold in reserve for later? Some school and classroom rules or procedures are best discussed directly and specifically at the beginning; others are better left to the context in which they apply. For example, how will you ask your students to hand in papers? This question is better left to the time when the first paper is due so that students can practice your procedure. On the other hand, your classroom entry procedures should be addressed immediately so that students follow established practice at the outset. Determining which procedures are essential the first day calls for thought before school begins. Once you have answers to the preceding questions, you are ready to move forward with your planning.

ACTIVITY 5.2

What Are the Rules? Rules for Your Class

Think of a rule (expectation) you would want your students to follow. State the rule in a positive form (for example, "Please push your chair under the table before you leave class," not "Don't leave class without pushing your chair under the table"). Now decide how you will teach that rule and explain its purpose to your class. Work with a peer to improve your rule and statement of purpose. Have the peer answer the following questions. Was it clearly stated? Specific? Stated in a positive way—avoiding *no* and *not?* Did the purpose make sense?

ACTIVITY **5.3**

Activities for Beginning the School Year

Using the following list, plan what you want to do during the first days. Ask your mentor or a peer to read the list and suggest activities you might have missed. Finally, divide the activities into two lists, those you will carry out the first day and those you'll save for later.

1. **Beginning the class**
   The roll
   > Absent students
   > Tardy students
   Expected behavior during announcements
   Distributing homework, instructional materials, or equipment
   > Textbook checkout
   > Supplemental texts and materials
   > Returning homework
   > Handout or other learning materials
2. **Activities during instruction**
   Focus activities at the beginning of class
   Teacher–student contacts
   Student movement about the room
   Signals for getting the students' attention
   Student signals for getting your attention
   Format of papers to be handed in
   > Headings
   > Location of name
   > Folding or stapling of papers
   Student talk during seatwork
   Activities to do when assigned work is completed
3. **Ending the class**
   Putting away supplies, materials, and equipment
   Organizing equipment and materials for the next class to enter the room
   Dismissal of the class
4. **Other**
   Student rules regarding the teacher's desk
   Food and drinks in the classroom
   Fire and tornado drills
   Lunch procedures
   Bathroom and locker passes

_____

_____

The Plan

Many experienced teachers put key points that they want to emphasize on paper; others do not. Many first-year teachers become nervous the first class day and forget what they planned, especially if it's not written. Unless you're absolutely sure you can remember all the points you want to share, we suggest that, at the very least, you list the key topics on paper to ensure "coverage" of them. To build a successful plan, think through the ideas you wish to transmit, share the major points with the students, and teach your rules. For instance, have the students rehearse or practice the procedures you've decided are important, and insist that students follow them (Evertson & Emmer, 1982b; Jones & Jones, 1995; Weinstein, 1996).

Entry into the Classroom

Although there will be variations based on the answers to the four preceding questions, most teachers should follow this scenario. Before class begins, position yourself near the doorway and greet the students as they enter your class. You are signaling the students that you welcome them and are monitoring their behavior. Although standing by the doorway is important, don't focus your entire attention outside the room. Position yourself so that those students who have already walked in are in your sight, knowing that inappropriate behavior such as pushing, shoving, or poking someone with a pencil can be noted. If the undesirable behavior is minor, you may ignore it until you have had a chance to establish your classroom entry policies and rules. If the inappropriate behavior escalates, you may need to attend to the undesirable behavior immediately. You may then indicate the expected behavior and the reason for it. Do *not,* however, assume that behavior problems will occur on the very first day. As suggested earlier, most students will enter your classroom with questions and will not create problems.

Starting the Class

All classes need a specific starting point. The teacher who fails to specifically call the class together on the first day invites random acts that will create difficulty in getting the class started later in the year. Generally, the most appropriate teacher action is to explicitly state, "Please give me your attention so we can get our class started." You want to appear organized and in control of the situation. Your nonverbal behavior at this time is also important. Begin talking further only when all students are quiet and attentive. Never talk over students who are inattentive or chatting. Wait! This beginning point is an appropriate time to clarify the type of behavior you expect as students enter the room. Generally, it is best to insist that they go immediately to their seats as they enter the classroom.

A second important entry issue is that of tardiness. Do the students have to be in their seats as the bell rings, or is it permissible to be just inside the room? Whatever policy you establish on the first day will be challenged by some students on subsequent entries. Therefore, it is generally better to establish your procedures in a minimalist atmosphere. By that we mean, give students little latitude initially. You can become more liberal as the weeks progress. Your tardy policy, like many others, may have schoolwide implications. Is there a school policy related to tardiness? Do the students have sufficient time to make it from one classroom to another? Many of today's secondary schools are so large and crowded that students are forced to scurry from class to class. If no schoolwide tardy policy exists, establish your own. We'd recommend that you make it clear that you expect students to be in their seats when the bell rings. Enforcing the in-your-seat rule for tardiness will minimize the arguments about whether or not the student is on time.

Welcoming Students to Your Classroom

Wong and Wong (1991) believe that it is especially important to start the first class by welcoming students and responding immediately to the uncertainties that Brooks (1985a) identified. Wong and Wong suggest posting in the hall adjacent to your door a sign with your name, the room number, the section or period if appropriate, the grade level or subject, and an appropriate greeting. Stand at the door and individually greet all students as they enter. Somewhere inside the room, write the same information as you posted in the hallway (e.g., your name, room number, and so forth). Then, collectively greet the students and reiterate the same information you had posted. Wong and Wong believe it is important to expose the students to the same information three times to reduce their anxiety and avoid confrontations.

Taking Roll and Establishing a Seating Chart

Virtually all secondary teachers are expected to take roll each class period. Taking roll and creating a seating chart should become your immediate concerns as your first class begins. Here again, local practices vary. Be sure you know what the expected roll-taking policies and procedures are. When will you have a class list of students who should be in your room? Some teachers establish a seating chart before the first class. Then, they can take roll on the first day while announcing the seating pattern to the class. Although many find an alphabetical approach to seat assignments to be the most convenient, teachers need to consider several factors, such as learning styles and disabilities, before assigning seats. Does a particular individual learn best when seated near the front? Does the student have a visual impairment that necessitates being close to the overhead screen? Without first meeting the students and getting to know them, teachers are not aware of their students' specific needs.

To minimize confusion if you are assigning seats, urge students to take any seat on entry into the room. Then make your seat assignments and permit all students to move to the appropriate seats at one time. When making the assignments, it is best to move up and down various rows, pointing to specific seats and announcing the name of the person who will be expected to sit at each. Moving around the periphery of the room will allow you to keep your eyes on the class. It is important to move so that you are establishing a habit for yourself and an expectation for your students that you'll be constantly monitoring their activity. If you expect to change the seating patterns later, this is a good time to indicate so; students will respond more positively to an assigned seat if it is clear that the arrangement is not permanent.

Secondary teachers often use self-selected seat locations as a privilege to be earned through appropriate behavior once the class organization has been established. If you plan to do this, announce it at this time. Still other teachers permit the students to sit where they'd like from the first day, making up a seating chart after class has begun. These teachers usually make it clear that self-selected seating is a privilege that can be lost by inappropriate student behavior.

Student Names

Steve, Jim, Jan, Frances . . . Starting class with a predetermined list of students and learning the students' preferred names, nicknames, and pronunciations is a major step in developing rapport. *Never* make light of someone's name pronunciation or preferred name to cover your embarrassment as you are reading unfamiliar names aloud from your class list. Our names are very important to us; they help establish our identity. Students are no exception. If you have an unusual name, you'll understand what we mean. Before calling roll, make it clear that you intend to call them by their preferred names and to pronounce their names correctly. Point out that you may not say their names correctly the first time, but that you want to learn to pronounce them. As an alternative, you may ask the students to introduce themselves first so that you can hear their preferred names and pronunciations. This technique works well and eliminates embarrassment for both you and your students.

Today's multicultural school environments present us with many opportunities for learning, but they also provide challenges because our mouths don't always pronunce the sounds of other languages easily. There is no shame in being unable to pronounce an unfamiliar name correctly the first time. There is shame in not getting someone's name right after a reasonable time. Practice, practice, practice; there's no substitute.

Working without a Class List

Another scenario that you may face on your first class day is the possibility that you'll not yet have a student roster. In that case, you may want to use 3 × 5 cards. Experienced teachers often find it helpful to distribute 3 × 5 cards and ask students to put certain information on them (Wong & Wong, 1991). Usually, the student's full name and a preferred name or nickname are written on one side of the card along with the parents' names, addresses, and home and work telephone numbers. Even if you have a class list in advance, you may want to have your students complete these cards. It is easier to gather this information on the first day rather than waiting until a problem arises before requesting phone numbers. Personal information such as hobbies, favorite musical group, or the best movie seen lately, is often asked. Or you may ask students to tell you what they want from this class besides an A. Of course, you will want to explain how the information will be used. Why did you ask for this specific piece of information? Did you have a reason?

If the 3 × 5 card approach is used, the seating chart can be made from the cards for the second class day. The cards then also become a convenient way to write special notes to yourself regarding the pronunciation of the students' names, or other pertinent information.

A Word of Caution

If instead of assigning permanent seats, you permit students to remain in the seats they took as they came into your room, you may need to be extra vigilant during your first class. Students will tend to sit near their friends so they can visit with them.

Rules and Procedures

Once the roll-calling issues are settled and seats assigned, you can proceed to your third task— explaining the classroom rules and procedures. Rules and procedures for your class should be viewed as positive guides so that time on tasks can be maximized. You can convey this message as follows: "I am looking forward to working with each of you this year. As we begin, I'd like us to discuss guidelines so that we can function appropriately and enjoy our time together."

Rules versus Procedures

Many teachers like to make a distinction between rules and procedures; others do not. Procedures specify such things as the method by which papers are collected and appropriate times to sharpen pencils. Rules directly state or imply specific do's and don'ts such as: "Be in your seat when the bell rings."

Often teachers prefer to involve students in setting the rules. If you choose to have students participate, and we suggest that you do, inform students that you too are part of the classroom scene and that you have certain rules and procedures that are "minimums" in your mind. Minimums may relate to safety issues, for example. Above all, be honest with your students about your expectations. If you want them to raise their hands, be certain they know that. Beginning teachers should carefully formulate their rules and procedures, share them with the class both orally and in writing via a posted list, explain the significance of each, delineate the consequences of failure to follow the established rules, and send the rules and consequences home to parents. In general, your rules should be: (a) positively stated, (b) few in number (limited to five to seven rules), (c) very public, and (d) accompanied by clearly delineated consequences.

Four Principles for Classroom Rules

Rules should be

1. reasonable and necessary
2. clear and understandable
3. consistent with instructional goals and what we know about how people learn
4. consistent with school rules

(Weinstein, 1996)

Brooks (1985a) describes five categories of procedures and rules that he indentified through his research in the mid-1980s.

1. *Entry:* "Be in your seat when the bell rings."
2. *Interactive:* "Always raise your hand when you wish to talk."
3. *Attention:* "Talk with others in the class with the teacher's permission only."
4. *Exit:* "When the bell rings, remain in your seat until I dismiss you."
5. *Classroom Procedures:* "In this class, sharpening pencils, going to the bathroom, or checking out equipment (procedures will vary with the nature of the class) will be handled in this way."

Stating the rule or procedure is not enough. The effective teacher also explains the "why" in student terms ("Why do we need to follow this rule or procedure?"). Providing a student-centered rationale for the rule or procedure is recommended. Jones and Jones (1995) suggest four basic steps to planning and teaching classroom procedures. These will vary somewhat depending on the students' ages.

1. Discuss the need for the procedure.
2. Solicit student ideas.
3. Have students practice the procedure until it is performed correctly.
4. Reinforce the correct behavior.

Using a nonthreatening tone, effective teachers explain the consequences for breaking rules. Good classroom managers never threaten students. However, giving practical examples of infractions to rules demonstrates to the students that you know how to communicate your expectations. Jones and Jones (1995) also assert that monitoring of rules and procedures at the outset is essential. They suggest that early in the year teachers respond to every violation by asking the student to state the rule or procedure being violated and then to demonstrate appropriate behavior.

Course Content

Introducing course content is another task to consider for the first day. Never assume that students understand your course or even know the nature of the class. A brief course introduction includes answers to the following: Why is this course offered? What can the student expect to learn? Will this course be different from or similar to courses the students have previously taken?

Starting with a puzzling question or thought-provoking demonstration is a good way to elicit interest. In one instance, a chemistry teacher took two beakers filled with liquids to class and mixed them in a third beaker, resulting in a liquid of a startlingly different color. He then asked the students to hypothesize about the reasons for the color change and the nature of the liquids. The teacher then used that inquiry as a springboard to explaining why it is important for students to study chemistry.

The final activity advocated is a preview of the materials needed for the next day and a brief comment about the course content and activities. What materials will they be expected to bring to class on a daily basis? What will they find when they come into the room? Will you have certain materials (handouts) located at a key spot that they'll need to pick up as they enter? How do they turn in homework?

Handing Out the Books

Schools often expect teachers to distribute class textbooks. Sometimes it is simply a matter of checking out the books to individuals and recording the student's name and book number. Other schools require teachers to collect "rental" fees as they check out books. Be sure you know the book distribution system and your role. Check with your mentor, department chairperson, or principal for the specifics regarding the textbook process. Also, you may need to locate the books you'll be distributing. Over the summer break they may have been placed in a storage room somewhere apart from your classroom.

Special forms are sometimes used to check out books to individual students. If no form is provided, you may want to create one for that purpose, or you may use your class list or grade book to record the textbook numbers if your class list is accurate and complete. In any event, you'll want to have the necessary forms. To reduce problems later, you will want to let your students know the replacement policies if they lose a book. What will the book cost if it's lost?

Grading and Grade Books

Experienced teachers usually address grading practices during their first class period. Students want assurances that the teacher will be fair and appreciate their efforts.

The first few days are often chaotic because students' schedules change frequently. Students may be added and removed from your classes. You may want to wait a few days before entering your class roster in your grade book. In fact, some school administrators require all teachers to set up grade books on a certain day. Also, they request that these books be turned in before teachers pick up their last paycheck at the end of the school year. It is a good idea to ask your mentor, other experienced teachers, or your department chair to explain your school's procedures.

ACTIVITY 5.4

Woes and Wonders of Grading

Think of one of your former teachers who used a fair, consistent grading policy. How did that teacher explain the assignments? Did you receive written explanations? Did the teacher use any student suggestions in creating the assignments? Why did you think the grading was fair? Write a two-page journal entry in which you explain how you will make your grading policy clear and fair.

ACTIVITY 5.5

It Isn't Fair!

Discuss the following scenario in class and decide on the best solution. According to Joey's IEP, he is mentally retarded and must receive a modified math test. You have decided that he will complete every other math problem on the test rather than the whole page. While telling Joey what is expected, another student, Pat, overhears your comments and screams out, "This isn't fair! Why does he only do half the work?" All eyes turn toward you. What do you do next?

Content Activities on the First Day

Teachers disagree about the value of content activities on the first day. Some want to send a clear message that class is a work environment, and they involve students in learning activities as soon as possible. Others prefer to wait a day because productive work may not be possible if the students' schedules change or if only a portion of the class is present the first day of school. Length of class also is often a determining factor.

If you decide to use a learning activity the first day, it should be one that will (a) arouse curiosity, (b) involve the students, (c) ensure a high likelihood of student success, and (d) call for whole class participation. Suggestions include a review game to refresh students' memory of the previous year's learning, a short demonstration of a concept that you'll be teaching, or content-related puzzles. The teacher's textbook guide is an excellent place to locate creative ideas.

If you have limited time, you may start an activity and conclude it in the second day's class. If you ask younger students to put something on paper during the first day's activity and they need it on the second day, it is best to collect the unfinished work at the end of class, otherwise they may forget to bring it. Plus, some students may not have lockers. In fact, some schools are no longer assigning lockers or allowing students to carry book bags because of safety issues. Therefore, it's highly unlikely that all students will return the next day with all materials. We recommend the model designed by Mary Bicouvaris (1999), a veteran high school government teacher who never gives up on her students. When they fail to complete or turn in an assignment she gives them zeros. But she'll be looking for that student the next day. She says, "I won't give up until I see the assignment. This tells my students that I'm not going to give up on them either" (Henson & Eller, p. 124).

Use the initial content activity to teach procedures that you want students to follow. For example, if you are giving directions or conducting a demonstration, let the students know what to do if they wish to ask a question. On the other hand, if they are expected to work on an assignment during class, let the students know how to request your help.

Whenever you introduce a new procedure to your classes, explain it and indicate your expectations. List complete procedures, step by step, on the chalkboard, overhead, or computer screen before demonstrating. Finally, when the students engage in the activity, monitor behavior and give immediate feedback—especially positive comments. The very first time students are to hand in class work have them practice the procedure you outlined. Perhaps you will have a box for each class period to turn in work rather than having papers scattered across your desk. Think about the procedure that is most efficient for your particular classes.

Wong and Wong (1991) suggest having an assignment posted on the board or on students' desks as they come into the room. The advantage is that it signals the students that you intend for this class to be a work environment and that there is nothing more important than learning activities, including taking roll and setting up a seating chart. One middle school math teacher divided a portion of the chalkboard into three sections: today's objectives, tomorrow's assignment, and today's warm-up activity. She used bright red tape to divide these three sections. Each day as students entered, even before the bell rang, they began copying the objectives and assignment in their notebooks. Then, they started working on the warm-up activity, which she promptly took up for a grade as soon as she finished checking roll. Students were seldom tardy to her class, and she rarely had discipline problems.

The Intercom

Secondary schools often have an intercom or public address system connecting classrooms with the administrative offices. Furthermore, many schools make daily schoolwide announcements, which often contain activity-related scheduling such as times for tryouts or practice for drama and music activities, cheerleaders, and athletic teams. Club meetings, student council activities, the lunch menu, and congratulations directed to specific student groups or individuals for their successes are also often heard. And sometimes teachers are asked to read bulletins to students, usually during the first hour of school.

Often students are visiting, talking, and generally ignoring announcements. Getting students to listen can be a trying process if not addressed directly at the beginning of the school year. Regardless of whether you are expected to read bulletins to the class or messages are delivered via the intercom, we suggest that one of your classroom practices be that all other class activity stops and everyone, including the teacher, listens carefully. (Remember, you are a role model.) Doing so will enable more students to hear the messages and save you teaching time because you'll have fewer students asking you questions about events or other information.

Ending the Class

The final act of your first day—dismissing the class—needs to be as deliberate as your first act. You may adopt a rule that the students never leave their seats as the bell rings. Rather, they leave when you have verbally dismissed them. There are several reasons for this. If students leave with the bell, they begin getting ready to leave a few seconds earlier each day. By late in the year, several minutes will be wasted each class period because the students quit work, chat, comb their hair, or stack their books in anticipation of leaving. At times, you may wish to distribute handouts as students leave. Therefore, we strongly recommend that you verbally dismiss the students at the end of each class.

Dismissal by the teacher demands two points. First, just prior to the bell, you need to be time conscious and alert the students to get ready to leave on time. You have a professional obligation to allow them to be on time for their next class. Second, you must enforce your dismissal policies. If one or more students leave their seats early, you'll need to firmly remind them that you'll be dismissing them and insist that they be reseated.

Whole Class Activity versus Individual Needs of Students

Although you'll want to meet the individual needs of students, we recommend that you engage the whole class in productive activities on the first day. Devote attention to the total group—especially if you have shortened periods and need to cover a fairly lengthy series of procedures. Simply ask any students who seek your individual attention to be seated and assure them that you'll discuss specific problems when everyone else is attending to the class tasks. Unless it is an emergency situation, delay your attention to the students' problems until the remainder of the class is on task and you feel you can comfortably turn your attention to the needs of individual students.

Students will get into the habit of raising issues immediately upon entering the room if you begin addressing individual concerns before starting whole class activities. Sometimes students use this tactic to get attention or distract you from the day's agenda. Henson and Eller (1999) describe incidents in which students encourage their teachers to discuss "war stories" to minimize the content covered on tests. If possible, resist the temptation to respond to individual students' needs, even if genuine, as they enter the room.

Often on the first day, students will not have materials needed for productive activity. Plan to have whatever the students need available. As suggested earlier, it is usually better to concentrate on helping your students learn whole class and seatwork procedures before trying more complex activities.

Day Two and Beyond

What will you do the second day and beyond? First, identify students who are new to the class. They will need to (a) complete any forms that you asked the class to fill out, (b) be assigned seats, and (c) receive any handouts that you've already given the class. If there are only a few new students, have them first fill out forms or your 3 × 5 cards. As new students are completing forms, you can review the class rules and procedures and reemphasize the daily class routine. You can also check attendance and complete other administrative duties.

On day two, insist that the students follow any rule or procedure outlined the first class day so that you signal to them, quite clearly, that you really meant what you said. Your follow-through is critical to good classroom management for the remainder of the year. To ensure that students understand the rules, some teachers give tests over them. Will an exam on rules and procedures be part of your second-day class meeting?

Summary

Research on classroom management suggests that teachers whose classes are well managed have habits in common. They spend more time providing a rationale for rules, procedures, and activities that they ask their students to follow. In these classes, students are not ordered to act in certain ways. They are firmly and politely *asked* to act in certain ways with a carefully thought-out rationale provided. We suggest that you begin school with a rationale for each of your rules and procedures.

The first few school days are pivotal for both teachers and students. They set the tone for the remainder of the year. Students ask many questions while their teachers are busy organizing and beginning the class. A few of the issues teachers must address as the school year begins include getting to know the students and having them meet one another, identifying rules and procedures, helping students become motivated, checking roll, and establishing seating charts. The procedures you establish in the first few days can be carried out in a positive, friendly, but firm manner. This is the kind of atmosphere you'll want to establish.

REFERENCES

Bicouvaris, M. (1999). A teacher's class. In K. T. Henson & B. F. Eller (eds.), *Educational psychology for effective teaching.* Belmont, CA: Wadsworth.

Brooks, D. M. (1985a). The first day of school. *Educational Leadership, 42*(8), 76–78.

Brooks, D. M. (1985b). The teacher's communicative competence: The first day of school. *Theory into Practice, 24*(1), 63–70.

Emmer, E., Evertson, C. M., Clements, B. S., & Worsham, M. E. (1997). *Classroom management for secondary teachers.* Boston: Allyn & Bacon.

Evertson, C. M., & Emmer, E. T. (1982a). Effective management at the beginning of the school year in junior high classes. *Journal of Educational Psychology, 74,* 485–498.

Evertson, C. M., & Emmer, E. T. (1982b). Preventive classroom management. In D. Duke (ed.), *Helping teachers manage classrooms.* Alexandria, VA: Association for Supervision and Curriculum Development.

Henson, K. T., & Eller, B. F. (1999). *Educational psychology for effective teaching.* Belmont, CA: Wadsworth.

Jones, V. F., & Jones, L. S. (1995). *Comprehensive classroom management.* Boston: Allyn & Bacon.

McIntyre, D. J., & O'Hair, M. J. (1996). *The reflective roles of the classroom teacher.* Belmont, CA: Wadsworth.

Steffy, B. E., & Wolfe, M. P. (1997). *The life cycle of the career teacher.* West Lafayette, IN: Kappa Delta Pi.

Weinstein, C. S. (1996). *Secondary classroom management.* New York: McGraw-Hill.

Wong, H. K. (1972). Dear class, I love you. *Learning, 1*(2), 20–22.

Wong, H. K., & Wong, R. T. (1991). *The first days of school.* Sunnyvale, CA: Author.

6   Managing Instruction

*Organization and planning
are the fundamentals of
successful teaching.*

OBJECTIVES

1. Design a systematic plan for improving your classroom instruction using the current
   knowledge base on teaching and learning.
2. Describe teacher behaviors that unwittingly serve as barriers to student learning.
3. Define such terms as *Premack principle, shaping,* and *fading* and explain how these help or
   hinder learning.

Arnold Grigsby has been teaching ninth grade mathematics and physical science for twenty-five
years. Each morning he arrives to class with his morning newspaper. A close inspection will
reveal that the paper carries today's date and has never been unrolled since the carrier rolled it
up the night before. Mr. Grigsby has a daily routine. Each day he enters the room, puts the newspaper on his desk, and copies the day's classroom assignment on the board. Next, he turns and
faces the class, reading through the roster and recording absences. After checking roll, Mr.
Grigsby bids his students good morning and calls their attention to the assignment on the board.
Like clockwork, he sits down, unfolds his newspaper, and begins reading it from front to back.

Meg Chapman teaches across the hall from Mr. Grigsby. Occasionally, Mr. Grigsby can be seen smiling as he watches Ms. Chapman arrive at her room. She is excited over her lesson. She, too, calls roll and turns immediately to the board. But, instead of giving a seat assignment, she writes three or four daily objectives and calls the students' attention to these objectives. Then the routine in her room ends.

On some days, Ms. Chapman has a simulation game prepared for her students. On others, she uses the case study method. Sometimes she assembles students into small work groups for cooperative learning exercises. At other times she has carefully planned discovery or inquiry lessons.

The student behavior in these two classes differs as sharply as the teacher behavior. Both classes are noisy, but Mr. Grigsby's students are busy arguing and poking at each other, whereas Ms. Chapman's students are working to achieve the three or four clearly stated daily objectives. Ms. Chapman usually circulates throughout the room unobtrusively and helps students. Even when responding to a student's question, it is obvious that she has her eyes and ears focused on the rest of the class.

As you read this chapter, remember these two teachers. Although they are fictional, their prototypes can be found in most schools. In fact, you probably recognize these teachers from your past experiences. Whether you will arrive at school each day like Mr. Grigsby, with the goal of getting through the day, or like Ms. Chapman, with a clearly defined, activity-centered lesson that will excite your students is up to you. A nationwide emphasis on academic accountability makes this chapter most important.

Overview

This chapter focuses on how classroom management is involved directly with improving teaching and learning. We first review how teachers have traditionally behaved and then introduce ways that teachers can act to ensure higher academic achievement among students. As mentioned in Chapter 5, today's teachers are expected to significantly improve the standardized test scores of their students.

Actually, the race to improve has already begun, and the competition to have your students achieve more than other teachers' students is growing. Berliner and Biddle (1997) noted that this country is already full of good teachers. You may be wondering whether you can really make a significant difference in your students' academic performance. The literature is very clear; teachers can and do influence student achievement (Leithwood, Menzie, & Jantzi, 1994).

Using the Knowledge Base

From the time this country was first settled in 1620 until the late nineteenth century, the methods of teaching remained fairly constant. But the late nineteenth and twentieth centuries brought a steady enlightenment regarding how teachers teach and how teaching practices can be altered to raise student achievement. The knowledge on good teaching practices has accumulated, first at a slow pace but during the past few decades at a highly accelerated pace, resulting in a strong knowledge base on teaching and learning (Biddle, Good, & Goodson, 1996; Christensen, 1996). By having an awareness of this information, using it in your classroom, and reflecting on your teaching and its consequences, you can become an expert teacher. An awareness of this knowledge base can empower you to make better decisions (Clark, Hong, & Schoeppach, 1996), if you are willing to reflect on your teaching to steadily improve your craft. Some teachers are afraid of failure and, therefore, refuse to experiment with new methods (Zlatos, 1994) but, throughout their careers, successful teachers reflect on their behavior to improve their teaching (King & Kitchener, 1994).

Enriching the Environment

Effective Teaching Varies

So far, it may appear that we have already answered an age-old question: "Is teaching an art or science?" It may appear that it is not an art at all, but a science because that is exactly what constitutes the work of a scientist: gathering data, examining them, making hypotheses, applying them, reflecting on the results, and drawing conclusions. Effective teachers (those who lead their students to high academic and social achievement) do use these skills, but contemporary educational psychologists inform us that there is an infinite variety of ways that teachers can use the existing knowledge base to improve student learning (Postner & Rudnitsky, 1997). Therefore, teaching is also an art and Steinbeck was right; it may even be the greatest of all arts because the medium is the human mind and spirit.

The importance of your experimenting with new methods cannot be stressed enough. Effective teachers are risk takers. Mistakes are valuable if we reflect on them and improve. Be an experimenter and risk taker. You must if you are to become an expert.

The Importance of Culture

Chapter 1 discussed the practices of many schools today that are developing learning communities. The learning community concept works because definite steps are taken to redefine the school's mission and craft a culture to meet that mission. The classroom should be a microcosm of the school's learning community.

The school has always been a product of its surrounding community, and even the classroom may be considered a miniature model of the school. In the past, however, most classrooms have not had the qualities essential for effecting maximum academic success. For example, teachers in traditional classrooms have relied on threats, punishment, ridicule, failure, and spankings (Krasner, 1976); however, today we know that a pleasant classroom and student achievement are closely related. Furthermore, the use of threats, criticism, and ridicule actually deters student achievement (Berliner, 1990).

You might ask, "How can I make my classroom a more pleasant environment for my students?" The following list offers suggestions.

Enriching the Classroom Environment
1. Examine your perceptions of students and, if necessary, change your perceptions.
2. Think of your students as individuals.
3. Use praise.
4. Issue clear and reasonable academic expectations.
5. Involve students with class work and homework.
6. Use monitoring to keep students on task.
7. Review.

Figure 6.1 shows a sample handout for policies and procedures.

FIGURE 6.1   Class Policies and Procedures

Ms. Christie McWilliams
Mance Park Middle School
Journalism

HELLO!!! Welcome to journalism. Below you will find information on the materials you will need and class policies and procedures.

Materials

Notebook paper	Black and/or blue pens
A notebook for notes and handouts	One computer disk
One spiral notebook (to use as a journal)	One clean manila folder

Grading Policy

Your grade for each six-week period will be determined by the following percentages:

Daily Grades (quizzes, rough drafts, short writing assignments)	40%
Major Grades (journal, tests, final drafts, projects)	60%

Homework

Any homework assigned will be handed in at the beginning of the class period on which it is due unless directed otherwise. Homework should be placed in the appropriate tray. I do *not* accept late daily work. Work turned in late for a major grade will receive a 30-point deduction. PLEASE GET YOUR WORK IN ON TIME!

Make-Up Work

You are responsible for checking the red binder the day you return to class to see what work you missed. If notes were taken, you are responsible for copying those notes from a classmate. Any handouts that you need should be on the counter. Finding out what you missed (and completing all of the work) is YOUR job, not mine. Make-up work should be completed and turned in within *one week* of returning to class.

Extra Credit Opportunities

I always allow opportunities to earn extra credit. For example, I collect mistakes found in newspapers, magazines, and junk mail for the "OOPS" bulletin board. For each mistake you find, I will add one point to a daily grade.

Journals

You are required to keep a journal. Journal assignments will vary. Journals are graded according to these standards:

- Did you complete the assignments?
- Did you freewrite for the entire time period?
- Did you follow directions?

If you write a personal journal entry (limit of two per six weeks), simply fold the page in half and write "personal" across the top. I will not read it, and you will still get credit. Your journal will count as one major grade per grading period.

Rules

1. Be prompt. (Three tardies = detention!)
2. Be prepared.
3. Listen.
4. Be polite.
5. Work quietly.

(continued)

FIGURE 6.1   Continued

Consequences
When you break a rule, you will be given a *verbal warning* and I will document your behavior in the green book. If the behavior does not stop, you will have a *conference* with me. I will call your parents, and you will be assigned a one-hour, after-school detention.

After this, there *must* be an obvious improvement in your behavior. If there is not, you will be sent to the office.

In addition, I like my room kept clean. The last five minutes of every class are spent putting up supplies, straightening desks, and cleaning your area. If I find trash in our classroom (that is not in the trash can) and I know it is yours, you will receive a detention to clean the room.

Rewards
(Individual) If you have not been written up in the green book at the end of a grading period, you will receive a homework pass good for a 100 on a daily assignment.

(Group) If there have been no more than three write-ups in the green book (per class) at the end of a grading period, we can plan a fun activity.

Restroom Passes
Each of you will receive two restroom passes per six weeks. After they have been used, you can forget about going to the bathroom, so save them for emergencies!

Reprinted by permission of Christie McWilliams.

Examine Your Perceptions of Students

Many people criticize students for doing poor work and for lacking commitment when they should understand the obstacles they face (Good, 1996). It is better to expect the best from all students. By focusing on individuals in the class, you will be far less reluctant to stereotype students negatively. Effective teachers feel a sense of responsibility to all students (Jones, 1996).

Use Praise

Most contemporary teachers do not use praise very much in the classroom (Postner & Rudnitsky, 1997). However, when used appropriately, praise makes learning pleasurable (Yelon, 1996). When a teacher praises a student's work, that teacher is showing care, and Shane's studies of the mid-1970s indicated that students' foremost desire was for teachers who really care about them. In addition, the Center for Research's study on the context of secondary schools in the early 1990s found that students carry a recurring message: They want teachers to care about them (Phelan, Davidson, & Cao, 1992).

Help Students Enhance Their Self-Concepts

Chapter 3 discussed the correlation that a sense of self-worth has to academic achievement. In essence, before students can truly succeed, they must feel themselves worthy and capable. One way to help enhance their self-concepts is by ensuring that students' needs are met (Miserandino, 1996). Henson and Eller (1999) offer the following suggestions for helping students improve their self-concepts:

- Avoid hasty judgments about students' self-concepts. Carr and Kurtz-Costes (1994) found that teachers' ratings of students' self-concepts are often wrong.
- Help students find personal meaning in academic studies (Miserandino, 1996).
- Include self-concept activities, not only in special time blocks, but throughout the day.
- Help students set reasonable goals for themselves.
- Teach students to praise themselves. Teachers should serve as models for students by occasionally praising themselves.
- Teach students to praise others.
- Allow teachers to become important people to students.
- Make specific and accurate comments when praising students' work.
- Assign tasks that challenge students and yet are within their ability ranges and give them the autonomy required to complete the tasks.
- Teach students to develop self-evaluation skills and to make realistic self-assessments.

Issue Clear and Reasonable Expectations

Teachers who make their expectations clear can anticipate higher achievement in their classes (Good & Brophy, 1997; Postner & Rudnitsky, 1997). Be careful not to set your expectations either too low or too high. Students often gauge their perceived abilities according to the level their teacher believes them capable of attaining. Conversely, if the goals are set too high, students may discount them automatically. Ideally, teachers should set realistic expectations and systematically move students toward these goals (Yelon, 1996). Studies by Rosenthal and Jacobson (1968) reported that expectations become a self-fulfilling prophecy and that through grading practices teachers may unwittingly help students reach the set level of expectations, but these studies were never verified.

Using Rewards

All people need rewards. Teachers have many ways to use rewards in their classes. One method that has been proven highly effective is a system known as the *Premack principle*. This reward system consists of students being rewarded with pleasurable experiences like listening to music or reading their selection of books or magazines *after* they have achieved the class objectives. In many instances where students have been permitted to earn additional free time, students have doubled or even tripled their rate of working (Jones & Jones, 1995). Students

ACTIVITY **6.1**

Let's Reflect

Examine the ten bulleted suggestions for nurturing students' self-concepts. Now think back to a class that you've enjoyed, a class in which you felt positive about yourself and your performance.

Remember the teacher in this class? If so, what do you remember most clearly about how this teacher treated you? Did your favorite teacher exhibit any or all of the behaviors shown in this ten-item list? Have you considered writing your favorite teacher a thank you note and actually mailing it? Write what you would say to that teacher. Now, find a stamp!

can even learn to reward themselves for academic achievement and, indeed, some educators insist that this should be the goal (Deci & Ryan, 1994).

Involving Students

The major cause of classroom behavior problems is failure to involve students (Glasser, 1990). Research has also found that students learn more when involved. But this is only true if students view what they are studying as relevant (Finn, 1993). Effective teachers plan content and activities that are right for students (Acheson & Gall, 1992). Homework as well as class study time can be used successfully to increase learning. Students prefer homework that they are involved in selecting (Haines, 1990). Have you considered how you will assign homework that is both stimulating and worthwhile? What assignments have worked best for you as a student? Thinking about answers to these questions will help you in determining what homework to give.

Monitoring: Keeping Students on Task

Students score higher on achievement tests when they spend more time on the lesson (Armstrong, Henson, & Savage, 1997). Another way of viewing this is by examining engaged time. Engaged time is the portion of the class hour that students spend actually completing the day's lesson. This implies a special role for teachers in monitoring class activities to ensure that students are staying on task. Postner and Rudnitsky (1997) have emphasized that effective teachers monitor everyone. Teachers often focus attention on the low achievers while ignoring those students who behave appropriately and are involved in academic tasks (Good & Brophy, 1997). These students, too, need praise and reassurance.

One skill used while monitoring students' classroom work is called shaping. *Shaping* is a procedure whereby desired behavior is taught by reinforcing successive approximations of the behavior (Becker, Engleman, & Thomas, 1975). In other words, don't expect those students who have poor work habits to be transformed immediately into good workers. Some students may have experienced so little prior success that you will want to praise them for effort alone, shaping their social behavior, while praising close but inaccurate answers until the accuracy improves to the desired level.

One middle school journalism teacher told us about Isaac, an eighth grade, low-achieving student. For most of the year, Isaac sat passively in class and turned in nothing, which caused him to fail miserably. When the teacher instructed the class to write a personal column over anything they felt strongly about, Isaac decided to vent his frustrations. He began, "Teachers, why do they have to be so mean?"

Although his column was poorly organized and filled with mechanical errors, Isaac earned an A on his paper. He accomplished the goal, to write a column that stirs the reader's emotion. And Isaac was so thrilled that he immediately began to work on a *second* column.

Fading, another helpful skill that keeps students on task and extinguishes misbehavior, is defined as the gradual removal of prompts, cues, or other helpful stimuli for responding. As students gain more confidence in their abilities, they may need fewer prompts to elicit the correct response.

A third method that helps students succeed academically is *questioning.* Teachers use questions while they are instructing large groups and monitoring class work. Unfortunately, they often direct questions to individuals but fail to give the students the wait time or help needed to provide an acceptable answer. The results of this practice are little or no learning (Ellsworth & Sindt, 1994) and often diminished self-concepts. A three- to five-second *wait time* seems like an eternity to most beginning teachers. Yet, students need time to formulate answers. You must practice the timing skill to be proficient. Good and Brophy (1997) recommend that at least 75 percent of teachers' questions should elicit correct responses. Furthermore, Mosston (1972) reminds us that once we direct a question to a student, we are obligated to help that student reach an acceptable answer.

You will also want to include mainly higher-order questions. On the average, a full 95 percent of teachers' questions are lower-level, usually requiring a yes or no response. Asking higher-order questions is easy. Follow up student responses by asking "why?" Not only do you want students to respond, "yes," when you ask whether George Washington was the first U.S. president, but also you want them to tell you "why" he was chosen.

Using Review

Because everyone forgets, it is helpful when teachers review. Yelon (1996) has commented, "Teachers should provide practice in recalling, thinking, performing, and solving problems to enable students to perfect their learning" (p. 3). Avoid reviewing all the information covered; only the most important concepts should be reexamined. By providing students a review sheet, perhaps with all the key concepts identified, you can aid them in preparing for exams. In addition to the sheet, the review game will help you write the test.

Along with reviewing material at the beginning and end of a lesson and at the end of grading periods, the returning of graded assignments is an excellent time to review. At such times, those items frequently answered incorrectly should be the focus.

Direct Instruction

Direct instruction refers to teacher-led learning that begins with a review of the previous lesson, followed by a clear set of objectives and a sequenced set of student activities aimed at helping students grasp specific concepts. When introducing the lesson, the teacher may use a combination of lecture and questions. The questions are carefully chosen to monitor student comprehension. The students are then assigned classroom activities to emphasize the

---

ACTIVITY **6.2**

The Review Game

Have you ever had your students write the test? Ask students to write one multiple-choice, one true-false, one short-answer, and one essay question. When reviewing for the test, take up the questions and pass them out randomly to students. Ask students to answer each other's questions. Then have them find "their teacher" to check their work. Afterward, have all questions returned to you.

One author guarantees her students that she will take one idea from each person in designing the exam. Therefore, her students have part ownership in the test, and few individuals complain. They not only take the test, but also they help create it. Try this approach; it works!

major concepts. During class assignments, the teacher monitors students to ensure that they are completing the assignments correctly, gives immediate feedback to let them know where their thinking is correct, and clarifies the task. Then lessons often end in a review.

Although there are variations of direct instruction, they all have several commonalities. The teacher makes the purposes clear and emphasizes major understandings to be developed. Students are given assignments to perform, and the teacher monitors students' behavior to ensure that they are on task and grasping the major ideas, reviewing at the beginning and ending of each lesson to provide further learning opportunity.

Mastery Learning

Mastery learning, another example of direct instruction, was developed in the early 1960s by a professor at Harvard University. Its originator, Dr. John Carroll (1963), introduced mastery learning in the journal *Teachers College Record*. Carroll believed that almost all students could learn any content well if they were properly motivated and given the time they needed and the opportunity to recycle (confront the material in a variety of ways without penalty).

Mastery learning programs vary. Some are teacher-paced whereas others are student-paced; some are group-based, and others are individually-based. One of the most highly perfected, tested, and successful mastery learning models was developed at the University of Chicago under Dr. Benjamin Bloom's direction. This model is called learning for mastery (LFM). A study of over 3,000 schools using mastery learning over a period of fifteen years found that students learned more in these classes than in traditional ones (Hyman & Cohen, 1979). For instance, in twenty-five studies researchers reported that mastery learning groups outlearned students in traditional classes (Guskey & Gates, 1986).

Other Teaching Strategies

In Chapter 1 we emphasized that teaching is an exciting profession because the main purpose is to help students confront knowledge. And today is an especially exciting time to teach because we now have a strong knowledge base about teaching, a warehouse of concepts that we can use to make our classrooms fertile grounds for learning.

Never before have we known so much about how students are motivated and learn. By having a strong repertoire of teaching strategies, you can use one that is appropriate to meet each lesson's objectives. Some of these strategies include lecture, inquiry, case study, simulations, and projects. Following is a discussion of each of these strategies. As you read about each one, look for its strengths and weaknesses. Pay particular attention to the teacher's role and ways to improve each method.

The Lecture

The lecture is the oldest, most used, and overused of all teaching strategies. A brief lecture can be great to introduce a new topic, summarize major points, and review material. The lecture is a good way to examine material quickly; it lets you give a quick overview.

However, as you know, the lecture can be boring. Poor students like it because it enables them to daydream or sleep. It certainly doesn't do anything to promote creativity or social skills.

You can improve lectures by introducing the lesson with an advance organizer, giving an overview of the lesson to get students mentally focused on the topic, and keeping it brief. In addition, having students apply their skills through activities and then following up with a brief discussion of the major concepts provides more student interaction.

The Inquiry Method

Watching the chemicals bubble in the test tube and trying to figure out the causes, researching how cloning works and debating the issue, analyzing what humans would need to live on other planets—these are inquiry lessons, often called problem solving or discovery learning. Students love this method because it lets them get involved, invites them to discover, and lets them use their creative abilities.

But inquiry learning is not for the teacher who drives in the fast lane, always worrying about covering content as quickly as possible. It's a slow process. You can make inquiry lessons more interesting by encouraging students to explore a variety of possible solutions and involving them in choosing or setting up the problems. Let them know that they are free to hypothesize and that no hypothesis is unreasonable. You can add creativity and social development opportunities to your inquiry lessons by making group assignments and then allowing students to pursue solutions without interference.

The Case Study Method

The case study method, a special type of problem-solving activity, presents a lifelike situation and gives students the facts to solve the problem (Kowalski, Weaver, & Henson, 1994). They are told various information and must choose a route to solve the problem.

Students enjoy case studies because the problems are authentic, and they analyze ways of handling these situations. Students often disagree and argue, and they usually find arguing to be highly motivating. The method also invites students to work together (develop social skills within their group) while competing with other groups.

Two drawbacks are that it's time-consuming and the teacher needs excellent managerial skills. Some teachers assign a case study to run the length of a grading period, which is usually several weeks. Plus, teachers are required to manage the class without interfering with group work. You can improve the case study method by encouraging students to be imaginative and by including superfluous information, which forces students to sift through the pieces and judge the relevance.

Simulations and Games

Let's face it; games are fun, and we never get too old to enjoy them. Take a good game and superimpose it on an authentic (real-life) situation and you have a simulation. Simulations teach students through using a replica of some aspect of the world (Alessi & Trollip, 1991).

Because simulations are exciting, they are also highly motivating. Furthermore, students tend to remember knowledge learned through simulations longer than they remember facts learned from other methods (Lucas, Postma, & Thompson, 1975). Ironically, because simulations are fun, they may cause such problems as noisier classes. However, you can exercise some control through selecting the appropriate classes for this activity and involving the group

ACTIVITY **6.3**

The Case of the Missing Discipline

Divide into groups of four. After reading the scenario, decide how you would handle the situation.

When you were absent one day, you left a lesson plan for the substitute requesting that she take your fourth period, eleventh grade English class to the library so that they could work on their research papers. On arriving at school the next morning, you found a note taped to your desk. It read as follows:

> Dear Ms. _____ ,
>
> I hate to be the bearer of bad news, but your students acted absolutely terrrible today. They exchanged names when I called roll, so I'm not really sure who was in class. Then, they wouldn't behave in the library. For instance, they told me that they couldn't find the right books, so several chatted all period. Also, two boys left ten minutes early, but I'm not sure who they were. Christie and KeKe were so loud that the librarian had to ask them to be quiet three times. She said that this class could not come back again. She wasn't going to babysit a group who didn't know how to behave.
>
> I'm sorry that I had to tell you about the problems, but I thought that you would want to know. I do believe that your class owes me an apology.
>
> Sincerely,
>
> Ms. Angel

When the fourth period class arrived, you were ready to scold them. How could they have acted so immaturely? What were they thinking? But before you could say a word, some of your best students began telling you about the awful substitute they had. She yelled at them to "sit down and shut up" while she checked roll. They exclaimed that she definitely had PMS. Then, she caused more commotion in the library. She constantly told them "no talking" even when they were discussing their research papers. They begged you never to be absent again.

How do you handle the situation? Should the students apologize to the teacher? Librarian? Or should the substitute apologize to the class? How will your students complete their research papers if your class is barred from the library? Should you talk to the principal? What is the best solution? Are you crying at your desk?

---

in choosing and designing the simulation. By giving students the responsibility to create the simulation, you encourage them to display more responsibility and trust in your teaching.

Some of the most effective simulations are modeled after television game shows. Have you considered playing games similar to *Jeopardy!* or *Wheel of Fortune* in your classroom? The teacher and sometimes students identify important content in their class and write questions based on that knowledge. When students help design the game, learning often results.

We encourage you to use some of these innovative teaching strategies. You may find this advice somewhat contradictory—a classroom management book that entices teachers to employ methods that may invite "planned chaos." But remember from Chapter 1 that we believe teachers should be risk takers. Initially, you may have noisier classes because you use

ACTIVITY **6.4**

Effective Teaching Strategies

Following is a list of effective teaching strategies. Use this list and the corresponding spaces to fill in the blanks.

Teaching Method	Strengths	Limitations	Teacher's Role
Lecture	_____	_____	_____
Inquiry	_____	_____	_____
Case Study	_____	_____	_____
Simulations	_____	_____	_____
Projects	_____	_____	_____

Next, try to recall another teaching strategy. List the strategy and the corresponding strengths and weaknesses.

Strategy	Strengths	Weaknesses
_____	_____	_____

Now, explain how you could improve this last method when using it in your class.

---

methods with high student involvement, but we believe that through reflecting on your classroom management strategies, you will learn to redirect inappropriate student behaviors. The risk is worth taking because it leads to increased academic achievement.

Homework

Many teacher education students are unsure whether to give homework assignments because they don't know whether these tasks really help students achieve academically. Studies show that homework usually raises academic achievement (Solomon, 1989). The literature also reveals that although homework tends to increase academic achievement in all subjects and at all middle and high school grade levels, the degree to which it affects achievement varies greatly across grade levels but not across subjects (Cooper, 1990). More specifically, Cooper found that homework does not significantly affect achievement for elementary students. Middle schoolers achieve most when given a total of one to two hours of homework each night. High schoolers seem to achieve more as they get more homework; that is, for high schoolers, the more homework, the better insofar as academic achievement is concerned.

During the late 1990s, the trend has been to give increasingly more homework. From 1986 to 1997, the percentage of parents who reported spending six or more hours a week helping their children with homework rose from 5 percent to 25 percent, a 500 percent increase (Rose, Gallup, & Elam, 1997).

Middle and High School

The teacher's role in giving a homework assignment often determines how effective it is on student achievement. Teachers who give homework must have a clear understanding of the assignment's purpose. Is it to introduce new material or to review previously introduced material? The latter of these two purposes is much more appropriate. Students become confused, discouraged, and frustrated when teachers give unclear or incomplete instructions regarding assignments. Conversely, students may appreciate tasks that enable them to practice skills learned in class.

It is extremely important that teachers check assignments by collecting and grading them immediately. When returning the work, teachers should praise extraordinary responses and review parts that were poorly done, correcting any misunderstandings. Returning homework promptly has advantages. It tells students that you perceive the assignment as important and enables students to learn from the homework while it's fresh. Undoubtedly, you can remember feeling more than a little disappointed when a teacher either returned your paper after you forgot about it or never returned it at all. One middle school student, Morgan, related the story of how she would always remember her seventh grade science teacher. She said that the teacher always knew who turned in what and who didn't and always had papers graded the next day.

Academic Projects

Every teacher is confronted with the possibility of either assigning students required projects or responding to students' requests to do a project, usually to earn extra credit. You can make an informed decision about whether to assign projects and to permit earning extra grade points if you know the strengths and weaknesses of academic projects.

The term *academic projects* is being used because any project that would affect a student's grade would have learning value. We believe that the same criterion should be used to decide whether to permit a student to complete a project for academic credit. To receive your permission, the student should be required to write a good rationale, a statement that convinces you that if permitted to complete this assignment, one outcome would be additional learning.

An evaluation scheme should be used to assess all approved projects. Points given for neatness and appearance should be limited or minimal and determined prior to giving the assignment. Following is one example of a project evaluation instrument.

	Points
Creativity	(0–20)
Appearance	(0–10)
Effort (time and energy required)	(20–40)
New knowledge generated	(40–60)
Cooperation (if collaboration)	(30–40)
Other	

Obviously, the points possible in this example exceed 100. That isn't important; you can adjust them so that you can use your own weighting preference, making the total 100 points.

The major precaution is that you think through each activity and decide its relative value and how the student will demonstrate competency. For example, to earn points for generating new knowledge, the student would be required to design a method to demonstrate this new understanding (write a paper, give a talk, hold a personal discussion with other collaborators). Our final suggestion is that you be generous in grading volunteer projects. Because their purpose is to promote learning, if this goal is demonstrated, then the resulting grade should reflect success.

Summary

Over the past century or so, the approach to classroom management has changed to reflect a shift in purpose. Prior to the late eighteenth century, the ultimate purpose of classroom management was to subdue misbehavior. Since then, the purpose has shifted to focus on learning. Contemporary teachers want to design strategies to produce as much learning as possible.

Generally, this shift can be described as a shift from negative to positive teacher behavior. A knowledge base has been accumulating showing that students learn more when in an enjoyable environment that helps them feel good about themselves. Teachers can increase the amount of mastery by using a variety of teaching strategies and learning each method's strengths and weaknesses.

Homework should be assigned only if it has a clear purpose. High school teachers assign more homework than elementary teachers because it has more potential to increase learning among older students. The subjects or disciplines do not affect the potential of homework to promote learning. One or two hours of homework per night seems to work best for middle level students, whereas high school students can profit from longer homework assignments. If assigned, however, they should be collected, graded, and returned promptly. You should discuss the correct answers to questions that were missed most frequently.

By choosing the appropriate instructional strategies, teachers can reduce discipline problems dramatically. Thinking of innovative lessons that keep students active, involved, and continually learning is part of an effective teacher's daily life.

REFERENCES

Acheson, K. A., & Gall, M. (1992). *Techniques in the clinical supervision of teachers.* White Plains, NY: Longman.

Alessi, S. M., & Trollip, S. R. (1991). *Computer-based instruction, methods, and development.* Englewood Cliffs, NJ: Prentice-Hall.

Armstrong, D. G., Henson, K. T., & Savage, T. V. (1997). *Teaching today: An introduction to education* (5th ed.). New York: Macmillan.

Becker, W., Engleman, S., & Thomas, D. (1975). *Teaching I: Classroom management.* Champaign, IL: Research Press.

Berliner, D. C. (1990, March). Creating the right environment for learning. *Instructor, 99,* 16–17.

Berliner, D. C., & Biddle, B. J. (1997). *The manufactured crisis.* New York: Longman.

Biddle, B., Good, T., & Goodson, I. (1996). *The international handbook of teachers and teaching.* New York: Kluwer.

Carr, M., & Kurtz-Costes, B. (1994). Is being smart everything? The influence of student achievement on teachers' perceptions. *British Journal of Educational Psychology, 64,* 263–276.

Carroll, J. B. (1963). A model of school learning. *Teachers College Record, 64,* 723–733.

Christensen, D. (1996). The professional knowledge—research base for teacher education. In J. Sikula, T. J. Buttery, & E. Guyton (eds.), *Association of Teacher*

Educators handbook of research on teacher education (2nd ed.). New York: Macmillan.

Clark, R. W., Hong, L. K., & Schoeppach, M. R. (1996). Teacher empowerment and site-based management. In J. Sikula, T. J. Buttery, & E. Guyton (eds.), *Association of Teacher Educators handbook of research on teacher education* (2nd ed.). New York: Macmillan.

Cooper, H. (1990). Synthesis of research on homework. *Educational Leadership, 47*(3), 85–91.

Deci, E., & Ryan, R. (1994). Promoting self-determined education. *Scandinavian Journal of Educational Research, 38,* 3–4.

Ellsworth, P. C., & Sindt, V. G. (1994). Helping "Aha" to happen: The contributions of Irving Sigel. *Educational Leadership, 51*(5), 40–44.

Finn, J. D. (1993). *School engagement and students at risk.* Washington, DC: National Center for Education Statistics, U.S. Department of Education.

Glasser, W. (1990). *The quality school: Managing students without coercion.* New York: Harper and Row.

Good, T. L. (1996). Teaching effects and teacher evaluation. In J. Sikula, T. J. Buttery, & E. Guyton (eds.), *Association of Teacher Educators handbook of research on teacher education* (2nd ed.). New York: Macmillan.

Good, T. L., & Brophy, J. E. (1997). *Looking in classrooms* (7th ed.). New York: Longman.

Guskey, T. R., & Gates, S. L. (1986). Synthesis of research on the effects of mastery learning in elementary and secondary classrooms. *Educational Leadership, 43*(8), 73–80.

Haines, J. M. (1990). A homework checking system: Maximizing the information, minimizing the time. *The Clearing House, 63*(5), 229–230.

Henson, K. T., & Eller, B. F. (1999). *Educational psychology for effective teaching.* Belmont, CA: Wadsworth.

Hyman, J. S., & Cohen, A. (1979). Learning for mastery: Ten conclusions after fifteen years and 3,000 schools. *Educational Leadership, 37,* 104–109.

Jones, V. (1996). Classroom management. In J. Sikula, T. J. Buttery, & E. Guyton (eds.), *Association of Teacher Educators handbook of research on teacher education* (2nd ed.) (pp. 503–521). New York: Macmillan.

Jones, V., & Jones, L. (1995). *Comprehensive classroom management* (4th ed.). Boston: Allyn & Bacon.

King, P. M., & Kitchener, K. S. (1994). *Developing effective judgment: Understanding and promoting intellectual growth and critical thinking in adolescents and adults.* San Francisco: Jossey-Bass.

Kowalski, T. J., Weaver, R. A., & Henson K. T. (1994). *Case studies of beginning teachers.* White Plains, NY: Longman.

Krasner, L. (1976). *Behavior modification: Ethical issues and future trends.* In H. Leitenberg (ed.), *Handbook of behavior modification and behavior therapy* (pp. 627–649). Englewood Cliffs, NJ: Prentice-Hall.

Leithwood, K., Menzie, T., & Jantzi, D. (1994). Earning teachers' commitment to curriculum reform. *Peabody Journal of Education, 69*(4), 38–61.

Lucas, L. A., Postma, C. H., & Thompson, J. C. (1975, July). Comparative study of cognitive retention used in simulation gaming as opposed to lecture: Discussion techniques. *Peabody Journal of Education, 52,* 261.

McWilliams, C. (1997). Class policies and procedures. Handout, Mance Park Middle School, Huntsville, Texas.

Miserandino, M. (1996). Children who do well in school: Individual differences in perceived competence and autonomy in above average children. *Journal of Educational Psychology, 88*(2), 203–214.

Mosston, M. (1972). *From command to discovery.* Belmont, CA: Wadsworth.

Phelan, P., Davidson, A., & Cao, H. (1992). Speaking up: Students' perspectives on school. *Phi Delta Kappan, 73*(9), 695–704.

Postner, G. J., & Rudnitsky, A. N. (1997). *Course design: A guide to curriculum development for students* (5th ed.). New York: Longman.

Rose, L. E., Gallup, A. M., & Elam, S. M. (1997). The 29th Annual Phi Delta Kappa/Gallup Poll of the Public's Attitudes Toward the Public Schools. *Phi Delta Kappan, 79*(1), 41–56.

Rosenthal, R., & Jacobson, L. (1968). *Pygmalion in the classroom: Teacher expectations and pupils' intellectual development.* New York: Holt.

Solomon, S. (1989). Homework: The great reinforcer. *The Clearing House, 63*(2), 63.

Yelon, S. L. (1996). *Powerful principles of instruction.* White Plains, NY: Longman.

Zlatos, B. (1994). Outcomes-based outrage runs both ways. *Education Digest, 59*(5), 26–29.

7 Parental Involvement

Parents, teachers, and students can work together to develop consistent educational and management goals.

OBJECTIVES

1. Communicate effectively through telephone calls, letters, and other means to make parents aware of what is happening in your classroom and school.
2. Design pre- and postconference plans.
3. Conduct different types of parent conferences.

Overview

Rachel's mom wants to know why you sent Rachel to in-school suspension. She never has problems at home. Can't you control your classroom?

Johnny's father is adamant that his son did not cheat on the calculus test. Although Johnny knew that other students were trying to look at his paper, he did not tell them that they could. Isn't it the teacher's responsibility to monitor tests? Who are you to accuse Johnny of cheating when it is really your fault?

Ms. Moore wants to set up a parent conference to discuss her daughter's new medication, Ritalin. Christie was diagnosed last week as having attention deficit hyperactivity disorder (ADHD). The mother seems overwhelmed and hopes that you can explain more about her parental rights and the services that must be provided according to the federal guidelines.

Ms. Mulsow called to say "thank you" for helping Frances on her project for the science fair. She's ecstatic that Frances won the $1,000 scholarship, and she wanted you to know that teachers do make a difference in their students' lives.

How can we, as teachers, work with parents to help all students learn and like school? This chapter examines ways to communicate with parents before a problem arises, to help you design preconference and postconference plans so that you can assess your effectiveness, and to demonstrate how to conduct an actual conference. Often parents of secondary school adolescents only arrive at school when there is a problem. What fifteen-year-old wants Mom and Dad to visit the school? It's just not cool. The parents usually assume that their child is being educated and that there isn't a problem until you make the initial contact. In the past, and even to some extent today, parents of children in primary school are more directly involved through parent–teacher organizations, room mothers, and other activities. Unless the parent is involved in the band booster club or raising money to send the cheerleaders to a summer camp, secondary teachers seldom see parents. In fact, there seems to be an inverse correlation between grade level and parental involvement: The higher the grade level, the less parents are involved. By high school, it has practically disappeared (Rioux & Berla, 1993). Newman (1997/1998) stated that "findings show that American parents of high school students are just as disengaged from school as their children are" (p. 100).

District and Schoolwide Plans

Many administrators today are trying to persuade parents to take a more active role because they now have a better understanding of the benefits. According to the U.S. Department of Education, "parents are their children's first and most influential teachers. What parents do to help their children is more important to academic success than how well off the family is" (p. 7). Such programs as Partners in Education (PIE) are growing throughout the country. For instance, two Texas school districts formed an alliance with parents, educators, and other community members to "make a positive difference in student achievement." Parents are requested to sign a pledge card, which states that they will support the districts' initiative to raise academic performance and achieve excellence. Parent responsibilities include insisting that all homework assignments are completed each night, meeting regularly with the teachers, reminding the student of "the necessity of discipline in the classroom—especially self-discipline," and discussing daily work with the student to emphasize content learned that day (Hammock & Monday, n.d.).

A districtwide and schoolwide systematic plan to involve the entire community aids both parents and school district employees in understanding how to contribute to this effort. Having staff development programs for all teachers concerning parent–teacher team building creates the right school climate. Videos, such as "Community Involvement: Working Together to Improve Schools" and "How Families Help Children Learn," can help generate discussions among faculty members and parents. And using creative ideas that other districts have tried may prove successful for you too. One school held a sit-down dinner on Back-to-School Night to entice parents to come; another had teams of teachers visit the "neighborhood churches on Sunday mornings to invite parents to the high school" (Weinstein, 1996, p. 241). To make their building parent-friendly, a third school offered free coffee each morning under a sign that invited parents to linger (Hoerr, 1997).

If several parents are dealing with similar problems, such as how to help their children who have learning disabilities, Felber (1997) recommends starting support groups and creating newsletters with family articles and stories about their experiences. The administrators at Bay Point Middle School in west central Florida discovered that a group of forty-one seventh graders had the majority of discipline referrals at their school. Most of the students came from single-parent homes, and the parents typically worked full-time jobs. Therefore, these teenagers were often left unattended. To combat behavior problems both at home and at school, the parents requested information about management and parenting techniques. Bimonthly workshops and a monthly newsletter were designed to provide information, list useful books and videos, and announce upcoming events. The most revealing result of this new program showed that "parents were immensely supportive and enthusiastic. In the final surveys, parents expressed their satisfaction with the project and wished it would continue" even though attendance was minimal at workshops and seminars (Gibbons, 1992, p. 38).

Designing a mentor program so that first-year teachers can ask experienced teachers for suggestions to handle that first conference and providing role-playing scenarios help eliminate some of the anxiety that beginning teachers face. Lee Canter believes that we should mentally rehearse what to say before a major behavior problem occurs (Wolfgang, 1995). What will you say if a student in your class is cheating on the exam? Stealing someone's book? Carving on the desk? Have you thought about how you will handle these situations?

Guess what, you may say to us, you are a new teacher who doesn't have input into the entire school program, at least you don't think you do. Anyway, at this point you are simply trying to learn how to swim. Let's throw you several lifejackets.

A Boy Scout troop on a nature hike ran across abandoned railroad tracks. They tried to walk on the rails. Each of them fell off. They could only walk a few feet. Two boys decided that they both could walk from one end of the rails to the other without falling. All of the boys claimed that that was impossible and bet them that they could not. The boys stood on a rail opposite each other and with one of their hands outstretched they balanced each other by placing the palm of that hand against the palm of the other boy's hand. Teachers and parents can work together just as these Boy Scouts did by reaching out to each other.

Communication

The most important aspect of working to achieve parental involvement is communication. As a general rule, the better informed the parents are, the more often involvement will occur. Secondary teachers tend to avoid contacting parents unless they have a problem. Parents want to hear about their child's work, and they want to hear positive messages. Think about your school experiences. How often did your parents receive calls about how well you behaved in school or how much you had achieved? Maybe we should ask *if* you behaved in school. If the

"That's the bad news. There isn't any good news."

Source: Phi Delta Kappan 79(1) p. 26. Reprinted by permission of Robert Vojtko.

parents receive positive messages from the teacher before being notified of a problem, they are more likely to support the teacher than if they only hear negatives.

Early Communication

The earlier the contact with parents, the better. Some secondary teachers have been successful contacting parents before school begins. If the class rolls are received prior to the opening of school, teachers might call, write, or visit the parents to express their excitement about this new academic year, explain the class goals, invite the parents to attend class, and provide a schedule of the conference period hours. Then, to maintain contact throughout the year, one new teacher handbook recommends sending monthly correspondence with a calendar of goals, plans, and topics for each week (Association of Texas Professional Educators, 1997).

Not only should teachers provide information to the parents, but also they need to ask for input. Felber (1997) recommends, "talk to parents, not at them" (p. 22). What suggestions do the parents have to ensure student success? Do they have any special talents that they would be willing to share with the class? For example, is Valerie's mom, a personnel counselor, interested in speaking to the senior English class about how to write an effective résumé? Is Bob's dad, an internal medicine specialist, willing to discuss AIDS and HIV in the health class? Do the parents have unique hobbies, videos of their trips, or artifacts from certain places that tie with your subject matter? When studying Chinese culture in your history class, the parent who can show the class a homemade video, coins, and dress of Inner Mongolia will make a larger impact than simply having the students read the textbook.

Many parents feel uncomfortable speaking to a group of secondary students. You can still involve these parents as chaperones at the senior party or field trip, as costume makers for the school theatrical production, or as bulletin board designers. It's "critical not to assume that poor parents, uneducated parents, or parents with limited English proficiency have nothing of value to offer" (Weinstein, 1996, p. 240). Think of all the possibilities for making the classroom a family gathering place rather than the off-limits arena that parents sometimes visualize today.

Along with asking for their help, you will want to know specific points about their particular child. What special interests or hobbies does the child have; what do the parents believe are the child's greatest strengths? By making these initial positive contacts, you produce strong working relationships between you and parents. Parents feel that teachers who get acquainted early and ask for input are willing to work directly with them in their children's best interest. One school staff began having "intake parent conferences" in September before the teachers knew much about their students. They told participants that they expected "parents to do the talking—and teachers the listening—75 to 80 percent of the time" (Hoerr, 1997 p. 41). To facilitate dialogue, teachers sent parents a list of questions to consider, such as "How does your child view school? What are your goals for your child this year? and How does your child solve problems at home?" (p. 42). Because these intake conferences have been so successful, the teachers have developed a second set of questions regarding ethnic, economic, and racial diversity. These questions include the following:

- What holidays does your family celebrate? Will any of these celebrations affect your child's activities at school?
- Would you share a bit of your family's heritage?
- What are some of the ways that your family has worked to help your child appreciate racial and ethnic differences? (p. 42)

Other means of gathering information include viewing the cumulative folder and talking to the students' former teachers. Teachers form professional opinions about students' needs based on an array of sources. *Use the information wisely.*

Resisting Involvement

Some parents resist any efforts by school officials to involve them. Mistrust of school and bureaucracies, poor self-image and feelings of inadequacy in school-related matters, unpleasant experiences in their own schooling, and limited English-speaking abilities are but a few reasons cited (Burden, 1995). Communicating with these parents takes extra effort and time. Being visible in the community, shopping at the neighborhood grocery store, and attending special holiday celebrations show them that you do care about who they and their children are. When one author taught in a writing lab, mainly used by adults of Arabic descent, the students would not readily come to the lab. However, she started teaching them English words and they taught her Arabic ones. Soon, word spread that it was all right to work in the lab. The students brought her their food and she shared hers. The lab overflowed with people. Twenty years later, some of these former students remain friends.

ACTIVITY **7.1**

Colleagues' Debate

There are certain issues that cause educators to have differing opinions. One such issue is debated here by two colleagues who teach university classroom management courses.

The question: Should teachers view the cumulative folder, read about a student's background, and talk to a student's former teachers prior to teaching that student?

WILLIAMS: I am concerned about teachers prejudging students prior to teaching them. In most instances, I believe that teachers should not read the cumulative folders or discuss students with other teachers prior to meeting the students. They should begin forming their impressions based on their initial contact. Often, a student who might be a terror in one class is an angel in another because of personality differences among teachers and students.

BARRETT: Think for a moment what that says about the professionalism of teaching. It assumes that teachers will let what they see in a cumulative folder or what they hear from a colleague influence them in such a way that they cannot work effectively with that student. If a teacher will allow information to bias judgment in a negative way, then that teacher is not a professional and should not be teaching.

WILLIAMS: I agree that they should not allow derogatory comments and hearsay to influence them, but we are dealing with humans. We are often influenced by what we read and hear. Why not get acquainted with the students first? Yes, teachers do need to know if a student must visit the nurse for a particular medication or if the student has a disability, but they don't need to know that Ms. Jones, the eighth grade science teacher, sent John to the assistant principal's office ten times last year because of excessive tardiness.

BARRETT: Let's suppose that you are referred to a specialist by your regular doctor because you have a unique medical problem. Would you want this specialist to have access to all of your records and discuss your problem with your doctor, or do you want him to start from scratch because he might prejudge your condition?

WILLIAMS: Those are different issues. We are not talking about a medical situation. We are discussing whether or not teachers are influenced by having information concerning past problems.

BARRETT: My point is that the medical profession is not unique. You could use any profession. If we as teachers allow information to influence us, then we do not deserve to be called professionals. Teachers should not be afraid to look at all data available on a student and ask everyone to share what they know. After a teacher has gathered all the possible facts, then she should decide what can be done to help that student succeed. The more we know about a student, the better the chances for success.

WILLIAMS: We are in agreement about gathering as much knowledge as possible, but we disagree on the time frame. I would wait until I got to know the student and formed my own opinion before viewing all the information.

What Do You Think?

Have a debate in class about this issue. What information is relevant? Does it make a difference if the teacher is a first-year or experienced educator? Have your teachers ever based their opinions about you on past experiences in another teacher's class? How did you feel about the situation?

Types of Parents

In most cases, parents willingly work with you to find solutions to problems, especially if they know that you care about their children. Darby (1979) identified seven types of parents you might meet. He also provided advice on how to handle each type.

- *Nonhostile, cooperative*—These parents will be the majority. You simply must work out a plan together.
- *Anxious or overwhelmed*—Encourage limiting the discussion to the student's strengths and weaknesses. Some parents "have personal problems and the best thing you can do upon discovering this is be a good listener. Arrange for another conference to discuss the child" (Darby, 1979, p. 1).
- *Self-absorbed*—These parents relate every comment about the child to self—a mirror image. You might ask the parent how the child feels about _____ . Do you think your child feels the same way about that?
- *In denial*—Avoid trying to prove the parents to be liars. Say that you are delighted that they are not having any problems and that perhaps the two of you can think of ways to solve the problems at school. Ask the parents to reward the student at home for behaving appropriately at school.
- *Resistant*—These parents typically ignore your advice, so don't give any. Instead, "toss the ball back to the parents and assist them in working out their plans" (Darby, 1979, p. 1).
- *Punitive*—These parents usually react to a call from school staff with a stern, "He's getting a good paddling." Many schools, districts, and states have outlawed corporal punishment. Avoid using swats even when the parents dictate that punishment. Work out a plan to reward appropriate behavior and withhold privileges when the plan is broken.
- *Hostile*—Darby (1979) recommends, "Caution! Defensiveness is your biggest enemy here. Let the parents vent without comment. If they are right, discuss the situation frankly and openly without arguing. Apologize and reassure as appropriate" (p. 1). Parents may on occasion explode about an incident. For instance, they may feel that you were unfair to their child. You are the professional educator, however, and must respond appropriately. Parents do not have the right to humiliate, belittle, or curse you. If a verbal attack occurs, end the conference promptly. Tell the parents that the meeting will need to be rescheduled. If they begin shouting obscenities, walk away from the scene. You are not required to take abuse. To diffuse such a situation, Lamb (1995) suggests seven steps to help you stay calm, controlled, and focused.
  - *Do the unexpected.* Rather than appear agitated as the parents walk in the door, welcome them as you would a guest. Smile, thank them for coming, and begin with a positive comment about their child.
  - *Listen and take notes.* By using active listening techniques, taking notes, and summarizing to the parents what you think they are saying, you can open communication lines. Sometimes Lamb (1995) "refers to these notes when [she] needs to redirect the discussion in a more constructive vein" (p. 26).
  - *Admit mistakes.* Sometimes we unintentionally hurt a student's feelings or make a comment in anger that we regret. For example, if we embarrassed a student in front of the class, we need to apologize. We need to let the parents know that we can admit mistakes.

- *Document problem behaviors.* By writing in a notebook the incident, date, and a brief description, teachers have an objective file on what happened at school. For secondary students, we recommend that the students do the writing. Then the teacher has documentation in the students' handwriting. However, if you decided to use an inappropriate behavior book, we suggest having an appropriate behavior book for students to sign and add documentation too.
- *Hold a three-way conference.* If parents don't believe you or are argumentative, you might include the student in the conference. After having the student "tell his side of the story, [I] question him in a nonthreatening way about the documented facts. Usually, the student will admit what really happened" (Lamb, 1995, p. 27). You may also want to invite the counselor, assistant principal, department chair, team leader, or principal to the conference if you believe it has a chance of escalating. Various school district administrators attend parent–teacher conferences, especially when there is a potential for violence or aggressiveness.
- *Display confidence.* Respond as a professional who is friendly and knows what to do. If parents don't understand why particular instructional strategies or materials were used, explain the reasons and cite examples of student successes.
- *Develop cooperative solutions.* Remember that "even though parents may be furious, their presence in the classroom is evidence of concern for their child" (Lamb, 1995, p. 27). Ask them for suggestions on how to handle the situation and together work out a plan. Let them know that both of you are working toward a common goal—helping their child achieve academic success.

Communicating Expectations in Written Form

Before school begins or within the first few days, teachers should send a letter home in which they emphasize that they are enthusiastic about working with students and look forward to having their children in class. When possible, Wong and Wong (1991) suggest personally taking the letter to the home to get acquainted with both parents and students *before* school begins. *Beware!* Most parents of secondary school-aged children will faint. They have never had a middle school or high school teacher conduct a home visit unless they were personal friends. In the letter, mention this year's goals, and include both academic and behavioral expectations, such as the homework and grading policies and class requirements. In designing your homework plans, reread the section in Chapter 6 and consider how you will communicate the following information to parents.

1. Rationale for assigning homework
2. Types of homework
3. Amount and frequency of homework
4. Grading of homework
5. Penalty for incomplete assignments
6. Policy for make-up work
7. Policy for extra credit projects
8. Expectations for parents

Have you ever wondered why university teachers assign particular projects, papers, or portfolios? What assignments are you to complete in your classroom management course?

Why? How will your homework be evaluated? Are there makeup and extra credit policies? How did your teacher explain them to you? Do you like classes more when you know what is expected at the beginning of the semester, rather than having a surprise research paper due at the end? Your students will have the same feelings. They will like the class more when they know you will treat them fairly. They have a *right* to know your academic requirements.

Behavioral expectations can be explicitly stated, but you will probably want student input before listing them. Plus, you will want them to be positively stated, clearly understood, and few in number. Who can remember twenty-five rules and consequences? Five to seven rules is an appropriate number for secondary students to follow, along with the requirements stated in the student handbook or code of conduct. Examples of class rules are as follows:

1. Classroom expectations
   a. Be on time. *Not* Don't be tardy. (too negative)
      Consequence—Student will receive one-half hour of detention for every tardy.
   b. Respect others by one person speaking at a time. *Not* Respect others. (too vague, too broad)
      Consequence—Teacher will call on another student whose hand is raised.
   c. Turn in homework at the beginning of class. *Not* Be prepared at all times. (too broad)
      Consequence—Student will receive a free homework pass that can be used in lieu of one assignment if all homework is completed for three weeks.

Now, complete the freewriting exercises in Activities 7.2 and 7.3.

ACTIVITY **7.2**

Rule Writing: Freewriting Exercise

Think of how you will communicate your expectations. Before discussing your rules and communication techniques with your peers, spend two minutes freewriting.

Rules for Freewriting
Keep your pen moving or your hands on the keyboard for the next two minutes, jotting down your thoughts. You cannot stop writing, even if you write the same word over and over again. You do not need to answer all the questions, and you may want to elaborate on a particular answer.

Questions to Ponder
What do you want your students to do? How much input will you allow them to give? Will you hold a class meeting to allow students to select some of the rules for *our* classroom? Or will you tell them what you expect because you are the "adult" in the class? How will you communicate your expectations to the parents? How will you gather parent suggestions? Will you invite parents to visit your class? As speakers? As observers? As helpers? As tutors?

Directions
After the two minutes of freewriting, break into groups of five or fewer, and discuss your ideas. See if your group can reach any consensus about well-written rules and parental input.

ACTIVITY **7.3**

Consequences for Breaking the Rules

Will you inform the parents about consequences for students who break the rules? What will your consequences be for the first-time versus the tenth-time offender? Will you first give a verbal warning? Will you ask parents to set limitations at home if students are misbehaving in class? For instance, will you ask that sixteen-year-old Rolanda not be given the car keys on Friday night? Do you have a right to ask parents for this type of support?

Will you have *natural* and *logical consequences,* or do you believe that *punishment* is more effective? Let us explain the differences among these terms. If a student trips and falls while running in the halls, the student has experienced a natural consequence. However, if the student is sent to the back of the lunch line because the student ran down the hall, this is a logical consequence. For a student who is caught running, the teacher may assign a one-hour detention, which would be punishment. Will you document any incidents? When will you contact parents? Will you call parents about good as well as bad behavior?

After outlining your plans for handling behavior problems, you might also consider the types of reinforcement or rewards to give.

How do you know what students want? Ask them. You might give students 3×5 index cards to specify what types of rewards they would like. When we asked middle school and high school students to complete this activity, they requested the following:

a. Leave ten seconds early for class or lunch
b. Receive a no homework pass (*Caution:* This reward should only be given for completion of academic work. For instance, students may be given a pass for finishing the last ten homework assignments, not for being in their seats before the tardy bell rings.)
c. Free food (hamburgers), candy, gum
d. Restroom and hall passes
e. Money (One substitute teacher could not keep the students active in the class discussion. In fact, he felt that he was giving a soliloquy. Then he pulled a dollar bill out of his pocket and gave it to the student who answered his question. Soon he had the full attention of all students and they willingly participated.) See Chapter 9 for a more in-depth look at rewards and consequences.

For documentation purposes, have parents sign a sheet to indicate that they have read the expectations and understand them. You should also include your scheduled conference period time and a phone number for parents to contact you with questions or concerns.

Positive Communication

When was the last time someone made a kind gesture or complimented you? We all remember those individuals as being considerate and thoughtful, yet we sometimes forget how much a positive comment means to a parent. Charles (1997) notes that "the ability to compliment genuinely is a behavior that receives little attention in human relations. It nevertheless has considerable power" (p. 248). For many parents, their children are the most important individuals in their lives. They need to hear positive feedback from teachers either through notes, phone calls, or e-mail. Yes, we do understand that many parents and, unfortunately, many teachers as well may not have ready access to computers. However, postcards can be designed on a computer for the whole school to use or purchased in quantities and placed in the school supply room. In one junior high school, all the teachers used cards with the following border inscription: "Something good is happening at school." What a surprise to parents!!!

When making contacts, you need to keep records so that you will have all required documentation. By creating a folder or filing system with a check sheet for each student, you can easily track your calls and messages. Be sure to add the parent's or guardian's and student's names because the last names are sometimes different. Approximately one-fourth of all children have one or more stepparents and one-third of all marriages are remarriages (Swap, 1993).

A C T I V I T Y **7.4**

Sample Letters

Write letters to parents expressing your academic and behavioral expectations. Then exchange letters with a peer. As you read each other's letters, decide whether they are *positively* stated, clear, and concise. Also, determine whether the letters included all the pertinent information. You may want to use the sample letters as guidelines.

Sample Introductory Letter

Dear Parents:

I am _____ (student's name) social studies teacher. I am excited about this school year and look forward to working with both you and _____ .

Last year, I graduated with a B.A. degree in history from State University and am enrolled in a master's level course this semester. My philosophy of teaching high school history is that the subject must be interesting and relevant to each student's life. I also believe that a teacher should maintain a structured, organized classroom, but be flexible enough to make changes to improve the class. You will find a calendar of events enclosed, including information about this year's Doe ISD History Fair. If you are interested in a specific era, such as the Civil War period, or have historical documents, please let me know. Students will be completing their projects for the fair by mid-November.

The students and I will be writing bimonthly newsletters to keep you up-to-date on what's happening in our classroom. In addition, please feel free to call me during my conference period, which is from 1:00 p.m. to 1:50 p.m. I can be reached at _____.

I appreciate your allowing me the chance to work with your child. Please contact me if you have any questions or concerns.

Sincerely,

Chris Morris
Ninth Grade Social Studies Teacher

(continued)

ACTIVITY **7.4**   **Continued**

Sample Homework Policy Letter

Dear Parents:

This letter will answer your questions about the homework that will be assigned this year. Homework is important because it reinforces what has been taught in class, prepares students for future lessons, and helps develop responsibility. Each student is required to complete all assigned work. Please read this letter, discuss it with your child, and return the bottom portion to me.

Most homework will be either textbook readings from _____ book or project assignments. Reading assignments will be given on Monday and Wednesday nights. Assignments should take approximately forty-five minutes per evening. A major test will be given every other Friday, and students are expected to study Thursday nights for the test. Most students should spend at least two hours preparing. In addition, we will complete multicultural projects for the history fair.

During the week, students will write short paragraphs regarding one of their reading assignments. These essays help students maintain their reading schedules, and I will know if they are understanding the important concepts. If a student is not able to write because of failure to read the assignment, then the student will complete a makeup assignment. If this occurs more than once, you will be notified.

Please ask _____ if the assignment is complete. You can make this a positive experience by offering your support. If there is a legitimate reason for missing an assignment, please send a note explaining the reason with your signature. I am looking forward to meeting you in person. Our next open house is scheduled for October 10.

Sincerely,

Chris Morris
Ninth Grade Social Studies Teacher

****

I have read and discussed this policy with _____. I will support my child in helping complete the assignments.

If you would like for me to contact you, please complete the following by checking the appropriate lines and filling in the blanks.

_____ I would like to schedule a parent–teacher conference before October 10.

_____ I would like to help chaperone the students at the State History Fair on November 15.

_____ I would be interested in speaking to the class about _____.

_____ I would like to attend the class on _____.

Signature _____

Date _____

Sample Letter about Behavioral Expectations

Dear Parents:

This classroom discipline plan will explain the behavioral expectations that will play a part in developing your child's self-discipline. It outlines rules, rewards, and consequences for appropriate and inappropriate behavior.

Rules

1. Be on time to class.
2. Follow directions the first time they are given.
3. Keep hands, feet, and objects to yourself.
4. Request permission before leaving the classroom.

Rewards

Verbal and nonverbal praise

Free selection of favorite classroom activity
(e.g., play computer game dealing with math
or trivia game in history)

Positive notes home

Positive phone calls

Consequences

First step—warning

Second step—last out of the classroom

Third step—after-school detention

Fourth step—contact parents

Fifth step—send to the assistant principal

If you have any questions please call me at _____. My conference period is from 11:00 a.m. until 11:50 a.m.

****

Please go over this plan with your son or daughter, sign the sheet, and return the form.

I have read the Classroom Discipline Plan and discussed it with _____ .

Signature _____   Date _____

Parental Contacts

Parent's Name	Student's Name	Phone Number	Date Contacted	Message

Within the folder, you may also add brief notes about "something good" that the student did. When a student warrants a positive note, pull your comments from the folder, write a note, and give it to the student to take home. Or have the card already addressed and simply place it in the mailbox. Secondary students will take positive notes home, even though they may not acknowledge your efforts. They often leave them for parents to find or casually pitch them on the table and say "Here's something from school."

When one author taught high school, she was required to send ten positive notes home before she received her last paycheck. The principal collected and mailed all the notes. Perhaps it would have been a better idea to send them periodically during the school year rather than waiting until the last day. In selecting the ten students, she chose several students who she knew would never receive a note because they were not the shining stars. They were not team or band performers, they had never been award winners, and they were definitely not honor society members. They were the unnoticed, "average" kids in a school with 3,600 pupils. One student, Hugh, a big red-headed student with an instant smile, received a note. He never made above a C on any English exam, never was a leader in any school-sponsored organization, never was mentioned in the school newspaper. But he participated in class and tried to improve his writing skills. He deserved a letter too. What a difference one note can make to a student, and a parent, when they are not expecting it. Also, when parents positively reinforce their child, the positive impact doubles.

Phone calls are another effective method if handled appropriately. Teachers are often reluctant to call parents because if they spend ten minutes on each call and talk to thirty parents, they have spent five hours voluntarily on the telephone (Becker & Epstein, 1982). There are some tips, however, to save time. With answering machines in almost every residence, it is simple to leave a brief, positive message. Or have a script prepared so that you will know what points you want to make and how you will break off the call before it becomes a lengthy parent conference. You are in control and should ascertain who is on the phone, deliver the positive message, and then close.

Communication about Problems

At times, parents must be notified about a problem at school. Teachers tend to be leery about contacting parents, especially during work hours, because they are concerned that parents will

---

A C T I V I T Y **7.5**

Scripting Messages

Script a positive phone message to a parent or write a positive note to be sent home. Refer to the following sample.

Sample Positive Phone Message

PARENT: Hello

TEACHER: Hello, this is Mr. Smith. I am Jimmy's biology teacher. Is this Ms. Morales?

PARENT: Yes, this is she. What's Jimmy done now?

TEACHER: Everything seems all right. I'm calling to tell you how much Jimmy's work has improved this past week. He turned in every paper and made a 95 on this week's test. Please tell him how much I appreciate his hard work. I know that you're very proud of all that he has done, and I wanted to keep you informed of his progress.

PARENT: (After a long pause from the parent collapsing on the floor) Thank you, I will.

TEACHER: Thank you for your time, Ms. Morales. Have a great day!

be agitated and uncooperative. One of the most important keys is to contact them before a problem escalates. Do not let the problem grow because you think it might disappear. When should you contact parents with a problem? The answer is as soon as you know there is a problem.

Parents who are contacted in the spring about a problem that has been going on all year have a right to be angry. How do you judge if the parent should be contacted? A good rule of thumb: Ask yourself whether or not you would want to be notified if this were your child. If the answer is a resounding *yes,* you have your answer.

Telephone Communication about Problems

Brief telephone calls can eliminate some problems. As the great child psychologist, Barney Fife, notes, problems may be "nipped in the bud." OK, we're showing our age. Do you know who Barney Fife is? If not, watch reruns of *The Andy Griffith Show* with Opie (a young Ron Howard), Andy, and Barney.

Sample Telephone Script

PARENT: Hello

TEACHER: Hello, Ms. Henderson, this is Rex's math teacher. I wanted to let you know that Rex's average so far this semester is a 90, and I'm sure you're very proud of him for raising his grades. However, I am concerned that he has not turned in his required homework for the past two weeks.

(Always begin by identifying yourself, making a positive comment, and getting straight to the point.)

I have told Rex that his failure to turn in his work will drop his grade one letter.

(State what you have done.)

I have offered to tutor him before or after school if he is having difficulty with these new math concepts. However, he has not been to any of the tutorials yet.

Is there anything you could tell me that will possibly give me a clue as to what is causing this problem?

(Ask the parent to share or suggest what might help.)

PARENT: I hate to hear this because I know he has been having some problems with his girlfriend, but I didn't know it was affecting his work.

TEACHER: Thank you for letting me know because it certainly helps to understand what has been happening. Please talk to Rex at home and see if you can get him back on track. I'll mention the tutorials to him again and provide one-on-one assistance if he is not understanding these new formulas.

(Suggest something that the parent can do at home and explain what you will do at school.)

PARENT: I will definitely talk to him, and please let me know what else I might do.

TEACHER: I'm sure together we can make a difference. Rex is a very bright student, and I enjoy working with him. I will call you next week. If you have any questions, feel free to give me a call. My conference period is from 11:00 a.m. until 11:50 a.m. each day, and my number is _____.

ACTIVITY **7.6**

Bud Nipping: Role Playing Parent Calls

Select a partner and pretend that one is the parent and the other is the teacher. Take turns switching roles with the following four scenarios. You, the teacher, received the following phone messages from Mr. Fitts, the parent, who called about his son, Steve. He asked you to return his call. How would you handle the telephone conversation? First, script the call using the format provided, then role-play the scenarios. How can you stop the problems before they escalate? Remember, teachers should be positive and professional.

Scenarios

a. Mr. Fitts believes that Steve's gym shoes were stolen from his locker. He doesn't want you to take off points for Steve not dressing out in class, and he was wondering who's going to pay for the next pair of shoes.

b. Mr Fitts wants to know why you confiscated Steve's water gun when he told you he wouldn't play with it anymore. Don't you intend to give it back to him?

c. Mr. Fitts received a message that you called him at work yesterday, and he wants you to know that he resents being taken away from his job. Can't you handle the situations at school?

d. Mr. Fitts wants Steve to read a more appropriate book than *To Kill a Mockingbird*. He thinks it is unsuitable for eleventh graders to study "trashy novels."

Telephone Script

You might script the call before making it. By writing what you intend to say, you will be much better prepared to have a successful phone call. The script is not intended to be read; instead, you should use it to give structure and substance to the call.

Begin with a brief introduction: _____

_____

Make a positive statement: _____

_____

State your concern and what you have done: _____

_____

Ask for parental input: _____

_____

Suggest what the parent can do to help: _____

_____

Make a positive statement, set a time for a return call, and close: _____

_____

(Close with a positive statement, and let the parent know what you will do next. This technique is called the sandwich. You begin and end with positive statements and put the meat of the conversation in the middle.)

The purpose of calling parents is to inform them of a problem early so that it can be corrected. Insignificant problems can develop into major infractions if not handled properly.

Parent and Teacher Conferences

At the agreed upon time, call the parent to explain what has been happening. If the student has improved, then thank the parent for the help and support. If the problem has escalated, then arrange a face-to-face conference. You may want the student present at this meeting to discuss what has occurred, to offer suggestions, and to help solve the problem.

Informational Conferences

Informational and problem-solving conferences require different strategies. An informational conference is usually held to let the parents know details about the class or to discuss a student's particular strengths and weaknesses. For example, during open house, parents are often given an abbreviated schedule of their children's classes and asked to visit each teacher during a particular time slot (Burden, 1995). Therefore, teachers may meet twenty parents within the same fifteen-minute time period. Planning what you intend to say is imperative. Along with giving a brief introduction of who you are, you might want to discuss class goals and policies, primary course topics, and your conference period time. Parents may then schedule a private conference to discuss their son or daughter at a later time. Avoid addressing major issues or being sidetracked by one or two overwhelmed parents who want to tell you specifically about their child's needs. Parents Night is designed for all parents, not just a few. Other informational conferences can be arranged later to answer particular questions about individuals.

Conferences about Problems

Another type, the problem-solving conference, can be used for either academic or behavioral problems: Haley doesn't understand how to do the calculus problems (academic), or Haley

ACTIVITY **7.7**

When Would You Invite the Student to Attend the Conference?

Discuss the following scenarios and decide whether or not the student should be invited to the parent–teacher conference.

1. Two seventh graders had a fistfight by the lockers during lunch. Would you ask the student who threw the first punch to meet with you and her mom? Or do you immediately contact the school police and let the officer take the student to jail? (Some school districts have now implemented a policy that states that all students involved in a fight will automatically be detained by the police until their parents arrive and pay a fine at the station.)
2. You suspect that a ninth grader cheated on his physical science test. He had an almost identical answer on the essay as the student seated next to him. Would you ask him to attend a conference with his father? Would you ask the two students and their parents to attend?
3. A tenth grade student called you a very unflattering name under her breath, as happened to one of the authors when she was student teaching. Do you pretend not to hear the comment or have a conference? Would you invite both the parent and child to the conference?

ACTIVITY **7.8**

Informational Conference Script

Think about a student you have worked with or a child in your family. Use the following form to script an informational conference. You can script the conference before meeting the parents. By writing what you intend to say, you will be much better prepared. The script is not intended to be read, but it will give structure and substance to the conference.

Positive beginning: _____

_____

Academic strengths: _____

_____

Academic weaknesses (if appropriate): _____

_____

Academic goals: _____

_____

Parental input: _____

_____

Social strengths: _____

_____

Social weaknesses (if appropriate): _____

_____

Social goals: _____

_____

Parental input: _____

_____

Additional issues: _____

_____

is constantly talking to her boyfriend in class (behavioral). You and the parents can use Gordon's steps, as outlined on page 67 to decide on solutions, consequences, and rewards. Parental input and support are vital. If Haley must attend tutorials after school, she will probably miss the bus. Her parents will need to make transportation arrangements, or she might walk home. And some schools have installed homework and tutorial hotlines so that parents can call each day to find out tonight's homework assignments and students can have questions answered.

This conference should always be set up when you have time and privacy. We know you're thinking, "When do I find this *time*?" As Emmer, Evertson, Clements, and Worsham (1997) have stated, "The chief drawback to parent conferences is the time and energy they require" (p. 159). Make a plan and sign a contract with yourself that you will follow it. Could you call eight parents each week and conduct one conference during your allotted time or after school? Many parents will tell you that they cannot visit during school hours. They are working too. You must decide how to handle this situation.

Can they come before or after school? Can they take off work for this important meeting? We suggest that you determine what is also in your best interest. You need a life too. You may not be able to accomodate every parent, every time. Plan the schedule so that you are not stressed out even more; you have enough to do within your first few years of teaching. By thinking your plan through, you will eliminate some of the stress. However, your plan must be individualized because each teacher has different responsibilities, stress thresholds, and time constraints. Decide what will work best for you and follow your action plan.

Furniture Arrangement

Comfortable, regular-size chairs rather than desks can be arranged so that you can sit side-by-side with parents. Sitting across a desk sets up a barrier and sends the message that you are the boss who intends to tell the parents what to do. If you need a place to show work samples, then sit at the end of a table so that only the corner will be between you and the parents. You may need to borrow chairs or conduct the meeting in a counseling area or administrator's conference room if your classroom is not suitable.

ACTIVITY **7.9**

My Contract with Parents

Please complete the following contract, then sign and date it.

I, _____ , will contact my students' parents or guardians in the following ways.

Place a check mark beside those steps you plan to take.

_____ Call eight parents each week. Busy signals don't count; left message do.

_____ Send a newsletter home about the class and school every other month.

_____ Conduct one parent conference each week.

_____ Write letters to all parents every other month.

_____ Send five positive notes home each week.

_____ Other ideas—please explain. _____

_____

_____

Teacher's Signature	Today's Date	Date for Review of Contract

Body Language

When a person shakes his head "no," but says "yes," what do you read? Nonverbal communication is what we most often read. You want to send the message that you are open and receptive. Make sure that the body language you send is positive.

Sit square and relaxed in the chair with no crossed legs or arms, leaning slightly toward the parents, and being attentive to what they have to say. Practice active listening by making eye contact and acknowledging that you understand.

Parents also send messages by the body language they display. If you see that their arms and legs are crossed, they might be showing that they are closed and not receptive. If they slouch or lean away from you, then they are probably uncomfortable. They may be expecting bad news, and in many cases parents have had unpleasant experiences at school and with teachers. If you send strong open messages with your body, you will help alleviate their fears. Be alert to the body language, and it will set the stage for a positive conference.

Verbal Communication

Word choice also sets the tone of a parent–teacher meeting. Because that child is often the most important person in a parent's life, feelings can be easily hurt when a teacher makes a seemingly derogatory remark. Rather than telling a parent that the child is disliked by his peers, you might state, "Steve needs help in forming lasting friendships." Or if the student needs to bathe more often, you might mention that "Diane needs guidance in developing good hygiene habits." When the student attempts to bully others, you may comment that "Dorothy has leadership qualities, but she needs to learn to use them democratically."

The successful conference does not just happen; it requires organization and planning well in advance. You should collect all documentation needed prior to the meeting. Burden (1995) recommends that these materials include the following:

1. sample work
2. sample tests and projects
3. grade book to show all the students' grades
4. textbook and other significant resource materials
5. an agenda for conducting the conference

Plus administrators, usually the assistant principal, should be notified if there is potential for conflict. Have the furniture arranged as suggested earlier. Script the conference ahead of

---

ACTIVITY 7.10

Choose Your Words Carefully

What if your student was insolent, lazy, rude, noisy, and dishonest? How would you phrase the sentences so as to inform, without offending, the parent? Is phrasing important, or should a teacher simply call the student a cheater or liar? How might parents react? List the phrases you would use and compare them with your classmates' word choices.

time so that you have a sense of what will be said. The script does not have to be followed exactly but will give you guidelines for what needs to be covered. When the parents arrive, welcome them as you would a guest in your home and begin with a positive comment about their child.

Sample Conference

TEACHER: Hello, Mr. and Ms. Wheeler, thank you for coming. Please have a seat. Would you like a cup of coffee or a cold drink before we begin? I am Jan's history teacher, and I enjoy having her in class. She is one of the brightest young women I have had the privilege of teaching. I'm concerned, however, that she is not completing her required work.

(Always begin by saying something positive about the student. Then state that you are concerned and state the problem.)

I have told Jan that her failure to turn in work will affect her grade. For the past week, Jan has met me during lunch hour to complete her work. Here are some examples, and I'm sure you will agree that she can do much better. (Show three incomplete homework assignments and two major tests with grades below 70.)

(State what you have done and share documentation.)

Is there anything you could tell me that will explain what is causing this problem?

(Ask the parent to share or suggest what might help.)

PARENT: I know she has continued to have problems because she's trying to work too many hours. She wants to buy another car because the one she's driving now is totally shot. We can't afford to help her pay for one. We have three other children, and two are in college.

TEACHER: I know we talked about this problem on the phone, but I didn't know the extent of it. What I will do is to continue to work with her at school and insist that she complete her work. I will also use positive reinforcement.

(Tell the parent what you plan to do at school.)

TEACHER: I know that Jan is going through a difficult time, and I want to support her as much as I can. I'm willing to tutor her any day this week to help her complete her unfinished work.

Is there anything you can do at home to make sure she is doing her work? Will you help her with her assignments or allow her to quit her job at MacBurger? I know that she has been working until 10:00 p.m. on some nights, and she does seem tired.

(Ask the parents what they could do at home, and suggest certain consequences when appropriate.)

PARENT: Well, we could ask Jan to cut back the hours, especially during the week. I know she wants another car, but schoolwork is more important.

TEACHER: Let's devise a plan. I will send a note home each night with Jan telling you if she has completed her work that day. Each night, please sign it and ask her to bring it to me the next day. If she finishes all her work during the week, then you might allow her to work until 8:00 p.m. on weekdays and later on the weekends.

PARENT: Well, this might work. She must finish school.

TEACHER: I'm sure together we can help Jan. I have other students with this problem, and I have seen this plan work in the past.

(Express confidence and let them know that you have dealt with similar problems.)

TEACHER: Let me make sure that I am clear as to what we are going to do. I will continue to work with Jan during the lunch hour if she fails to turn in assignments,
and I will also use positive reinforcement when she does complete her work.
Each day I will send home a note to let you know how she is doing. So that I am
clear, what are you going to do at home?

(Check for understanding by asking the parents to explain what they intend to do.)

ACTIVITY **7.11**
Problem-Solving Script

Use the following form to script a conference. Think of a problem that a senior in high school
may have.

Examples: Breaking up with that significant other
Working long hours to pay for a car, the rent, or family needs
Being bullied by gang members
Skipping school or being tardy every other day
Having senioritis (college seniors sometimes fall prey to this disease too)

Positive opening and concern statement: _____

_____

_____

State what you have done: _____

_____

_____

Ask for parental input: _____

_____

_____

State what you will do: _____

_____

_____

Suggest what the parent could do to help: _____

_____

_____

Check for understanding and close: _____

_____

_____

PARENT: We will read the note and sign it. If she has not completed her work, then she will cut back her hours during the week and on weekends.

TEACHER: I will call you next week to make sure everything is going well. I appreciate your visit. Feel free to call me if you have any questions or if there is a problem. I enjoy working with Jan because she is one of those students who always participates in class and is friendly to everyone. I know you are very proud of her, and I feel that we have made tremendous progress today.

(Close with a statement that you will call the parents back to reevaluate the plan.)

As you prepare for, conduct, and follow up on parent–teacher conferences, you might find a rubric helpful to reflect on what worked and what didn't.

General Rubric for All Conferences*

Directions: Examine each conference tip that follows and then rate your own skill on each item. Scale: 1 = rarely ever happens to me, 3 = applies half of the time, 5 = applies to me most or all of the time. Add your scores for each item and compare your total with ranges on page 131.

Preparing for the Conference	*Rating Scale*
1. (Doing Your Homework!) Before the conference, I reflect about the child's interests, needs, and actual work in school. It is helpful for me to write out some ideas I plan to discuss with the parents.	1 2 3 4 5
2. (Partnership) Unless proven otherwise, I believe that the parents and I are concerned with the same basic goal—*helping the child.*	1 2 3 4 5
3. (Differences in Judgment) I realize that there may be legitimate, honest differences of opinion about working with children. I write my basic beliefs and assumptions on paper to clarify my own point of view. Then I try to determine parents' beliefs during the first conference.	1 2 3 4 5
4. I don't consider parents' concerns as a personal attack or an affront to my integrity. Part of my job as a teacher is helping parents to better understand their children and the school.	1 2 3 4 5
5. (Impromptu Conferences) I don't get into "conferences" at PTO, open house night, or the grocery store. I listen to parent concerns and then make a specific appointment to meet to discuss the problem.	1 2 3 4 5
6. (Keep Administrators Informed) Prior to any conference, I inform my team leader or principal of any concerns or questions I may have.	1 2 3 4 5

*Reprinted by permission of Grace Quantock, Former Assistant Principal, Huntsville High School, Huntsville ISD.

Preparing for the Conference   *Rating Scale*

7. I identify specific examples of student work and bring them to   1 2 3 4 5
   conferences so I will not be talking about casual impressions.

8. If the conference is likely to involve discussion of standardized   1 2 3 4 5
   test scores, I examine student folders and talk with the counselor
   ahead of time so that I can explain test data accurately and in
   nontechnical language.

Conductng the Conference   *Rating Scale*

1. I am straightforward in my communication—neither aggressive/   1 2 3 4 5
   demanding, vague/mysteriously aloof, nor apologetic/
   uncomfortable. I am myself and help parents feel relaxed as well.

2. I am prepared to listen to parents' questions and concerns.   1 2 3 4 5
   I ask questions for clarification when I am uncertain about
   their "true" concern.

3. I avoid comparing a child with other siblings or friends,   1 2 3 4 5
   and I encourage parents to think of each child as a unique
   individual as well.

4. I always remember that teachers and parents observe children's   1 2 3 4 5
   behavior in different settings; therefore, we may observe
   different behaviors. I probe for examples/illustrations from
   settings that are different from the classroom (e.g., outside
   clubs/groups, family activities) that may lend additional
   information about the child.

5. In talking with parents, I focus on the child's behavior/   1 2 3 4 5
   performance and my own observations/concerns instead
   of what the parents may believe the problem to be.

6. I focus on how we can best work together to help the child   1 2 3 4 5
   rather than on polarized attitudes (the school versus unreasonable
   home demands).

7. I emphasize the child's work, feelings, and behavior. I deal with   1 2 3 4 5
   evidence of the child's work.

8. I am alert to the strengths and weaknesses of a child and relate   1 2 3 4 5
   both types of information to parents.

9. I never criticize parents personally. I avoid defensiveness and   1 2 3 4 5
   hostility on their part *and* on mine.

10. I work diligently at each conference to help parents (and myself)   1 2 3 4 5
    define specific problem statements (skills/concepts to be learned
    this year, behavior problems) and then to develop a definite plan

Conducting the Conference	*Rating Scale*

of action. I make sure that my responsibilities in each case are
clearly delineated.

11. I end each conference with a summary of major points, plans, and   1   2   3   4   5
consensus. I set plans for a follow-up evaluation conference, either
in person or by phone, to evaluate progress on a problem situation.

Follow-Up after the Conference	*Rating Scale*

1. If concerns discussed at a conference have not been resolved to   1   2   3   4   5
my satisfaction or that of the parents, I share my feelings candidly
and set up a second conference with other people present
who may be able to help. This action is an appropriate step in
difficult cases and does not reflect on my ability to conduct
conferences effectively.

2. I am willing to think about parents' ideas, suggestions, and   1   2   3   4   5
comments and incorporate them into compromise solutions in
an effort to avoid polarization.

3. I am not threatened and do not respond angrily toward a parent   1   2   3   4   5
or child when disagreements arise.

4. I seek specialized assistance when a problem is particularly   1   2   3   4   5
challenging. I know I am not the "single-handed master solver"
of every problem.

5. I keep written records of my conferences, plans, and follow-up   1   2   3   4   5
evaluations so I can continuously monitor progress of students
and my conferencing skills.

110–120	You are superior at dealing with parents in problem situations.
75–109	There is probably some friction and misunderstanding in your conferences.
24–74	Your conferences probably do more harm than good.

Summary

Parents want to know that their children are receiving the best education possible. They seldom question a pediatrician because the doctors are skilled, trained professionals. However, sometimes teachers, especially beginning teachers, are not confident in their abilities. A beginning teacher has had many experiences working with students. In fact, with both early field experiences and student teaching, secondary teachers can honestly say that they have worked with hundreds of youngsters. If you have carefully thought out what is best for a student and have scripted what you will say, then you should feel confident in dealing with parents. You are working toward a common goal: to educate tomorrow's future leaders.

REFERENCES

Association of Texas Professional Educators. (1997). *New teacher handbook: 1997–98.* [Pamphlet]. Austin: Author.

Becker, H. J., & Epstein, J. L. (1982). Parent involvement: A survey of teacher practices. *The Elementary School Journal, 83*(2), 85–102.

Burden, P. R. (1995). *Classroom management and discipline: Methods to facilitate cooperation and instruction.* White Plains, NY: Longman.

Charles, C. M. (1999). *Building classroom discipline* (6th ed.). New York: Addison Wesley Longman.

Darby, C. (1979). Parent conferences. [Handout from summer graduate course at Sam Houston State University].

Emmer, E. T., Evertson, C. M., Clements, B. S., & Worsham, M. E. (1997). *Classroom management for secondary teachers.* Boston: Allyn & Bacon.

Felber, S. A. (1997). Strategies for parent partnerships. *The Council for Exceptional Children, 30*(1), 20–23.

Gibbons, M. F. (1992). Student success through home/school collaboration. *The Delta Kappa Gamma Bulletin, 58*(4), 35–38.

Hammock, B., & Monday, J. (n.d.). *Walker County partners in education: PIE* [Brochure]. Huntsville and New Waverly, TX: Huntsville/Walker County Chamber of Commerce with Huntsville and New Waverly Independent School Districts.

Hoerr, T. R. (1997). When teachers listen to parents. *Principal, 77*(2), 40–42.

Lamb, C. (1995). 8 ways to defuse hostile parents. *Learning, 23*(5), 26–27.

Newman, R. (1997/98). Parent conferences: A conversation between you and your child's teacher. *Childhood Education: Infancy through Early Adolescence, 74*(2), 100–101.

Rioux, J. W., & Berla, N. (1993). *Innovations in parent and family involvement.* Princeton Junction, NJ: Eye on Education.

Swap, S. M. (1993). *Developing home-school partnerships: From concepts to practice.* New York: Teachers College Press.

U.S. Department of Education (1986). *What works: Research about teaching and learning.* Washington, DC: U.S. Government Printing Office.

Weinstein, C. S. (1996). *Secondary classroom management: Lessons from research and practice.* New York: McGraw-Hill.

Wolfgang, C. (1995). *Solving discipline problems* (3rd ed.). Boston: Allyn & Bacon.

Wong, H. K., & Wong, R. T. (1991). *The first days of school.* Sunnyvale, CA: Author.

PART THREE

Understanding Student Behavior and Applying Consequences

The adolescent years are the most awkward and confusing times of our lives. Growth means change, and change brings confusion. Exacerbating the problem, different kinds of growth occur—physical, psychological, social, and emotional. Further intensifying the problem, growth among these areas is uneven. If teachers are to work effectively with teenagers, they must understand why appropriate and inappropriate behaviors occur. Every behavior has a cause. Chapter 8 examines behaviors that characterize this age group and helps the readers understand why adolescents behave as they do.

Effective classroom managers must take this investigation further and learn how to stimulate appropriate behavior and extinguish inappropriate behavior. Chapter 9 gives several teacher actions that reinforce desirable student behavior and suggests effective ways of responding to inappropriate student behavior.

Chapter 10 provides techniques and strategies to help teachers deal with solving social problems of youths who join deviant groups. Both schoolwide and classroom solutions are discussed.

8 Understanding the Behavior of Secondary Students

Adolescence can be an exciting but also turbulent period that finds expression in a variety of behaviors and activities.

OBJECTIVES

1. Interpret the following statement: "The adolescent is facing a dilemma that presents frustration and confusion."
2. Write a brief, exact statement concerning the general trend of the adolescent crime rate in this country.
3. Draw a graph to show the relationships among a particular student's social, emotional, psychological, and physical growth rates.

Nelson McPherson, a veteran social studies teacher, looked up from the paper he was grading as Marge, a second-year English teacher, arms loaded with papers, literally stumbled into the teachers' lounge. Having just faced a rowdy class of seventh graders, she was already showing signs of exhaustion, and three-fourths of the day was still ahead. With nineteen years of teaching behind him, Nelson had just about seen it all. Seeing Marge's frustration, he smiled kindly when she uttered the all-to-familiar teachers' lounge expression, "Teaching would be great if it weren't for the students."

Overview

We hear Marge's words too often from teachers, even though most of them give "a love for working with young people" as their reason for choosing the profession. Once on the job, most teachers find that they are continuously in situations that make them wish they had a better understanding of adolescents. As a future teacher, you need to know what motivates students' behavior and why that behavior is changeable and unpredictable.

Adults cannot view the world as adolescents do, but they can understand the perspective better if they are aware of the forces that motivate adolescents either to accept and adjust or to reject and rebel. You will need to know about their value system and how they select those things that they prize most. What obstacles delay, limit, or even prevent their learning? These are a few of the questions that we shall examine in this chapter. As you read, try to remember your own teenage experiences; then picture yourself helping your future students solve problems and appreciate and enjoy your classes.

Meeting Our Needs

Adolescents and adults share the same basic needs, but adolescents often feel these needs more intensely. In fact, teenagers experience so many needs simultaneously that they are typically confused and frustrated. The teacher who understands the basis for such feelings can

---

ACTIVITY **8.1**

Identifying Your Needs

Throughout life, we look to groups to help us meet our needs. Some needs remain constant as we outgrow and discard others. Think about your daily needs and, in particular, those for which you look to various groups to supply. List the most important groups in your life and identify at least one need that each group satisfies (for example, family, cheerleading squad, campus organizations, religious groups).

Groups	**Needs**
1.	1.
2.	2.
3.	3.
4.	4.

find ways to help students achieve their desires or learn to cope without achieving them. Satisfaction of personal, social, and psychological needs is often necessary before the student can become free to concentrate on classroom lessons. Two of the most basic needs are belonging to groups of other human beings and learning to value and appreciate oneself. The teacher is in a key position to help students achieve.

Though individuals feel a need to be accepted by others, some show this need very intensely, whereas others appear to experience it in lesser degrees. Yet all people need other people. Because, in their rapidly changing lives, there are many people whom they have to please, adolescents often find themselves in serious dilemmas; for example, some behavior that will please their friends may alienate their parents. One of the authors remembers "borrowing" her parent's car when she was in junior high school, not knowing how to drive. Her friends wanted to go riding, and she decided to deal with the consequences later. She soon discovered that this wasn't a smart move. She was grounded and the phone was taken out of the house so she couldn't use it. Angry parents sometimes do strange things too.

Dealing with Bullies

Peer Group Pressure

At no other time in life do people experience the closeness of their peers as they do in adolescence. And because this is a time of rapid development, adolescents admire those who seem best to understand their uncertainties and anxieties—their peers. How often do parents hear adolescents explain their reason for doing certain things with "Everybody's doing it"? "Everybody," of course, means their peers. Peers are intolerant of anyone who is different. As Levine (1998) explains, "Intolerance in school often takes the form of bullying, or putting another person down through physical threats or verbal taunting" (p. 34).

Bullying is often seen as a part of growing up, but as Barone (1997) explains, it is serious and widespread, and although solutions require effective preparation, it is preventable. "Students who are the victims of bullies and school officials who hold the power to stop them have very different perceptions of the problem. This difference has hindered effective prevention efforts" (p. 81).

In 1993, Barone (1997) surveyed 847 eighth graders and 110 counselors, teachers, and administrators in the same schools as the students. He defined bullying as "a situation when a student or group of students is mean to you over a long period of time (weeks or even months). Bullying can either be physical (hitting, kicking, and so on) or it can be verbal (threats, name calling, gossiping, or ignoring)" (p. 81). Barone asked the school's staff members to estimate the percentage of the students who had been bullied. The responses indicated that 16 percent of the students had been victims of bullies. When asked whether they had "ever been bothered by a bully or bullies while you were in middle school," 58.8 percent of the students said they had.

The discrepancy suggests that teachers are not always aware of the bullying that occurs in their schools. Surprisingly, according to the students' own perceptions, the majority (53 percent) of the victims of bullies are girls. This bullying usually is verbal abuse, as contrasted with physical bullying among boys. However, sometimes girls do receive physical abuse, even serious enough to require hospitalization. Of those students allegedly injured by a bully, 76.5 percent were boys.

ACTIVITY **8.2**

What's Wrong with This Picture?

A middle school creative writing teacher related this story to us. Dennis, a new student with an Americanized name, had recently moved from Russia to the United States. Even though he spoke English quite well, he was constantly bullied because he was different. One day, as the teacher monitored the hall between classes, she noticed a group of girls poking, pushing, and threatening Dennis. They were making fun of his clothes and hair, bumping into him so that he'd drop his books, and laughing at his accent. They kept saying "excuse me" as they hit him.

What should the teacher have done? What would you do in this situation? Would it matter if you didn't know any of the students? What would you do about your class that is about to begin? Have you ever seen girls bully boys? (Yes, this happens.) What should happen to the bullies? Any consequences?

As Paul Harvey would say, here's the rest of the story. The teacher quickly told Dennis that she needed to talk to him about something. Then she put her hand on his shoulder and reeled him into the room. The girls immediately walked off, but she reported them to the administrators. Did she handle the situation correctly?

Effective Remedies

Barone (1997) asked the respondents to name the three most effective ways of solving bullying problems in school. Teachers recommended "tougher discipline" (41.4 percent), followed by "better supervision" (33.7 percent). Students, however, most often recommended "more counseling." Both groups recommended closer supervision. Barone concluded that stronger discipline codes, closer supervision, and sterner repercussions are needed to hold students accountable.

Also important is the location of the supervision, for example, in hallways, recreational areas, and locker rooms. The majority of bullying was found to occur in the hallways. Interestingly, only 10.6 percent of the staff surveyed felt that most of the bullying in their school takes place in the hallways.

Intervention Programs

Daniel Olweus (1991) describes an intervention program in Norway designed to diminish bullying in schools. Throughout Norway, a 32-page booklet is used to educate teachers, other school officials, and parents about bullying. This program reportedly creates a warm and positive climate, sets firm limits on unacceptable behavior, consistently applies sanctions against bullying, and helps adults act as authority figures.

The Norwegian program blends close supervision of strict and straightforward rules, rewards and praise, parent encouragement of student friendships, and nonphysical punishment to children who misbehave. Roland (1983), also of Norway, uses reading to diminish bullying. He has a class read and discuss a story about bullying. Students must reflect on the story and express their feelings and thoughts about being bullied. The students then pair up and role-play, often reversing the role of the bully and the victim. Students act as peer sponsors, who assume responsibility for looking after younger children. And finally, Roland uses class meetings in which the group assumes responsibility for the well-being of all its members. An evaluation of the program, following twenty months of implementation, showed a fifty percent decline in bullying.

St. John-Brooks (1990) describes a school in North London where all students are required to tell someone when they have been bullied. This school takes the position that students have a right to come to school without being afraid and that they have an obligation to report all bullying. Some British schools have established "bully courts" to try and sentence offenders (Stead, 1990). A faculty advisor and four students meet weekly to read descriptions of bullying behavior and administer such punishment as after-school detention and eating lunch in isolation. Mellor's (1990) study of bullying in Scotland outlines some proven strategies for combating bullying. The school must acknowledge ongoing bullying problems; acknowledge that bullying hurts students; condemn bullying throughout the school; and involve parents, teachers, and pupils in formulating an antibullying policy so that they will have a vested interest in making it succeed.

Greenbaum (1989) discusses ten prevention and intervention strategies that schools can employ.

1. Use a questionnaire to determine the scope of the problem.
2. Communicate clear standards of behavior and consistently enforce them.
3. Monitor playgrounds closely.
4. Establish a recording system for incidents of bullying.
5. Provide students with opportunities to discuss bullying.
6. Never overlook intentionally abusive acts.
7. Contact the parents of both the victims and the bullies when a problem occurs.
8. Establish intervention programs.
9. Encourage parent participation.
10. Provide support and protection for victims.

Bullying does not have to be part of a child's school experience. It is not "part of growing up," nor is it a "rite of passage." By working together, schools and parents can make going to school an experience that students will enjoy, not dread.

Adolescent Wants and Needs

Peer pressures on a student's behavior will become obvious to you as a teacher. You will see students look to each other for approval. When you ask a question, students may look to others before responding; if not, they may hear groans or hisses. Recall times when you hesitated to ask a question for fear of appearing stupid. You knew that your response would be judged by the group. Or how many times did you decide not to purchase a particular shirt or pair of shoes because they weren't "in"? At one high school, students cut the labels out of coats and sweaters, replacing them with a brand name acceptable to their peers. At another, a high school student was robbed and killed for his name-brand shoes. Often students will purposefully work to receive certain grades (either high or low) to please their peers. In some groups an F is a disgrace; in others an A is an equal disgrace. Therefore, the adolescent is faced with trying to conform without even knowing the standards. With a combination of unknown and ever-changing standards (what's "in" at age fourteen can be totally taboo at age fifteen) and conflicting standards (what my friends expect me to do are often those things that my parents would dread the most), it is no wonder that the adolescent is often confused and anxious.

ACTIVITY **8.3**

What's in Style?

Visit the local teenage meeting place. In some areas it's the mall, the parking lot of a fast-food restaurant, or the teen night club in town. Observe students and write a list of what seems to be "in" today. Pick two students whom you have never met and start a conversation with them. If possible, find students you would probably never talk to unless you were doing this activity.

- What are the students wearing? Do they all have designer labels on their clothes?
- If they are old enough, what types of cars do they drive?
- What are the newest slang words? Have the "in" words changed since you were in high school? (The answer is yes.)
- What does this age group want to talk about?
- How did they treat you as an "older" person?

Write a two-page summary of what you have learned from this experience.

Challenges and failure within the secondary schools can add to this anxiety and hostility (Silbergeld, Manderscheid, & O'Neill, 1975).

Another strong need of adolescents is to be very close to a few people. The fortunate ones find this need met in their homes, but millions of youths do not have the home lives that provide this close relationship. In fact, many home environments are so bad and the relationships between youths and their parents are so poor that two million American youths leave home every year. Young people who do not find warmth at home look to their classmates and teachers to find acceptance and deep mutual respect. The maturing adolescent also begins to look more and more toward members of the opposite sex for close friendship ties.

A study by the National Education Association queried ninety-five secondary students as to what they thought might be done to improve their schools and their schooling (Shane, 1977). They expressed three major concerns. They wanted schools that would help them learn to *cope* in a world that they find frustrating, distressing, and sometimes frightening. Between 1984 and 1994, the number of young people charged with killing another young person increased by 144 percent (Dohrn, 1997). Second, they wanted schools that *cared* about them as people. Because many parents today seem to substitute things rather than giving of themselves, the students looked to their teachers for warmth and personal concern. Finally, they wanted their schools to teach them how to *communicate* their feelings, hopes, and concerns. Although parents may value most the 3R's, students clearly value most the 3C's—coping, caring, and communication.

In addition to providing students with some needed attention and friendship, some teachers are offering special courses on coping. These courses appear to be working very well. For example, when a junior high school offered four courses in coping with stressful situations, the results were highly satisfactory. Afterward, the students who were in the courses had fewer interactions with classmates, but those discussions were longer, more personal, and had more content (Silbergeld & Manderscheid, 1976). The potential of such programs can be increased by including experiences that help students learn to use their own adaptive assets. In fact, according to one expert (Hamburg, 1974), coping skills programs are crucial.

As a beginning teacher, you will want to find out whether your school already offers courses in coping, and, if so, whether you will have the option of recommending some of your students whom you feel might benefit. If your school is not currently offering such a course, you may discuss with your administrators and colleagues the possibility of developing one.

Independence

In direct conflict with adolescents' needs for acceptance and approval is their need for independence. Since early childhood they have been gradually learning independence, which is natural and necessary for good mental health, and even for intellectual growth. Emotional independence from others has been found to correlate highly with the ability to establish relationships with peers, to master intellectual requirements, and to rely on one's own conscience (Cronbach, 1963). Of course, learning to rely on one's own conscience is itself a type of independence. Today's teachers and school programs give much attention to helping all students learn to develop and understand their own set of values.

Here, then, is another dilemma for adolescents. They are bound by a need to earn the approval of others and yet have an equally strong need to become independent. Indeed, this is the basis for much of their frustration, for many situations appear impossible to solve without disappointing either themselves or their friends. They need to find alternative ways of responding that meet the approval of their friends, teachers, and parents and yet are acceptable to their own values.

The need for independence increases as adolescents grow older. Often the automobile becomes a means of expanding the physical environment, which they feel is trying to smother them with demands and expectations. It becomes not only a symbol of freedom and independence but also a way of achieving them.

Growth Patterns

Adolescent Development

Several characteristics of the growth patterns of adolescence make this a very complex process. The adolescent is growing physically, mentally, emotionally, and socially. Although the rates of growth in the separate areas are different, they are not at all unrelated because one's growth in one channel can significantly affect the rates in others. For example, the adolescent portrayed in Figure 8.1, Jerry, is physically more mature than most others. Physical maturity

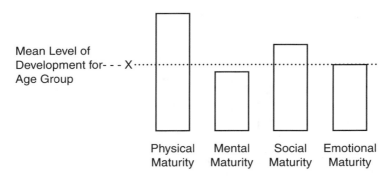

FIGURE 8.1 Channels of Adolescent Development—Physical (Jerry's Profile)

can lead to acceptance and even popularity because it enables the student to compete in sports and may increase favorable attention from members of the opposite sex. The fact that this adolescent's mental growth is slightly below average does not seem to affect his emotional stability. His large physical size or coordination probably overcompensates for this lag, leaving him confident about himself.

Physical Growth

Physical maturity is extremely important to teenagers. Size and muscular coordination are important, not only for competitive sports but also for everyday situations. The teenage boy who lags in physical development may be ridiculed for his awkwardness or bullied because of his small stature. Girls may experience similar abuse if they become too buxom or too tall (Shakeshaft, Mande, Johnson, Sawyer, Hergenrother, & Barber, 1997). Thus, it is not uncommon to see a teenage boy stretch to appear taller and a teenage girl slump to appear shorter. Girls whose physical development rates lag behind those of their classmates may find themselves left out during social events, and boys may be ridiculed if their voices remain at a high pitch longer than usual.

Modern medical science has developed substances that, through injection, can increase the growth rate significantly. Much is to be learned about such treatments, but many possible side effects may result that are yet unknown and, thus, are unpredictable.

Mental Maturity

There is more to mental maturity than the accumulation of knowledge or the increasing of one's intelligence quotient. Swiss psychologist Jean Piaget studied how the mind develops and described levels of cognitive ability in terms of the mind's capability of performing certain feats. Piaget found that as mental development progresses, the individual learns to complete increasingly complex types of operations. The learner cannot bypass one level and jump to a higher level. In other words, there is a predictable sequence of stages.

The student profiled in Figure 8.2 is smaller than other classmates, but the adolescent's mental skills are superior. Because this teenager, whom we'll call Kevin, can think in more abstract terms, he may become very frustrated when he can conceptualize certain things that his body cannot do. For example, the ability to play certain sports or musical instruments may

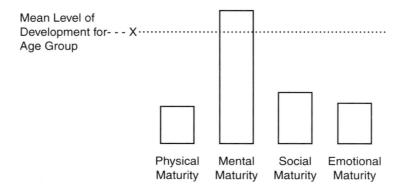

FIGURE 8.2   Channels of Adolescent Development—Mental (Kevin's Profile)

seem simple; however, when he tries he discovers that he does not have the psychomotor control necessary to succeed. His friends may criticize and tease him because of his size. And this ridicule may be hard to accept if he is in other ways more mature than his friends. His mental maturity may win the approval and respect of classmates or it may even alienate them, depending on how he uses or misuses his mental superiority. Peer rejection or isolation can lead to feelings of insecurity and eventually may lead to emotional problems. This student who is capable of performing complex mental operations may even develop a feeling of superiority and exhibit snobbish behavior; thus, his social development is curtailed. Although the ability of an adolescent to meet the expectations of his family, friends, and teachers is very important, it is no more significant than the ways he chooses to use his abilities.

Social and Emotional Maturity

The teenager's social and emotional growth rates are very closely related. Failure to live up to others' expectations can eventually lead to emotional problems and social rejection. By age eleven or twelve, youths develop the ability to conceptualize about their own thoughts. Because peer pressure is great and adolescents are often egocentric, they fail to differentiate between what others are thinking about and their own mental preoccupations. Instead, they assume that other people are as obsessed with their behavior and appearances as they are (Elkind, 1974).

Ironically, adolescents' concern for what others may think of them can become so intense that it can blind them to what those expectations really are. Their preoccupation with themselves can undermine their social acceptance. Conversely, the student, Susan, whose profile is shown in Figure 8.3, relates well to peers and is well received by them. Therefore, she is likely to feel emotionally secure and confident.

ACTIVITY **8.4**

Who Am I? Yesterday and Today

Think of your seventh grade school year and draw a profile of who you were at the time. Make a graph that includes the four areas: physical, mental, social, and emotional maturity. Now answer the questions: Who are you? What helped you become more mature? Did any teachers play a part in your maturation? Were you ever teased or ridiculed? Write about that incident.

Average Maturity
Level for Age---X ---
Group

Physical   Mental   Social   Emotional

See page 142 for an example of a graph.

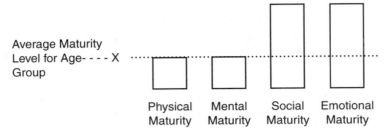

FIGURE 8.3   Channels of Adolescent Development—Social and Emotional (Susan's Profile)

The ability to adjust socially and emotionally requires an adequate, positive view of oneself. This view comes from an accumulation of successful experiences and an attitude toward problems as challenges rather than as threats. The teacher's role in providing experiences essential for systematic social and emotional growth seems clear. Teachers can take several proactive actions to ensure more positive self-concepts among their students.

Conflict and Violence

Adolescent psychologist Erik Erikson (1968) has described adolescence as a time of identity crisis. He lists the following seven conflicts that arise during adolescence:

1. Temporal perspective versus time confusion.
2. Self-certainty versus self-consciousness.

ACTIVITY **8.5**

My Personal Goals

Review the list of ways to develop students' self-concepts on page 97. Then write a lesson plan in which you describe activites to teach students how to set goals. You can have them design goals either for "our" class or for their individual needs.

Sample Plan
Objective: Each student will identify one personal goal to achieve and describe how to attain it.

Activities: Have students read books about outstanding individuals, such as Helen Keller and Christopher Reeve, who have excelled in some area. Break the class into groups and have them illustrate on butcher paper ways these individuals have succeeded. Put these papers on the classroom walls.

Have students freewrite for two minutes on the topic: "My Personal Goal for This Year Is . . ." Have them choose their most important goal.

Evaluation: Ask each student to complete a chart that states the following:

- My personal goal for this year is _____
- I will achieve it by _____
- I will check my progress on _____

3. Role experimentation versus role fixation.
4. Apprenticeship versus work paralysis.
5. Sexual polarization versus bisexual confusion.
6. Leader-and-followership versus authority confusion.
7. Ideological commitment versus confusion in values.

A brief look at this list gives the reader a feeling for the intense frustration of adolescence. Given the nature of adolescent life, it is not surprising to learn that in this country 43 percent of all serious crimes are committed by young people within the ten to fifteen year age group or that the peak age for committing violent crime is fourteen. By the end of the ninth grade, 20 percent of adolescents will have a drinking problem (Hurd, 1979). Although many adolescents vent their frustrations on society, others direct their anger at themselves. Among young people between fifteen and nineteen years old, suicide is one of the leading causes of death (Sartore, 1976). And the United States has 75 percent of the child murders in the industrialized world (Dohrn, 1995).

For a decade now the National Center for Education Statistics of the U.S. Department of Education has conducted surveys every three years, sampling 50,000 public school teachers. The results, presented in Figure 8.4, show that teachers perceived increased school violence in five out of the seven categories measured. These areas were physical conflicts, robbery or theft, student possession of weapons, vandalism of school property, and verbal abuse of teachers.

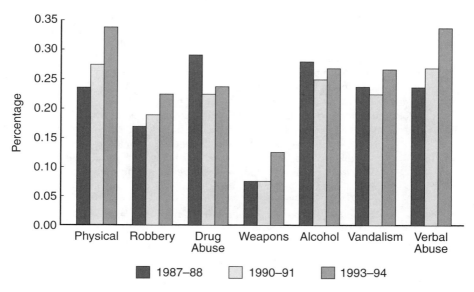

FIGURE 8.4 School Problems over the Past Decade: Percentage of Teachers Who See Problems

Source: U.S. Department of Education, National Center for Education Statistics.

Seeking Solutions

What Can You Do?

Obviously, the growth in school violence is rapid and should be of great concern to all teachers. Litke (1996) provides the following suggestions.

- *Be proactive in dealing with student violence.* If violence is not a problem at your school, do not assume that it cannot become a problem. Make safety part of your mission and values. Have a clear policy in place, and notify all stakeholders about it.
- *Use a multifaceted approach to dealing with student violence.* No one factor contributes to bullying and other acts of harassment or violence. Zero-tolerance policies, therefore, are not enough. Educators need to increase supervision throughout the school, teach values of tolerance and respect, increase student ownership, and build interpersonal relationships in the school. Consider involving other agencies such as the police department in your plan.

> Thus far this year, incidents of fighting are rare, and the number of fights has gone down significantly. Expulsions, suspensions, and reported incidents of bullying have also decreased. (Litke, 1996, p. 80)

- *Form an advisory program.* If your junior high school or middle school does not have an advisory program, take steps to implement one. . . . [T]eaching values, fostering acceptance, and building relationships are essential elements in building effective schools. Advisory classes provide the perfect forum for these types of activities.
- *Be aware of group dynamics.* In our situation, a number of the students who caused trouble were reasonable, articulate young people when dealt with on a one-to-one basis. In a group situation, however, they became less than reasonable and dangerous to other students. When planning strategies to deal with intimidation and bullying, be sure to look at the effects of group behavior.
- *When in the middle of a crisis, take action; don't philosophize.* I understand that many educators would have definite problems with some of the top-down decisions that we made during our year of turmoil. Establishing a bottom-up consensus about antiviolence policies and procedures would have been preferable. If you have a mission statement and goals that include a belief in a safe school, however, you'll probably receive support for taking swift actions. We received very little criticism from the public for enacting harsh consequences for violent actions. The harshest criticism often comes from perceived inaction rather than action.
- *Remember that good reputations take many years to build and only a short time to tarnish.* We are doing a better job in dealing with problems of violent behavior than any period during my seven years at this school. Community perceptions about bullying in our school, however, have not been quick to disappear. There is still negative talk in the community. Restoring our reputation is proving to be as big a challenge as restoring order in the school. (pp. 79–80)

ACTIVITY **8.6**
Read All about It

For two weeks, collect newspaper and magazine clippings that are stories about teenagers. Make a class bulletin board on which everyone adds articles that depict youth in a positive light. Count the number of positive versus negative articles. Discuss how teenagers are portrayed in the media. Is this an accurate portrayal? How can teachers help society view youth in positive ways?

Underachievers

Many of today's youths suffer from a severe lack of energy and commitment needed to succeed academically. The Carnegie Corporation's report, *Years of Promise* (1996), reflects the seriousness of this problem.

> Make no mistake about it: underachievement is not a crisis of certain groups; it is not limited to the poor; it is not a problem afflicting other people's children. Many middle- and upper-income children are also falling behind intellectually. Indeed, by the fourth grade, the performance of most children in the United States is below what it should be for the nation and is certainly below the achievement levels of children in competing countries. (p. 9)

Consider the mental and emotional condition that youths face when they lack both the motivation to achieve and the achievement level needed to feel good toward themselves. Rimm (1997) describes this quality that is found throughout school-age youths:

> Underachievers don't have internal locus of control, nor do they function well in competition. The lack of internal locus of control translates to a missed connection between effort and outcome; underachievers haven't learned about hard work. Underachieving students are often magical in thinking; they expect to be anointed to fame and fortune. They want to be professional football players even when they have never played football; they strum the guitar hoping their unique sound will be discovered by a passing talent scout. They know they're smart because they've been told that by almost everyone. They just don't know how to be productively smart. If they put forth effort, they no longer have an excuse to protect their fragile self-concepts. They've defined smart as "easy" and anything that is difficult threatens their sense of being smart.
>
> The competition problem is less obvious because underachievers often declare that they are good sports. It is their behavior that tells you that losing experiences make them feel like losers. They avoid any risk of losing and choose only activities or interests at which they are best; but when they hit the proverbial "walls," they quit, drop out, or choose something else. (p. 18)

Rimm (1997) offers teachers the following five-stage strategy to help underachievers overcome their losers' syndrome.

- Overreaction by parents to children's successes and failures leads them to feel either intense pressure to succeed or despair and discouragement in dealing with failure.

- Children can learn appropriate behaviors more easily if they have an effective model to imitate.
- Deprivation and excess frequently exhibit the same symptoms.
- Children feel more tension when they are worrying about their work than when they are doing that work.
- Children develop self-confidence through struggle. (p. 22)

High Expectations, Parent Support, and a Work Ethic

Although there is no simple answer to the complicated question of underachievement, we can use the Trifocal Model as a framework for some principles that we know underlie good learning. If parents have realistically high expectations, if they respect teachers and teachers respect them, and if children can be taught a healthy work ethic, despite the multiple problems in our society, resilience and achievement can be taught. We need to emphasize the words, *realistically high expectations*. Some parents inhibit their children's academic success by raising the bar too high. These parents want their children to be stars, and when they don't meet the parents' expectations, both the parents and students see themselves as failures. As parents and educators, we must accept our leadership responsibilities. If we can build students' confidence and competencies, we can empower them gradually as they grow in maturity and wisdom.

Summary

Adolescents experience the same basic needs that all humans share, including (1) the need for safety, (2) the need to belong, (3) the need for esteem, and (4) the need for self-actualization. Often, though, they may experience these needs much more intensely, because they are forever trying to adjust to changing demands. It brings a changing environment as well as internal changes; therefore, adolescence is often described as a period of uncertainty, frustration, and even depression. The advent of puberty and a need to display appropriate sexual behavior often accentuate feelings of awkwardness, fear, and depression. The teacher who is aware of these conditions may be able to accept the student and understand the problems.

Adolescents' strong need for approval leads to many conflicts. The various people from whom they seek approval may expect opposing kinds of behavior. Further accentuating the dilemma, at the time in life when they most need acceptance from others, they are experiencing an increasing need to become independent. When these two needs are in direct conflict, they must try either to please others or themselves. Sometimes the teacher can help them find a third alternative, which will be acceptable to those whom young people wish to please and still let them be true to their own values.

As a teacher, your primary responsibility for the adolescents in your classrooms is for their learning; hence, you need to understand *how* they learn. Many schools of thought are at work today trying to explain how this process occurs. You will be wise to take an eclectic approach, trying to gain as much understanding as you can from each field. Chapter 9 will help you begin to develop the essential skills needed to become an expert teacher.

REFERENCES

Barone, F. T. (1997). Bullying in school: It doesn't have to happen. *Phi Delta Kappan, 79*(1), 80–82.

The Carnegie Corporation of New York. (1996). *Years of promise: A comprehensive learning strategy for America's children. Executive Summary.* New York: Carnegie Task Force on Learning.

Carr, M., & Kurtz-Costes, B. (1994). Is being smart everything? The influence of student achievement on teachers' perceptions. *British Journal of Educational Psychology, 64*(June), 263–276.

Combs, A. W. (1962). The positive view of self. In Arthur W. Combs (ed.), *Perceiving, Behaving, Becoming* (pp. 99–117). Washington, DC: Association for Supervision and Curriculum Development.

Cronbach, L. J. (1963). *Educational psychology* (2nd ed.). New York: Harcourt, Brace, and World.

Dohrn, B. (1997). Youth violence: False fears and hard truths. *Educational Leadership, 55*(2), 45–47.

Elkind, D. (1974). Egocentrism in children and adults. In *Children and adolescents: Interpretive essays on Jean Piaget* (2nd ed.) (pp. 74–95). New York: Oxford University Press.

Erikson, E. (1968). *Identity, youth and crisis.* New York: W. W. Norton.

Greenbaum, S. (1989). *Set straight on bullies.* Malibu, CA: National School Safety Center.

Hamburg, B. A. (1974). Coping in early adolescence. In G. Kaplan (ed.), *American handbook of psychiatry, Vol. 2. Child adolescent psychiatry, sociocultural and community psychiatry* (pp. 385–410). New York: Basic Books.

Henson, K. T., & Eller, B. F. (1999). *Educational psychology for effective teaching.* Belmont, CA: Wadsworth.

Hurd, P. (1979, April). Hurd reports new data on adolescence. *ASCD Newsletter 21.*

Levine, D. (1997). Someday that might be me. *Educational Leadership, 55*(2), 33–35.

Litke, C. D. (1996). When violence came to our rural school. *Educational Leadership, 54,* 77–80.

Mellor, A. (1990). *Bullying in Scottish secondary schools.* Edinburgh: Scottish Education Department.

Miserandino, M. (1996). Children who do well in school: Individual differences in perceived competence and autonomy in above average children. *Journal of Educational Psychology, 88*(2), 203–214.

Olweus, D. (1991). Bully/victim problems among school children: Basic facts and effects of a school-based intervention program. In Debra J. Pepler and Kenneth H. Rubin (eds.), *The development and treatment of childhood aggression* (pp. 411–418). Hillsdale, NJ: Erlbaum.

Rimm, S. B. (1997). An underachievement epidemic. *Educational Leadership, 54,* 18–22.

Roland, E. (1983). Strategy against mobbing. Oslo, Norway: Stavanger Universitetsforlaget.

Sartore, R. L. (1976). Students and suicide: An interpersonal tragedy. *Theory into Practice, 15* (December) 337–39.

Shakeshaft, C., Mande, L., Johnson, Y. M., Sawyer, J., Hergenrother, M. A., & Barber, E. (1997). Boys call me cow. *Educational Leadership, 55*(2), 22–25.

Shane, H. G. (1977). *Curriculum change toward the 21st century.* Washington, DC: National Education Association.

Silbergeld, S., & Manderscheid, R. W. (1976). Comparative assessment of a coping model for school adolescents. *Journal of School Psychology, 14* (Winter), 261–74.

Silbergeld, S., Manderscheid, R. W., & O'Neill, P. H. (1975). Free association anxiety and hostility: View from a junior high school. *Psychological Reports, 37,* 495–504.

Stead, D. (1990, January 7). British bullies toppled from the pulpit. *New York Times Education Life.* Section 4A, p. 7.

St. John-Brooks, C. (1990). The school bullies. *New Society, 6,* 1984.

9 Using Consequences and Positive Reinforcement

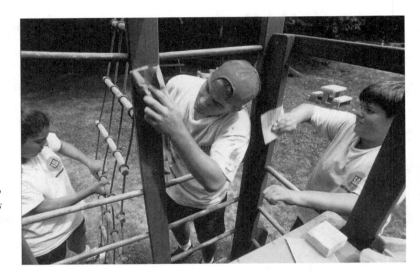

Finding positive solutions to student misbehavior, such as having students repair playground equipment, teaches students responsibility and improves their self-image.

OBJECTIVES

1. Distinguish between discipline and punishment.
2. Develop expectations for your classroom.
3. Develop a discipline hierarchy with a set of consequences.
4. Select natural and logical consequences.
5. Use positive reinforcement.
6. Identify the goals of students' misbehavior.
7. Confront severe or chronic misbehaviors and change those behaviors.

It's Tuesday morning and that means math quiz day. As you hand out the test in second period, you see two students in the back passing notes. You immediately question Neslon and Anthony about what's happening, and the note quickly disappears. Now they have made you curious. You walk toward the students and ask for the note. Both students deny that they have anything, but finally Anthony grudgingly hands you the piece of paper. It's the answers for the quiz that someone in first period gave them. You wonder how many others already know the answers before seeing the test, but you go ahead and give the test anyway.

Later as you're grading you become infuriated. Over half the class made 100, and you suspect rampant cheating. Do you discipline or punish the whole class? Do you reward those students who made less than 100? Now what's the next step?

Overview

After discussing self-discipline and student choice, we will describe consequences and reinforcement techniques with emphasis on those used in secondary classrooms. We will then address ways to handle severe and chronic misbehavior.

Defining the Terms

discipline /ˈdɪsɪplɪn/ *n. & v.*
n. control or order exercised over people or animals, esp. children, prisoners, military personnel, church members.
v. t. punish, chastise.

punish /ˈpʌnɪʃ/ *v. t.*
1. cause (an offender) to suffer for an offense.
2. abuse or treat improperly.

consequence /ˈkɒnsɪkw(ə)ns/ *n.* the result or effect of an action or condition.

reinforce /riːɪnˈfɔːs/ *v.* strengthen or support, esp. with additional personnel or by an increase of numbers or quantity of size etc.

reward /rɪˈwɔːd/ *n.* a return or recompense for service or merit.

Source: The Concise Oxford Dictionary, Ninth Edition, 1995.

Distinguishing between Discipline and Punishment

According to Bettelheim (1985), "The original definition of the word discipline refers to an instruction to be imparted to disciples" (p. 54). He contends that acquiring discipline and being a disciple are closely connected.

> Probably the only way for an undisciplined person to acquire discipline is through admiring and emulating someone who *is* disciplined. This process is greatly helped if the disciple believes that even if he is not *the* favorite of the master, at least he is one of the favorites. (p. 54)

Whereas discipline (i.e., guidance and training) teaches students self-discipline, punishment is *inflicted* on someone. Many people equate *discipline* with *punishment* and interchange these terms. We believe that there is a distinct difference and will use the terms as defined. Students are *subjected* to punishment. According to Hoover and Kindsvatter (1997), punishment is "imposing an aversive condition that is so unpleasant that it presumably will deter future behavior. Examples include giving harsh reprimands or ridicule, having the student perform onerous tasks such as writing a phrase repeatedly, or copying from the dictionary . . ." (pp. 164–165). Some teachers make students run laps for being tardy to physical education classes and then wonder why students are not excited about the jogging unit. When teachers use academic activities as punishment, whether it is writing one hundred sentences, doing push-ups, or running laps, they are sending mixed messages. How can the activities be enjoyable learning experiences one day and punishment the next?

To develop self-discipline, teachers must teach students how to make choices and allow them to do so. Whereas punishment closes choices, consequences provide students a way to control the discipline process. Are we having more discipline problems in schools today because we have limited the use of punishment (i.e., the paddle)? Answers to this question often fuel the public's uproar. In addition, teachers cannot agree about paddling. In the teachers' Gallup poll, approximately one-half of the teachers reported that paddling is effective in the earlier grades (Elam, 1989). If 50 percent of the teachers want it, are they right? Does it work? Authoritative literature suggests that mild forms, such as isolation, work, but physical punishment does not.

Self-Discipline and Choice

What choices did you, as a citizen, make today? Did you drive under or over the posted speed limit? Citizens choose to obey certain traffic codes or they usually face consequences (fines). You received a handbook and passed a test prior to receiving your driver's license.

Imagine that the "real world" of traffic laws operates as many secondary classrooms. We are expected to be "good citizens" and "safe drivers." Police decide if someone is not being a "good citizen" or "safe driver." No speed limit is posted, and each citizen must discover the speed limit by trial and error. If the police officer gives a ticket, then the citizen was driving too fast. Different police officers would interpret being a "good citizen" and "safe driver" as following different speed limits. Citizens would guess at the expectations.

Should teacher expectations and consequences be published or posted for students? Our laws operate this way in society, and secondary students should have the same rights inside the classroom. Burden (1995) recommends to "teach the rules as if they were subject-matter content; this could include a handout, a transparency, discussion, practice, and even a quiz" (p. 113).

Consequences

If students break rules, they are making choices to receive the consequences. Wong and Wong (1998) believe that "**Consequences are what results when a person abides by or breaks the rules. . . .** It may be better if less time is spent discussing rules and more time is spent discussing consequences **because a person's life, at any given point, is the result of that person's actions**" (p. 152). Secondary teachers must carefully select those consequences that act as a deterrent, something that students do not want to have happen. Does it need to be horrible?

No. Do teachers need to be consistent? Yes. If students know that consequences always follow, they often choose to behave appropriately. Examples of consequences include:

1. *Last Out.* Misbehaving students leave the classroom last. This consequence is immediate and effective. Precious minutes between classes give students opportunities to communicate with friends. Simply inform students to wait at their desks until dismissed. *Caution:* Teachers must allow enough time so that students are not tardy to their next classes. Otherwise, the teachers are infringing on someone else's right to begin class when the bell rings.

2. *Detention.* Detaining students either before or after school, during lunch, or on Saturdays works. Students are assigned for a specific amount of time, ranging from fifteen minutes to all day Saturday, to sit quietly and remain on task. If the school does not have an organized detention system, then the teacher may choose to keep the detention for a definite amount of time. During this time, teachers often talk with students about their misbehaviors, restate their expectations, and express confidence in the students' abilities to change. However, teachers must decide if they have the time and desire to maintain detention on their own. Don't use this technique if it creates a burden for you.

An alternative to regular detention is detaining students after class for fifteen or thirty seconds. This technique is effective because it again delays students. They either sit at their desks or stand beside the teacher as the teacher times the detention.

3. *Isolation.* Students can be isolated for a specific period of time. The isolation area can consist of a chair or desk located away from the other students and placed so that the student can see the board or overhead. Isolation is *not* in the hall. Students should remain in class where they can be seen and not miss academic work. Albert (1989) suggests that "an effective time-out could be another classroom of the same grade. The students in another classroom usually aren't interested in being an audience for someone they don't really know, so they probably will ignore the misbehaving student" (p. 76). If you use this method, however, be sure to prearrange it with the other teacher and reciprocate when you are needed.

4. *Writing.* Students can write letters to explain their side of the story rather than verbalizing the reasons for their actions. This provides an avenue for students to think about what has occurred and gives teachers a chance to consider how to handle a situation. For instance, one teacher said that he always had students who were arguing with each other write about what had happened. He would not let them scream above each other's voices to tell him their side of the story. By the time the adolescents had finished writing, they were much calmer and the problem could be resolved quickly. However, teachers *should not* assign themes, require students to copy the dictionary, or write sentences. Writing is equated with punishment when this occurs.

5. *Lunch Sign-In.* Students can come to the teacher's room and sign in before going to lunch. This would delay the students enough to make this an effective consequence. Lunch time is also precious to the students, and a consequence that cuts into that time is effective.

6. *Contact Parents.* Teachers contacting parents, especially by phone, aids communication. Teachers can call parents at home, or in some cases it is more effective to call them at work. An emergency number may be called if there is no phone at home and the parent does not work. As a last resort teachers can send a certified or registered letter. When possible, both the student and teacher talk to the parent on the phone. Teachers always begin or end the conversation and students simply state the misbehavior. One middle school teacher has her students call their parents on her cellular phone immediately when there is an infraction. They step into the hallway and make the call. This consequence is much more effective if the teacher has previously established a positive parent–teacher relationship as explained in Chapter 7.

7. *Send to the Office.* Students can visit the assistant principal, principal, or in-school suspension staff if that program is implemented. Queen, Blackwelder, and Mallen recommend having an intensive care unit (ICU) in a small area such as a seldom used office, storage space, or hallway. When secondary students do not take responsibility for their actions, teachers complete a referral form and contact the office. An ICU staff member then escorts the student from the classroom to the unit. Students are monitored so that no talking takes place in the unit, and they fill out an exit form before returning to class. This form includes areas to explain what "my irresponsible actions are" and what "my commitment to become a responsible student is" (p. 164). This consequence should be reserved for severe, repeated misbehavior. Administrators don't want to be bombarded with referrals. One secondary school teacher's contract was not renewed because he had referred students to the office more than sixty times in one year.

In selecting consequences, teachers need to feel comfortable with their plan and follow school policy. When the student handbook requires that teachers send the students to the office for being tardy three times, they must uphold these guidelines.

Discipline Hierarchy

In order to promote self-discipline, teachers must explain to students what consequences will occur if students choose to misbehave. As in the analogy about traffic laws, teachers should hand out or post classroom rules and consequences. Students are aware of the expectations and can then make choices; teachers simply enforce the consequences.

Classroom expectations are established so that students know what is required. Expectations or rules for the classroom must be *observable, positively stated,* and *few* in number. Glasser (1990) refers to boss-managers and lead-managers in discussing rules. He believes that "boss managers accept the cliché that workers do not want to work or that students do not want to learn, and they depend on rules to keep them on task" (p. 123). On the other hand, lead-managers and lead-teachers use "minimal rules because they know that as soon as they are put in a position of trying to enforce a rule, they risk becoming the adversary of the rule-breaker" (p. 123). Examples of posted rules are:

1. Be in your seat before the bell rings.
2. Bring your textbook, pen, and paper to class each day.

Avoid negative words such as *no* and *not.* For instance, "Be on time" is a better rule than "Don't be tardy." Review Chapter 5 before creating your rules.

A discipline hierarchy is an effective way to deal with minor misbehaviors. Any time students break rules, they choose consequences. These become tougher as students move down the hierarchy. Most begin with a warning and end with removal from class. For additional information about consequences and a discipline hierarchy, read *Assertive Discipline, Positive Behavior Management for Today's Classroom* (Canter & Canter, 1992).

Consequences—Sample Poster Board

1st Misbehavior—Warning

2nd Misbehavior—Last out of the classroom

3rd Misbehavior—Last out and 30-minute detention

4th Misbehavior—Last out, 30-minute detention, and parents contacted

5th Misbehavior—Last out, 30-minute detention, parents contacted, and student sent to the
      assistant principal

As noted previously, the consequences are cumulative. Teachers select consequences from the examples presented earlier in the chapter and develop a hierarchy that meets their needs. They also develop a system for keeping track of infractions so that they can apply the

ACTIVITY 9.1
Designing a Discipline Plan

Every teacher needs to design a discipline plan. Write your expectations or rules in the space provided. Remember the guidelines. Rules should be

1. positively stated
2. few in number (4–7 rules/expectations)
3. observable, specific
4. easy to understand

_____

_____

_____

_____

What consequences would you require if students break your rules? Design your own discipline hierarchy according to guidelines listed in this chapter. These rules and consequences will be useful as you develop your comprehensive management plan in Chapter 13.

_____

_____

_____

_____

_____

next level if necessary. Some teachers put the number of the rule broken by the student's name in the grade book. They then have documentation showing what rule was broken and the date. Others use an inappropriate behavior book, usually a spiral notebook, and have the student write what happened and the date. This system provides documentation in the student's handwriting.

Although some management experts suggest writing the misbehaving student's name on the board or transparency, we suggest other means. Why give a student attention for acting inappropriately? Plus, you don't have time to interrupt your class. By simply stating, "John, you broke rule two" and continuing with the activities, you have not lost the momentum of the lesson. If John begins to argue with you, state in a matter-of-fact tone that "we'll discuss this later." Sometimes students will still badger you by making comments such as "You're unfair," "I didn't do anything," or "This class sucks." When this situation occurs, you may need to walk over to the individual's desk and politely ask the student to refrain. If the individual continues, another consequence may be added. Yes, some students will push your buttons if they can, and you may send a student to the office or call a parent. However, the other students will know that you mean what you say and you will follow through with your plan. That's essential!

Natural and Logical Consequences

Rudolf Dreikurs and William Glasser suggest that students receive natural or logical consequences for misbehaviors (Wolfgang, 1995). They state that this allows students to experience consequences that relate directly to their actions.

Natural consequences refer to the natural flow of events without intervention. If a child refuses to eat, the natural consequence is hunger. Logical consequences are applied to the situation. For instance, if students are splashing paints in art class, they need to clean the room, not receive detention time.

These consequences can be very effective in some cases, but there are many misbehaviors that have no logical or natural consequences. For instance, there is no logical consequence for chewing gum in class, passing notes, or making inappropriate noises. If teachers can think of logical consequences for a misbehavior, then they are most appropriate to use. Some examples of misbehaviors and logical consequences for secondary classrooms are shown in Activity 9.2.

ACTIVITY **9.2**

Logical Consequences

Misbehaviors	Consequences
leaving paper on the floor	pick paper up
talking out of turn	lose privileges of participating
forgetting equipment	not allowed to do activity
being tardy	detention

List three additional misbehaviors and their logical consequences.

Positive Reinforcement

Positive consequences are used when students do what they are expected to do. This positive reinforcement can also be referred to as rewards. Many secondary teachers feel that positive reinforcement or rewards are inappropriate for secondary students. The thinking seems to be, "Why should students be rewarded for something that they should be doing anyway?" Consequences are usually thought of as only referring to negative actions, but consequences can be positive as well. If students do what is expected or go beyond what is expected, should they receive a positive consequence for their action? Do teachers receive paychecks when they perform their professional duties? Is this a reward?

The business community has found that positive reinforcement of workers results in increased production. The following quotes are from two of the best-selling books addressed to corporate managers.

In Search of Excellence

Positive reinforcement also has an intriguing Zen-like property. It nudges good things onto the agenda instead of ripping things off the agenda. (p. 69)

B. F. Skinner found that negative reinforcement will produce behavioral change, but often in strange, unpredictable, and undesirable ways. Positive reinforcement causes behavioral change too, but usually in the intended direction. (p. 68)

Positive reinforcement, on the other hand, not only shapes behavior but also teaches and in the process enhances our own self-image. (p. 68)

The One Minute Manager

People who feel good about themselves produce good results. (p. 19)

Help people reach their full potential; catch them doing something right. (p. 39)

Weber, Crawford, Roff, and Robinson (1983) reviewed the classroom management research and found that studies often indicate that positive behavior is a powerful strategy for modifying and maintaining student behavior.

Dreikurs and Cassel (1972) make the point that we are too negative with children. We want them to be perfect and not make mistakes, so we are constantly stressing the negative and do not allow them to have human frailties. A series of television commercials for a religious group illustrates Dreikurs's point. One commercial has a little girl running into the house and slamming the screen door behind her while she is waving a report card above her head yelling, "Mommy, Mommy, I made all A's!" The mother's voice can be heard from the back, "I told you not to slam that door!" We expect our students to do the correct things while being scolded or reprimanded. Students need to be positively reinforced when they are doing what they are supposed to be doing.

We all need positive reinforcement. The teachers who believe that students should just work because they are supposed to are the same teachers who want their principal to compliment their work. Everyone needs to be positively reinforced. Secondary students may at times act as if they do not like to be noticed, but they do.

Some high school teachers use smiley faces, scratch and sniff stickers, and other elementary-type reinforcers. For instance, one high school band director gave gold stars to individuals for practicing and playing their instruments well. These stars were placed on a poster at the front of the class. Students vied for gold stars because it became a competitive venture. They wanted to show their teacher and peers that they knew they were capable. One author tried a similar technique in her classroom management college course. She first asked the students if they would like stickers for answering the discussion questions correctly. A few students politely raised their hands to not offend her. She then told them that three stickers equaled a free journal entry. They write fifteen journal entries throughout the semester. The interest level automatically jumped. Now the entire class, composed of university juniors and seniors, wanted those stickers. Would you work extra hard if your professor gave you a no homework pass as a reward?

The teenage version of stickers is the patches (letters) placed on jackets and sweaters for winning athletic and music competitions or individual awards. Did you have a letter jacket in high school that you still own today? Many adults have fond memories of receiving these patches; they are symbols of success.

How can teachers discover what students want? Ask them. Give students 3" × 5" index cards. Have them write a reward that they would enjoy. Examples we collected from secondary students include:

Individual Rewards

a. Leave fifteen seconds early for next class or lunch
b. Have one free hall pass to be used whenever the student needs it
c. Get a free movie rental
d. Run errands—work as office helper
e. Receive iron-on decals
f. Receive money

Group Rewards

g. Have class outside
h. Go on field trips
i. Receive food—popcorn, pizza party, lunch picnic, candy, Coke
j. Write problems they are having and discuss problems as a group
k. Receive tickets to a special event (e.g., football game, school play)
l. Watch a film
m. Sign the bulletin board when the student makes a good grade or achieves in some other way

One junior high science teacher has five stars on her bulletin board, one for each class period she teaches. Students sign the stars for academic achievement, improvement, attitude, attention, and excellence. They may sign the star for nonscience activities, such as winning the football game, or for academic improvement and paying attention in class.

Be creative in planning rewards. Contact local businesses, such as local video rental companies or fast-food restaurants. Often owners will provide prizes and coupons for students. Although teachers may not be able to give money frequently, they can occasionally use this reward. Why not give one dollar to the person who helps straighten your classroom bookshelves or answers the most questions correctly during discussion? Emmer, Evertson, Clements, and Worsham advise that if you are using group activity rewards, be sure that they are "contingent on specific desirable behaviors; if the group cooperates, they will receive the incentive. If not, they will lose some or all of the time in the activity" (p. 120). See the reward suggestions g through m on page 158.

Secondary teachers can verbally reinforce a whole class or individuals on a regular basis. The following ways are suggested:

1. Stand at the door as students enter the classroom, be courteous, and compliment them as they enter. Think about what you like best about individual students. Glasser (1990) contends that "courtesy is the core of how a lead-manager [lead-teacher] deals with workers which sets an example for everyone" (p. 122).
2. Walk around the room and individually reinforce students as they work. Make specific comments about what students are doing right.
3. Reinforce students individually and privately as papers are handed back.
4. Praise correct answers during classroom discussions.

Rather than simply saying "OK" or "very good," teachers should be more specific. What is very good? Students need to know precisely what the teacher means. You may want to keep the following list on your desk as a helpful reminder.

Twenty-Five Ways to Say "OK" or "Very Good"

1. Thought-provoking comment
2. Excellent analysis
3. Creative interpretation
4. Clever point
5. Thorough analysis
6. Careful examination
7. Useful scenario
8. Powerful reasoning
9. Dynamite question
10. Major consideration
11. Fine-tuned performance
12. Logical solution
13. Sound advice
14. Persuasive argument
15. Correct assumption
16. Well-chosen words
17. Positive approach
18. Concrete solution
19. Specific details
20. Plausible explanation
21. Fresh idea
22. New twist
23. Perfect opening
24. Right response
25. Clear description

Another technique that has proven effective in reinforcing secondary students is to call parents or send positive notes or postcards home (see Figure 9.1). Again this can be done without fanfare. Secondary students will accept this type of positive reinforcement if it is not openly discussed in class but is conducted in private between the student and the teacher.

There are times that the whole class needs to change a behavior. To reinforce an entire class, Canter and Canter (1992) have advocated the use of the now famous "marbles in a jar." Teachers put a marble in a jar whenever they catch the entire class behaving appropriately. Secondary teachers are often turned off by the marbles routine; however, there are other ways to use this technique effectively. In one junior high class, a student teacher in English tried the popcorn jar technique. Whenever the class stayed on task, the students in each period selected the student with the largest hand. That student took as much popcorn as possible from the plastic bag and added it to the jar. When the popcorn reached the top, these junior high students ate the popcorn and watched the movie *Sounder,* based on a novel that they had just finished. Not only was this reward fun, but also the peer pressure kept the students working toward a common goal over several weeks.

Something good is happening
at school!!!

_____
Teacher's Signature

_____
Date

FIGURE 9.1   What's Happening?

Other whole class activities appropriate for secondary students include playing the radio during individual work time, such as while completing an art project, and providing structured free time to visit the library or computer center. *Caution:* Avoid giving free time without a purpose. Students are to learn to their maximum potential. If they are simply goofing off or sleeping in class, a teacher is not fulfilling the duties assigned. In addition, chaos often reigns. When the teacher and students have decided what the class will earn, then they need to determine the recordkeeping method. For instance, students can make a poster and chart the number of times that the class has correctly performed the required behavior.

Whatever the reward, it should be logically tied with what has occurred. For instance, students should receive no homework passes if they have turned in all assignments on time for the past four weeks (see Figure 9.2). These passes should not be given because students did not chew gum in class. And the passes should be received after the four weeks. Parents usually do not allow young children to eat their dessert before the main course. Well, at least many parents don't. Teachers should not give rewards before students have completed the task. Weinstein (1996) agrees that rewards should be "contingent upon completion of a task or achieving a specific level of performance. If you reward students simply for engaging in a task, regardless of their performance, they are likely to spend less time on the task once the reward is removed" (p. 86).

FIGURE 9.2   No Homework Pass

No Homework Pass

I, _____ , may use this pass in place of one homework assignment

for the week of _____ .

_____   _____
Student's Signature   Teacher's Signature

ACTIVITY **9.3**

Behavior Modification Reinforcers

Divide into teams of four. Give each team a topic, such as Activity, and see how many reinforcers they can think of for secondary students within five minutes. The winning team members receive a no homework pass.

Social	Activity	Tangible	Token
Smile	Pass to computer lab	Hamburger $1.00 (Yes, we've seen this idea used.)	5 purple dots = free library time

Severe or Chronic Misbehavior

Wong and Wong (1998) advise, "Always deal with the behavior, not the person. You leave a person's dignity intact when you deal only with the behavior or the issue" (p. 162).

What about students who continually act inappropriately, often defying the teacher's authority? These students must be handled differently. Teachers working with special education students follow an IEP (individualized education plan); teachers with severe and chronic misbehaving students should design an IDP (individualized discipline plan). There are four steps involved.

Step One

The first step is to determine that there is a problem. If students are misbehaving on a regular basis, or if behaviors could be considered severe, these students should be dealt with individually. This sounds much easier than it is. Some teachers, by their actions, force students into this type of behavior. For instance, personality conflicts cause some teachers to perceive particular students as major discipline problems. Being sarcastic even when kidding often makes students retaliate by saying something derogatory to the teacher. Then the problem escalates.

Chronic misbehavior may be defined as constantly misbehaving even if this includes numerous minor infractions. An apathetic student who refuses to complete work or participate is one example. Often regular consequences will not or have not worked. In addition, students who destroy property, harm others, refuse to do what the teacher directs them to do, or totally disrupt the class are showing severe misbehavior signs.

Step Two

After deciding what specific behaviors occur frequently, teachers need to determine the *goal* of the students' misbehaviors. Dreikurs et al. (1982) state that all behavior is goal directed, and a student who exhibits severe or chronic misbehavior does so to attain a goal. According to Dreikurs et al. and Charles (1999), there are four goals of student misbehavior.

Four Mistaken Goals of Misbehavior
1. Students seeking *attention* from the teacher or class often want approval or attention even if it's negative.
2. Students seeking *power* or *control* over the class or teacher want control of the situation.
3. Students seeking *revenge* feel hurt and want to hurt others.
4. Students displaying signs of *inadequacy* are discouraged easily and often have a low self-concept.

Teachers typically respond emotionally to these students. Because students react emotionally, teachers can read those emotions to determine students' goals. *The key to determining misbehavior goals lies in recognizing how the teacher feels.*

Teachers need to analyze their emotional responses to students, and through that analysis determine whether students are trying to gain power. If students demand *attention,* teachers are usually *annoyed.* When students attempt to *control* the situation or seek *power* through confrontation, teachers typically feel *angry.* Students who display feelings of *inadequacy* and refuse to work make teachers feel *frustrated;* when they seek *revenge,* teachers feel *hurt.* By using these important clues to understand, teachers can identify what is happening and why.

Step Three

To handle the students' misdirected goals, follow these steps:

Goal: *Attention*

Avoid giving attention-seekers negative attention, such as telling them to "sit down and be quiet" in front of the class. Teachers should provide consequences in ways that will not call attention to these students. When attention-seekers act appropriately, teachers should make positive comments or indicate approval through body language, a smile, a nod, or praise.

Goal: *Power or Control*

"I told you to sit down or else. . . ." What is "else"? Do not get into a power struggle and feed the power. Teachers who attempt to assert their power usually cause an argument or confrontation to occur. Arguing sparks the fire. Simply provide consequences in a calm manner, and if necessary, remove these students from the group. If teachers need to confront students, wait until a private conference time.

ACTIVITY **9.4**

Analyzing Your Feelings

Pretend that the following scenarios occurred between you and your student. How would you feel?

Annoyed—Attention-getting
Angry—Power
Hurt—Revenge
Helpless—Inadequacy

1. Lakia has not turned in a single assignment this six weeks. She usually walks into class and puts her head on her desk to sleep. You have tried to cajole her into doing the work, but she says she doesn't care if she fails.
2. Michael constantly blurts out answers to every question during class discussions. He does know the subject, but you'd like others to have a chance to speak.
3. Alice bluntly told you, "If you want this work done, do it yourself. You can't make me do anything."
4. You tell Don to "get back to work" instead of chatting with Fred. As you turn around, you hear him, under his breath, call you a ***. (You can fill in the words.)

Write your own scenario, pass it to a partner, and see if you agree on how the situation would make you feel.

Goal: *Revenge*

Remember the time your best friend in high school "stole" your significant other. If this didn't happen to you, it did to many others in your class. A typical response is wanting to retaliate. You were hurt and wanted to get even.

Those who get hooked into revenge often lash out in defense. As teachers, we need to realize that these students have been hurt and are trying to hurt others. They attempt to show strength by using fear and bullying tactics. See Chapter 8 for a more in-depth view of bullying. Often these students have little self-confidence.

Goal: *Inadequacy*

"I simply can't get through to this kid" is a pretty common statement. Apathetic students make teachers feel as if they are hitting their heads against a brick wall. Nothing seems to work. One author recommends to her student teachers to select one of these apathetic students. Then make a plan to change the attitude. Numerous student teachers are now "adopting" one student each semester. Wouldn't it be worthwhile if every teacher in the world selected one helpless student each year? What changes could we make?

One such student, Chris, was a classic case. Before he arrived in his eighth grade journalism class, his first-year teacher had already been warned: "He's a loser. Don't even bother with him; he won't do anything and always fails." On the author's urging, the teacher decided to adopt Chris. At first, Chris tried the typical behavior—sleeping, being absent, not completing work. She started talking to him more about his interests and finally persuaded him to write an essay. Miracle! His writing was much better, more creative than any other student's.

Soon, he was doing more in class because she praised his efforts. He dropped by between classes and sometimes came in after school. She selected him as editor of the newspaper and discovered he had true leadership qualities and was an excellent artist. He began making A's in her class and even started working in his other classes. Some of his friends started teasing him because he now dressed preppy, cut his long hair, and stopped taking drugs. By year's end, the school had the best newspaper ever, and Chris was a hero, at least to some.

During the summer, the teacher became a camp counselor for a gifted and talented program. She called Chris's mother to ask if he could attend if accepted. He completed the application materials, was selected, and became a leader there too.

Even though Chris has gone on to high school, he still stops by, send letters, and calls his favorite teacher occasionally. Unfortunately, he's not doing as well in high school and has shifted back into some old patterns. His former teacher is looking for a high school teacher who will adopt Chris once again.

In determining whether or not the goal is inadequacy, teachers must first determine if students truly cannot do the work or if they are playing the learned helplessness game. When the assignment is too difficult, teachers need to revise their lessons. However, if students are apathetic and unmotivated, they must realize that consequences do occur. Aid the students in understanding the assignment, but do not complete it for them. After working the first few problems, walk away and let students work on their own for a time. Some students have learned to play "helpless" so that they can manipulate teachers into doing their work. Consider trying the Jones (1987) PPL method discussed in detail in Chapter 4.

Step Four

Planning a conference outside of class time solves problems without interference from others. Several useful guidelines aid teachers in preparing these meetings:

1. Plan ahead of time. Rehearse what you intend to say. Have materials, such as documentation, available. For instance, keep a record in the grade book that indicates how often rule infractions have occurred.
2. Meet when both parties are *calm.*
3. Meet in private—use an office, conference room, or classroom when other students are not present.
4. Begin and end on a positive note.

During the conference, solicit the student's responses to find out the underlying problem. Ask specific questions in a friendly, nonthreatening manner and observe the reactions. After determining how you feel about the behavior (annoyed, angry, hurt, or helpless), ask the student the appropriate questions. Dreikurs suggested the following questions.

- Could it be that you want me to pay attention to you?
- Could it be that you want to prove that nobody can make you do anything?
- Could it be that you want to hurt me (or others)?
- Could it be that you want me to believe you are not capable? (Charles, 1999, pp. 49–50)

As you're asking these questions, look for a recognition reflex, a verbal or nonverbal clue that you may have hit a nerve (Wolfgang, 1995). The reflex may be eye contact, a nod, or a shrug. You may not notice anything. This technique takes practice.

If the problem seems to be lack of attention, think of ways you can give the student attention for positive actions. In some instances, you may ignore inappropriate behavior rather than reinforcing it. For power-seeking students, find avenues to give them chances to make decisions and hold leadership positions.

Being understanding and patient toward students who are vengeful is often difficult, but persistence is necessary. They will probably at first reject your efforts to help, regardless of how sincere. It may take time to show that you are accepting and caring, but you cannot allow a revenge-seeking student to be spiteful toward you or peers. Those who feel helpless are often the hardest to reach. They have given up on school and sometimes life. Instead of reinforcing their feelings of inadequacy, teachers need to support and encourage them for even small accomplishments (Charles, 1999).

Praise versus Encouragement

Dreikurs draws a major distinction between praise and encouragement. He believes that praise centers around how the teacher feels, whereas encouragement acknowledges the student's feelings (Dreikurs & Cassel, 1972). Therefore, he emphasizes that we should use encouraging words whenever possible. According to Burden (1995), "encouragement statements help students see what they did to lead to a positive result and also help them feel confident about their own abilities" (p. 44).

Logical Consequences

We addressed consequences earlier in this chapter. However, we want to emphasize that Dreikurs believes that teachers need to follow through with logical consequences (Charles, 1999). To ensure that you understand rewards and consequences, we have included a sample

---

ACTIVITY **9.5**

To Encourage or To Praise?

Change the following praise statements to encouragement.

Example: I'm so proud of you. (Praise)
You must be so proud of yourself for making the tennis team. (Encouragement)

1. I really like the way you sing. (Praise)
2. You did a super job on that oral report. (Praise)
3. I'm so pleased that you made a 100 on that test. (Praise)

Select one of the following statements. For two minutes, use a freewriting exercise to state your opinion.

I like praise more than encouragement because . . .

or

I like encouragement more than praise because . . .

Discuss in class whether praise or encouragement is more effective. Should you use both in a classroom?

A C T I V I T Y **9.6**
Behavior Contract

Name _____ Date _____

Statement of Situation _____

_____

_____

Rewards and/or Privileges _____

_____

_____

Consequences _____

_____

_____

Date for Progress Review _____

_____

_____

_____   _____
Student's Signature   Teacher's Signature

Practice writing a contract. What situation in your life would you like to change? Lose ten pounds? Finish all assignments before the due date? Clean your house and wash clothes? What rewards or privileges will you give yourself if you follow the contract? What consequences will occur if you don't? Select a day to review your progress. Then have a friend or family member sign the contract to "keep you honest."

behavior contract in Activity 9.6. As you complete the exercise and relate it to your life, you will develop a clearer understanding of how to use contracts in your classroom.

Confrontations should only occur after teachers have determined that students' misbehaviors are either severe or chronic, and they have identified the goals of the misbehavior. Confrontations are intended to be a hierarchy of dealing with these problem students. If after carefully following all the steps, students continue with the misbehaviors, teachers should attempt to seek help from other professional sources, such as school counselors, psychologists, and psychiatrists.

Summary

This chapter investigated the use of consequences and positive reinforcement in the secondary classroom. The more positive secondary teachers are, the fewer discipline problems occur. The chapter also discussed perhaps the biggest concern of secondary teachers, how to work with students who exhibit severe and chronic misbehavior.

REFERENCES

Albert, A. (1989). *A teacher's guide to cooperative discipline: How to manage your classroom and promote self-esteem.* Circle Pines, MN: American Guidance Service.

Bettelheim, B. (1985). Punishment versus discipline. *The Atlantic Monthly, 256*(5), 51–59.

Blanchard, K., & Johnson, S. (1982). *The one minute manager.* New York: William Morrow.

Burden, P. (1995). *Classroom management and discipline: Methods to facilitate cooperation and instruction.* White Plains, NY: Longman.

Canter, L. & Canter, M. (1992). *Assertive discipline, positive behavior management for today's classroom.* Santa Monica, CA: Author.

Charles, C. M. (1999). *Building classroom discipline* (6th ed.). New York: Addison Wesley Longman.

Dreikurs, R., & Cassel, P. (1972). *Discipline without tears.* New York: Penguin-NAL.

Dreikurs, R., Grunwald, B., & Pepper, F. (1982). *Maintaining sanity in the classroom: Classroom management techniques.* New York: Taylor and Francis.

Elam, S. (1989). The second Gallup/Phi Delta Kappa poll of teachers attitudes toward the public schools. *Phi Delta Kappan, 70*(10), 785–798.

Emmer, E. T., Evertson, C. M., Clements, B. S., & Worsham, M. E. (1997). *Classroom management for secondary teachers* (4th ed.). Boston: Allyn & Bacon.

Glasser, W. (1990). *The quality school: Managing students without coercion.* New York: Harper & Row.

Hoover, R. L., & Kindsvatter, R. (1997). *Democratic discipline: Foundation and practice.* Upper Saddle River, NJ: Merrill.

Jones, F. (1987). *Positive classroom discipline.* New York: McGraw-Hill.

Peters, T., & Waterman, R. (1982). *In search of excellence.* New York: Harper & Row.

Queen, J. A., Blackwelder, B., & Mallen, L. P. (1997). *Responsible classroom management for teachers and students.* Upper Saddle River, NJ: Prentice-Hall.

Thompson, D. (Ed.). (1995). *The concise Oxford dictionary* (9th ed.). New York: Oxford University Press.

Weber, W., Crawford, J., Roff, L., & Robinson, C. (1983). *Classroom management: Reviews of the teacher education and research literature.* Princeton, NJ: Educational Testing Service.

Weinstein, C. S. (1996). *Secondary classroom management: Lessons from research and practice.* New York: McGraw-Hill.

Wolfgang, C. (1995). *Solving discipline problems* (3rd ed.). Boston: Allyn & Bacon.

Wong, H. K., & Wong, R. T. (1998). *The first days of school.* Mountain View, CA: Author.

10 Youths in Crises: Solving Social Problems

Adult involvement can provide a positive influence in the lives of today's youth.

OBJECTIVES

1. Identify Maslow's hierarchy of needs.
2. Distinguish among cliques, gangs, and cults.
3. Examine colors, clothing, and initiation rites to reflect differences between cults and gangs.
4. Analyze ways to handle violence in classrooms and schools.
5. Analyze ways to handle crises, such as through a crisis management team.
6. Evaluate alternative programs used to work with students who need special counseling services.

Overview

On your first day of class, you anxiously await the arrival of your new students. You have prepared a dynamite, cooperative learning lesson, arranged all the bulletin boards, placed a welcome sign on the blackboard, and are now waiting to greet them at the door. The teacher from next door approaches to ask you if you need any help. She tells you that she has been teaching in that same classroom for twenty years and knows "all the kids and their parents." You show her your class attendance sheets, and she exclaims, "Oh no, you have Roberto and José in the same period; that'll never work. They're in rival gangs and despise each other." The students are supposed to arrive in less than ten minutes, and you feel that the air has just been let out of your tires. What will you do? What will happen if you ask class members to work together? How do you stop a fight?

How do you handle gang or cult members in your classes? The answer: the same way you work with any other eleven-, fourteen-, or sixteen-year-old. Students are individuals and we must help meet their needs. Being a gang or cult member, worshipping Satan, and practicing rituals are not illegal activities. In fact, the Church of Satan's followers have the right to religious freedom protected by the Constitution. The authors, however, believe that teachers and parents should be aware of reasons students join groups and ways to aid youths who are involved in crisis situations.

Each day, newspaper and television stories about juvenile crimes fill the pages and airwaves. How often have you read about violence, gangs, and cults in today's paper? What did the news report mention last evening?

"Gangs: They're in the Suburbs Now," *Houston Chronicle*

"Four Students and a Teacher Killed in Jonesboro, Arkansas—Two Students, Eleven and Thirteen, Charged in Killings," CBS, ABC, NBC Nightly News Reports, March 26, 1998

"Three High School Seniors Charged with Cult Slayings," *Scranton Tribune*

"Officer Works to Keep City's Gang Activity at Bay," *Huntsville Item*

History

Globally, "gang activity can be traced back to the 1400's. By the 1700's, gangs had arrived in the United States. One of the first reports of gang activity centers around a group of juveniles who adopted a name and wreaked mischief in a Pennsylvania town. In the 1800's, the National Guard had to be activated because of the Irish and Caucasian gang members in New York" (Bolin, Funk, Flesch, & Osborne, 1998, p. 64). Compiling exact figures for the number of gangs and members is impossible. According to Hubbard (1998), a campus police sergeant, in 1960, there were gangs in 58 U.S. cities; by 1990, organized gang activities had reached 769 cities. And in 1998, the reporting is tenfold what it was only eight years ago. The National Institute of Justice (NIJ) estimates that there are 4,800 groups and 250,000 gang members (NIJ, 1997); FBI figures indicate that there are approximately 400,000 gang members nationwide (Bayles, 1997). On a local newscast, a reporter stated that as of June 1998 the mayor's Anti-Gang Office reported that there were 13,000 gang members and 424 gangs in Houston. Even though the numbers have risen, there has been a 43.6 percent drop in Houston's gang crime (Walker, 1998). Our need as teachers is to understand reasons that students join deviant groups and to provide other options that fulfill students' needs.

To discover more about adolescents in today's schools, you might consider interviewing the experts. For instance, visit places, such as the malls or night spots, where students "hang

ACTIVITY **10.1**

Interviewing the Experts

Interview one of the following individuals, ask specific questions, and keep a journal about your perceptions: campus police officers, teachers, parents, administrators, counselors, probation officers, and gang or cult members.

a. What do the terms *gangs* and *cults* mean?
b. Have you had contact with a gang or cult member?
c. How do juveniles join these groups? What are the initiation rites?
d. What influences a student to join?
e. Are juvenile gangs and cults different today than a decade ago?

OR

a. Who did you interview and what is the individual's title? Where is the person employed?
b. What are the duties of the individual on a daily basis? Are the duties in writing? If so, where?
c. What are the procedures used to send a student to the office? How many students does the person typically see in one day? Does the person visit with parents often?
d. What can the individual tell you about the particular school that will help you as a new teacher? What makes the district unique?

Interview Questions*

1. Who did you interview and what is his title? Where is the individual employed?
I interviewed Officer Calvin Jones. Officer Jones is the Student Assistance Officer. He is a member of the Tomball Police Department. He has an office at Tomball Junior High School in the Tomball School-Community Guidance Center. He visits all of the schools within the Tomball city limits except Tomball High School, which has its own officer.

2. What are the duties of this individual on a daily basis? Are the duties in writing? If so, where?
Officer Jones visits schools as requested. He goes to juvenile court anytime a student is arrested whether the crime occurred on a campus or not. He regularly reviews the court dockets to determine if a student is involved in any upcoming cases. He gives courses to students on such topics as tobacco use and shoplifting. He also provides in-service to faculty and staff on such topics as gang symbols and activities. He participates in regularly scheduled special programs like TPASS—Tomball Police After School Special. This is a program for students who are considered at risk for criminal activity and/or dropping out of school. It is limited to twenty-five students and usually has a waiting list. He provides after-school activities for the students from the hours of 2:30–5:30 P.M., helps them with homework, gives them rides home, etc.

Officer Jones's salary is paid by three sources—the police department, the school district, and a grant given by the Community Guidance Center. His duties are defined by the Community Guidance Center under a grant from the Safe and Drug-Free Schools. The Tomball School-Community Guidance Center is located on the Tomball Junior High School campus. Its purpose is to locate and assist students and their parents who are experiencing difficulties interfering with education.

3. What are the procedures used to send a student to his office? How many students does he typically see in one day? Does he visit often with parents?
Officer Jones does not routinely handle discipline problems, although he sometimes participates in conflict resolution. Students are referred to him by teachers, parents, or themselves. He usu-

ally sees four to five students a day. Seventeen was the largest number he recalled seeing in one day. He does visit with parents fairly often, but most of his time on campus is spent with students.

4. What can the individual tell you about the particular school that will help you as a student teacher? What makes this district unique? (Example: special programs that are offered, staff development programs)

Officer Jones told me about several things that make this district special. The school has recently instituted team D-halls, which are handled by the team teachers rather than the deans. This is an intermediate step for minor problems. It is useful for a student teacher to know that there is more than one way to "write up" a student. He also gave me a copy of a brochure that was used for a staff development program on gang activity and symbols. As an art teacher, I had encountered student work that appeared to include gang symbols. One student even etched them on a beverage glass before I had seen the pictures in the brochure. He also told me that the in-school suspension program had been revised this year to include an actual curriculum of hard work that had to be done while the student was in ISS. He said that the change has cut down ISS by one-half.

5. Review a faculty handbook and a student handbook (or a student code of conduct). List three items in each handbook relating to a teacher.

From the *Student Code of Conduct and Handbook:*

    Dress code—Teachers must be aware of and enforce student dress code.

    Hall passes—Teachers must provide a hall pass to students leaving their classrooms during class hours.

    Discipline options—Explains such options as discipline reports, team D-Hall, and after-school detention

From the *Tomball Junior High School Teacher Handbook:*

    A few useful items: school year calendar, staff roster, who to see for . . . , school map

    A note on the importance of duty schedules. Because of the interpretation now being given liability laws as related to education, it is especially important that teachers be present and performing their assigned duty appropriately.

    Section on discipline describes procedures to follow, things to consider—i.e., a copy of a discipline report is sent home, be careful what you put in writing.

*Reprinted by permission of Nancy Nordquist.

---

out." Talk with three or more students and record your impressions. Other means include interviewing experts, such as campus police officers and probation officers, if you want to know about the difficulties that many young adults face.

Are our schools a reflection of our communities? Do you or family members have security systems in your houses and cars? Should metal detectors and school police officers be in every school? Why do we need crisis management teams now when they virtually did not exist twenty years ago? These are questions to ponder as we think about how we, as teachers, can combat violence in schools and have a positive influence on students who might join or who have joined gangs or cults. Rather than becoming frightened by students who have gang affiliations, we need to have a better understanding of their reasons for joining. To do this, teachers must understand Maslow's hierarchy of needs, presented in Figure 10.1. According to this theory, we all have basic needs that must be met. In interviewing police officers, a former Los Angeles gang member, incarcerated juveniles, and teachers who work with youth offenders,

ACTIVITY **10.2**

Visit an Alternative School

Visit a local alternative school and record your impressions in your journal.

1. What type of programs do they have at the school? Who are the administrators? How many teachers are employed? What classes are taught?
2. How many students are enrolled, and what is the age range?
3. What are the students' impressions of the campus? Teachers' impressions?
4. Why are the students enrolled at the alternative school?
5. What is the environment like at the school? Friendly? Hostile?
6. What have you learned from your visit?

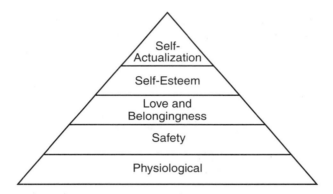

FIGURE 10.1   Maslow's Hierarchy of Needs

Source: A. Maslow, (1943), "A Theory of Human Motivation," *Psychological Review, 50*(4), 370–396; and A. Maslow (1954), *Motivation and Personality,* New York: Harper.

we discussed several basic premises. They often relate stories about unmet needs. As we view Maslow's pyramid, we will relate several of these stories (Maslow, 1943, 1954).

Maslow's Hierarchy

As homeless shelters constantly sprout across this nation, fewer individuals are getting their basic needs of food, water, and clothing. Many of these people have little hope for finding a better life. Gang and cult affiliations often pay, at least for a short while, because they can buy what they could not previously afford. Selling drugs, robbing, and other illegal activities are prevalent in many gangs. Safety needs tie in directly with the physiological needs because a safe place to live is another major concern. If students are not secure at home, if there isn't a home, or if family life is in turmoil, there is little chance that these individuals will be studying for tomorrow's math exam. Typical "reasons usually given for joining a gang include pressure from the environment, self-esteem, protection, belonging, money, shelter, power, sense of family or a family member belongs to a gang" (Bolin, Funk, Flesch, & Osborne, 1998, p. 65). One junior high gang member from the 28th Street Gang in Las Vegas came to a rural town in eastern Texas to live with his grandmother. The Nevada court system had suggested that he be relocated. The police detective described the Hispanic male as a small, slender young man who had neatly cut hair with a small tail in the back. He typically wore a baggy, black silk shirt and black pants with a silver chain draped across the front. Because he dressed differently, he attracted the attention of his peers. And his teachers described him as a nice, polite student who regularly attended church.

Soon he began recruiting for his gang by beating two boys who happened to be brothers. Whenever he found them alone, he would start a fight and always win. He then told them that he would stop the fighting if they would join him in beating others. They did. Within a few months, the Rolling 28's gang membership had grown to over twenty-five teenagers, even though the founder was returned to face criminal charges (with a one-way ticket to his former home, compliments of the Texas police). This gang caused havoc in this rural community (Collins, 1994).

Some gang initiation rites include being kicked and jabbed while walking through lines of gang members on each side. If a person can make it through, the individual is considered tough enough to be a member. Not only does this apply to male members, but also female gang members have similar activities. For example, as noted in police videotapes, the 28th Street Gang's female members will beat a recruit while she counts to 28. If she makes it, she can then join their organization. Having sexual relations with every male gang member (being "sexed in") is another prevalent initiation passage. One of the scariest rites is having sex with an HIV positive male. Three young girls in Dallas, ages eleven through fourteen, reported that they had done this in order to join.

Once involved, these individuals form a bond similar to a dysfunctional family. They will protect each other because loyalty is paramount. However, if someone decides to quit, that individual's life can be in grave danger. As one former Los Angeles gang member explained, he had to take on a new identity. His entire family had been affiliated with this group for generations. As a child, he had been groomed to be a part of this organization. By leaving, he was putting his and his family's lives in peril. Of course, security and protection were always available as long as he remained faithful.

Along with safety needs, gang membership helps some find love and belongingness. In fact, the gang term, "get love," means intense loyalty. To show their love, members will even scar their bodies. They may use cigarettes to burn the Pachuco mark, three dots on their arm or hand. One fourteen-year-old girl, Stephanie, heated a knife and coat hanger to burn an upside-down pitchfork, a sign of the Crips, on her leg. However, she was so high on drugs that she put it on the wrong leg. Gangs have very specific codes. They often tattoo only one side of their bodies to indicate what group they belong to. Because she had made this grave mistake, she was attacked by her "friends." She confided to Hubbard, a police officer, that she intended to remove the pitchfork by cutting her skin and putting the tattoo on the other side (Hubbard, 1998). Although each may feel weak as an individual, gangs provide strength in numbers. Peer pressure to follow, even when it goes against individuals' fundamental beliefs, controls their lives. Without this dysfunctional family unit, they feel alone and hopeless. The gang provides a false sense of security. In fact, senior gang members and leaders are often held in high esteem. If anyone appears disrespectful, other gang members will retaliate. Therefore, even new gang members quickly learn to conform and usually follow the unwritten, unspoken, but

A C T I V I T Y **10.3**

Meeting Your Needs

Reflect upon your background and list examples of how you have met your needs. Were all your needs met when you were a youth? Did your teachers help you to meet your needs? If so, how?

Physiological _____

_____

Safety _____

_____

Love and Belongingness _____

_____

Self-Esteem _____

_____

Self-Actualization _____

_____

Can teachers help students meet their needs if the teachers still have many unfulfilled needs to meet?

well-known rules. Typical gang members are followers who feel powerless without their counterparts. Therefore, self-actualization, an understanding of and contentment with their identity, is unattainable.

Meeting Needs through Schoolwork

How can we, as teachers, help students meet their needs so that they will not need the support of deviant groups? First, we need to understand the various types of groups students often join.

Defining the Terms

gang /gaŋ/ *n.* a band of persons acting or going about together, esp. for criminal purposes.
cult /kʌlt/ *n.* a system of religious worship esp. as expressed in ritual.
clique /kliːk/ *n.* a small exclusive group of people.

Source: The Concise Oxford Dictionary, Ninth Edition, 1995.

Whereas secondary students often band together to form cliques, these social circles can help them develop essential skills. When groups become detrimental, such as when students refuse to work with anyone outside their friends, teachers can find ways to circumvent the problem. How do teachers break up cliques and gangs in classes? They can use a variety of cooperative learning strategies to arrange class members in groups (Kagan & Kagan, 1998). One such technique includes having students number off from one to eight. Ask all the number ones to be in one group, the number twos to a second group, and so forth. Then each group member can be assigned specific tasks. Everyone has a part. Example tasks include the following:

- *Leader*—take everyone's suggestions and help the group make decisions concerning how to complete the work.
- *Checker*—make sure that all the steps are being completed.
- *Monitor*—keep the group, and individuals within the group, focused on the task.
- *Summarizer*—tell the entire class how the group completed the project's goals successfully.

By using this technique, teachers are not singling out individuals to work together. They are merely organizing class work. An idea that Wolfgang (1995) suggests is to mix secondary students by using a sociogram. Have students write the answers to the following questions: Who is the most popular student in class? Who is the most academically able student in class? With whom do you like to work in a pair situation? Have them hand in the papers without sharing their responses. Next, draw a sociogram that depicts the class and use this chart to arrange group work (see Figure 10.2). For instance, pair isolates, those students who are ostracized, with the most popular students. Switch group membership for various activities.

In this sociogram, Jan appears to be one of the brightest, most admired students in class. However, Rex and Randy seem to have few friends. They are the isolates. Therefore, the teacher needs to pair these isolates with popular students, such as Frances. Also, by having Randy and Jan work with other students at times, cooperative learning and socializing are being fostered. Because the teacher is not sharing the diagram with the students, no one will be embarrassed or feel shunned. Through varying grouping patterns, all individuals have a chance to work together and, therefore, get to know each other. Types of grouping can include interest, tutoring, and activity groups.

Preparing a Sociogram

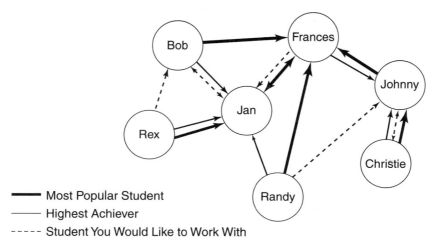

Can you make a sociogram of a secondary classroom?
Ask your mentor teacher if you can try this project.

FIGURE 10.2 Preparing a Sociogram

ACTIVITY **10.4**

Can You Read Gang Graffiti?

Identify the following gang symbols and explain their meaning (Hubbard, 1998). Then, check your answers against the explanations that follow.

1. Spider web
2. Pachuco mark
3. Teardrop
4. Pitchfork pointed down
5. 3 dots with "Mi Vida Loca"
6. Pitchfork pointed up
7. Eight ball

Spider web. This symbol is found in most gang graffiti; gang members easily recognize it.

3 dots with "Mi Vida Loca" (3pv). "Mi vida loca" means "my crazy life."

Pachuco mark. This means "We are everywhere: North, South, East, and West."

Pitchfork up. Sign of the Crips gang.

Teardrop. This means "Cry for my crazy life," and it's usually placed near the corner of the eye. According to campus police, "If it's colored in, it means that you have served time [in prison] or that you have successfully executed a drive-by shooting."

Eight ball. The eight ball signifies drugs, type of lifestyle, or that a person is carrying a weapon.

Pitchfork down. This is the Bloods gang sign. The pitchfork is the primary symbol for identifying individual gang affiliation.

Teachers may retort, "Yes, this is fine for most of my students, but what about gang members? They won't work in groups or participate." Yes, they can and will make worthwhile contributions if they are accepted and encouraged. Through class team work, they are having some of their love and belongingness needs met. When they truly believe that the teacher is caring and accepting, some will shine. Two success stories illustrate this point.

One former Texas "Teacher of the Year," who was also named as one of the top four teachers nationally, Meliane Christie, told us about her math student who failed countless times. José was supposed to be in high school, yet he was still in the eighth grade. Because of his age and his constant visits to the assistant principal's office, he was simply biding time until he could become another statistic, a dropout. José was associated with the local Low Riders, a Hispanic group. Because it was seen as cool to be totally apathetic toward school and learning, he had alienated most of his teachers. They felt it was impossible to reach him. However, Christie refused to give up. She showed a sincere interest in his learning math, included him in all class activities, even when he balked, and recognized his class contributions. One day, José did not show up for lunch, and the assistant principal assumed that he had skipped once again. While combing the school, this administrator found José in the computer lab. No, he was not trying to install viruses; he was working on his math problems. He was proud of his accomplishments and wanted to know if it would be acceptable to skip lunch so that he could come directly to the lab from now on (Williams, 1985).

Another success story occurred in a suburban district. A well-known gang member became the school's office helper because he could be trusted. Even though his gang had caused the community problems, school personnel decided to give him a chance to prove that he could be a help rather than a hindrance. He enjoyed his duties and wanted to remain in this job; therefore, he became a role model for other gang members. It was "cool" to be "doing the right thing." His self-esteem needs were being met. Can all students be turned around this easily? No. Is it worth trying to have more success stories? Yes.

Similarities and Differences between Gangs and Cults

We have discussed gangs and cliques within the chapter, but what about cults? They do have commonalties, which make them first appear to be identical, but they are not. Teachers need to become aware of signs to help distinguish between wannabes, dabblers, and hardcore members.

Defining the Terms

Wannabes   pretend that they are gang members, easy to recruit; sometimes dangerous because they are trying to prove that they are worthy to join.

Dabblers   pretend that they are in cults, dabble in occult activities, are learning rituals, sacrifices, heavy-metal lyrics. (We do not believe that all students who enjoy heavy metal are interested in cults.)

Hard Core   considered a member of the group and has completed the initiation rites.

Generalized Similarities and Differences between Some Groups

	Gangs	*Cults*
Purpose	Money, power	Religious control
Leaders	Charismatic, demand devotion	Mind control
Initiation	Criminal activity; "quoted," "jumped in," "beat in," or "sexed in"	Sacrifices
Symbols	Graffiti, territorial	Pagan, satanic
Clothing	Conformity, signals (e.g., green jacket—symbol for drug dealer in California)	Robes, hoods
Colors	Same colors, sports insignia	Black, white, purple, red
Affiliations/Ethnic Group	Racial lines, causes (e.g., hatred toward certain groups)	Religious groups
Secretive	Loyalty based on fear	Mystical, mind control

Not only are those differences prevalent, but also the tattoos and drawings help teachers recognize the groups with which their students are affiliated.

Graphics, Symbols, and Language

Incarcerated juvenile gang members produced pictures similar to the ones in Figure 10.3. We decided not to add too many of these graphics because they are constantly changing as new gangs are formed and as styles change. Not only does the graffiti change, but also the clothing styles reflect that what was "in" yesterday is passé tomorrow. For some time, symbols, such as sports insignia, have been used by numerous gangs. Some of the symbols and clothing reflect the type of gang. For example, a hate gang member will wear insulting language and symbols, such as a Nazi swastika, to raise the ire of others. Gangs can typically be divided into four categories:

- *Delinquent youth gangs.* Groups who hang out together. They typically wear similar clothing, colors, and use particular hand signs. Often these members engage in undesirable behavior to attract the attention of school officials and law enforcement personnel. However, most have not committed serious offenses yet.
- *Turf-based gangs.* Groups associated with a particular territory that they defend against rival gangs. Similar to delinquent youth gangs, these groups have leaders, dress alike, and communicate through their graffiti. However, members have often grown up in these gangs as a rite of passage, with relatives having been involved for generations. Therefore, young people usually find it difficult, if not impossible, to break away unless they move a great distance from the neighborhood.
- *Gain-oriented gangs.* Groups organized for economic gain. These groups want money, and will engage in various criminal activities, such as selling drugs, robbing, and steal-

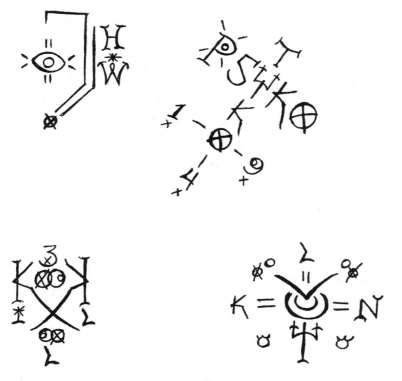

FIGURE 10.3 Gang Graphics and Symbols

ing, to satisfy their goal. Some of these gangs have extensive, sophisticated networks across the country.

■ *Violent/hate gangs.* Groups formed to promote animosity, hostility, and malice against persons belonging to a racial, ethnic/national origin, or sexual orientation group that differs from that of the gang's members. Violent acts against certain groups or types of individuals often cause serious bodily injury or death to individuals who the gang believes are unacceptable members of society (Morales, 1997).

Cult members typically form groups to practice their religious beliefs, and some use *The Satanic Bible,* written by Anton LaVey (1969), as their guide.

One student teacher related a story about a student in her high school English class who didn't do any work and drew satanic symbols such as a goat's head, the number 666, and a pentagram on his notebook and papers. Charlotte, the student teacher, was told not to bother the student because he had been threatening to commit suicide. The school psychologist had recommended that the student be left alone and not pressured to do any schoolwork.

Charlotte decided that she could not let the student just sit idly. Each day, she bent down at his desk, tried to make eye contact, and spoke to him. He rarely acknowledged her. Instead, he kept drawing Satan and other satanic symbols, wore only black, and never turned in work. One day, as she approached him, he rolled up his sleeve to show her the straight pins he had stuck in his wrist. He wanted a reaction; she didn't accomodate him. She simply smiled and

A C T I V I T Y **10.5**

Do You Know Street Language?

Match the following street gang language with the definitions. The Conroe ISD Police Department Gang Intelligence Unit provided us with the terms and definitions (Hubbard, 1998).

1. Ace kool	a. Expulsion from the gang
2. Boned out	b. Shoot someone
3. Break down	c. To fight
4. Courting out	d. Attempt to provoke a fight
5. Dis	e. Quit, left, chickened out
6. Do a ghost	f. Ugly girl
7. Drop a nickel	g. Best friend or backup
8. Get down	h. Leave before police arrive
9. Lizard butt	i. Shotgun
10. Talkin' smack	j. Humiliate or insult

1. (g)   2. (e)   3. (i)   4. (a)   5. (j)
6. (h)   7. (b)   8. (c)   9. (f)   10. (d)

How many did you define correctly? We did not write a long list because the words change as police officers, teachers, and others discover the meanings.

---

continued with her lesson. Yet, she was determined never to give up. On her last student teaching day, the students were all saying their goodbyes. Once again, she leaned down by this student's desk. He slowly took a page from his notebook and placed in on the desk. On the page was written "God bless you." She had made a difference in this young man's life.

The Cult Awareness Council publishes a list of warning signs for parents of teenagers. These include the following.

- Withdrawing from family and known friends.
- Being secretive and noncommunicative.
- Wearing more subdued, dark clothes and jewelry with occult designs.
- Showing signs of rebellion and aggressiveness.
- Showing interest in occult literature. They "may begin with their own 'Book of Shadows.' This can be a spiral notebook with their own rituals written in code" (Cult Awareness Council, n.d.).
- Collecting occult items, such as skulls, bones, ritual knives, candles, and silver chalice bowls. "Some teenagers have constructed satanic altars in their bedrooms, closets, or outdoors" (Cult Awareness Council, n.d.).
- Missing pets or animals in the community.

The Council advises parents "to educate themselves about the methods adult satanists use to secretly coerce, manipulate, and exploit teenagers" (Cult Awareness Council, n.d.). One way to learn more is to read Cassiel's *Encyclopedia of Black Magic*. Along with examining the occult history, the author explains numerous rituals and sacrifices. The name " 'Cassiel' is

ACTIVITY **10.6**

Satanic Rituals

LaVey, the founder of the Church of Satan in San Francisco, describes devices used in rituals. Can you explain the symbolic meaning of the following?

1. Black robes worn by men: _____
2. Illuminated black candles: _____
3. Silver chalice: _____
4. Sword: _____
5. Parchment made from sheep skin: _____

Answers
1. Black robes are the symbol of darkness.
2. Black candles represent power and success.
3. The chalice represents ecstasy.
4. The sword is symbolic of aggressive forces.
5. Parchment "is used because its organic properties are compatible with the elements of nature. . . . The parchment is the means by which the written message or request can be consumed by the candle flame and sent out into the ether" (LaVey, 1969, pp. 139–140).

Can You Identify Occult Symbols?

1. 666   2.   3.   4.   5.

Answers
1. 666 is the sign of the Antichrist.
2. The inverted cross is the symbol of Satanism.
3. This is the symbol displayed in *The Satanic Bible* for the Church of Satan.
4. The pentagram is the religious symbol of witchcraft.
5. The goat's head inside an inverted pentagram is the basic symbol of Satan.

Discuss the following as a class.

a. Is it important for teachers to know about cults and rituals? Why or why not?
b. Should we have school-sponsored programs for presenting this information to teachers and parents?

---

the nom de plume of an internationally recognized authority on ritual magic of both the black and white varieties; on voodoo; and on strange cults—east and west, past and present" (Cassiel, 1990, book jacket cover).

Even though we have identified some of the ways to recognize gangs and cults, you, as a teacher, may still be asking, "So what? These students are in my classes, and even if I can

ACTIVITY **10.7**

Attend a Juvenile Court Session: Journal Entry

Attend a session in juvenile court and record your impressions in your journal.

1. Who was in court?
2. What types of hearings did you attend?
3. How old were the juveniles? Had they been in trouble with the law previously?
4. Who was representing them?
5. Were other family members present? If so, who? What was their demeanor?
6. Do you think that any of the juveniles were in gangs? Why? Why not?
7. What was the judge's decision?
8. What did you learn from this experience?

identify the symbols, I still want the students to learn and to behave appropriately. What do I do after I have learned the signs? How do I make all students feel that they are a part of our class?" By visiting a juvenile court session, you will become more aware of your community.

Preventing Violence in the School

Within the school, teachers can help determine whether or not they will be victimized by violent acts. According to Garrison, a national expert on crime and violence in today's schools, if students feel that the teacher is a person rather than an object, if students feel respected as human beings, then violence against that teacher rarely occurs. In investigating violent school-related incidents throughout the country, he found teacher victims to be shut off from the rest of the school. They did not interact with students much inside or outside of the classroom. Instead they insulated themselves from their students and the community in which their students lived. For instance, they did not sponsor activities or attend special school functions. In addition, they knew little about the parents or the community. In fact, they took flight from that neighborhood as soon as the afternoon school bell rang (R. Garrison, personal communication, May 11, 1993).

Perhaps you are thinking, "Well, that's not me. I sponsored the music festival last year, and we sang musical pieces to celebrate the cultural heritage of the majority of my students." You are on the right track, but there's more to do. One day, or one week, of celebration is not enough. Can you think of other creative ways for students to study about cultures throughout the year? Can you have both students and parents involved in planning these various activities rather than one group? What do you know about the community? Have you ever asked businesspeople to be active in school-related affairs? How many homes have you ever visited? Did you attend the local festival, the town hall meeting, the local church? Do you know the names of your students' parents? These are a few questions we must ask ourselves if we are concerned with school safety.

One school tried to involve the predominantly Hispanic population in school functions, but most parents would not come to the school. The school personnel realized that this school did not offer a very welcoming atmosphere to many of these parents, especially because a large number could not speak English and had been alienated by their own school experiences. In fact, most had dropped out at an early age and did not see the value in formal education. To make the school the "in" place to visit, the principal and staff met with community leaders. They decided to hold evening tutorial sessions for adults seeking GEDs, use the hallways as a walking track for parents and their baby strollers because the neighborhood was unsafe to walk, especially at night, and even installed washers and dryers to accommodate parents who could not afford such luxuries at home. By making these significant but not very costly changes, the community now takes pride in its school. School has become the "in" place to be, both day and night.

A somewhat similar plan helped the Farrell Area School District in Pennsylvania avoid bankruptcy and kept the community involved. Before a community member is born, the school steps in to help arrange services, not paid directly through school taxes but through social agencies. The school system in this poor area decided to help the community members locate jobs, receive prenatal care, and find appropriate clothing and nourishing food. For instance, they offer complete makeovers for women who have just delivered a baby. What?! Isn't that too costly, and anyway, that's not part of school business. Good points, but let us explain the school superintendent's reasoning. He argues that by having these women come to school for a special treat in a friendly atmosphere, they will feel free to visit on other occasions. By making everyone feel that the school is a part of the community, less violence will occur around the school property, and neighbors will become crime stoppers who will contact the school if they see problems occurring. To pay for this expensive social program, the superintendent and his staff asked government and private agencies to provide community members services such as job hunting (most of the adult providers in the area were unemployed). Therefore, the superintendent has not asked for a raise in school taxes, yet the community now supports the school system (Sava, 1994).

Other districts use different plans to gain more parental support. Administrators in one suburban district rent rooms in nearby apartment complexes so that parents can easily stop by with questions and students can receive tutoring. They believe that if parents will not come to school, the school can come to them. In poor, rural Donaldsonville, a local university professor recruited ministers to preach about the importance of reading. A local bar owner became interested in the program and informed "mothers who patronized his establishment that they would no longer be welcome unless they put as much time into learning how to read to their children as they spent enjoying themselves at the bar" (Edwards & Young, 1992, p. 78).

To increase school support, ask business leaders to provide mentoring and after-school jobs. When teenagers can understand that the school relates to their lives, and that they are acquiring necessary skills, they have a reason to want to attend. They begin to value an education. Having businesspeople talk to classes and organizations helps both groups become better acquainted. Have you thought about switching places with a businessperson for one day each semester? Ask the individual to teach your classes while you conduct the business's operations. What an eye-opener for both parties! One author used a similar plan by switching places with secondary teachers while they taught her university education classes for the day. Everyone learned from these experiences. For example, she knew that she needed to handle disruptions appropriately if she taught college courses in classroom management (Williams & Harris, 1988).

Some students will say that they are not impressed by these business leaders or university faculty members, or the salaries they can receive, because they can make a pocketful of money dealing drugs. One high school drug dealer shook a fistful of money in his teacher's face when she confronted him about his illegal activities. He then asked her how much she was making. It will not be easy to convince these young minds that the quick fix is not the answer, but it is worth doing. Teaching students that contributing to the community, being lawful citizens, and making a difference in others' lives are more significant activities than that large dollar sign is a difficult task. Gang members warn adolescents that teachers will tell them that they shouldn't belong to a gang. Then, when they hear teachers preaching about the evils of gangs, the warnings of the gang members are reinforced (Hubbard, 1998). Some students do not see any future for themselves or their friends. When asked what they will be doing in twenty years, many will reply, "doing time in prison or dead." Yet, with mentors who do take an interest in students' lives, with teachers who truly care about their students' survival, and with community members who envision the neighborhood as a family unit, positive changes can happen.

Preventing Violence in the Classroom

We have been discussing ideas you as a teacher can incorporate in your school. Now let's turn specifically to your classroom and ways to prevent violence. Again, being a human being who cares about all students is a somewhat simplified answer, but it has merit. Beginning on the first day, greet your students as you would a guest coming to your home. Put a welcome sign on the door or chalkboard, have the room arranged in a comfortable, orderly manner with plants, and tell them that you are glad to meet them (if you are). For many students this will be an unusual occurrence in their lives. Other people often dread the thought of seeing them. You are already starting on Maslow's hierarchy of meeting their love and belongingness needs. Having students provide input and showing them that the class is "ours" instead of "mine" can make a huge difference in preventing disasters. What decisions will they make in your room? If they do not have any rights, then how can it be "our" classroom? Will they make choices about the class? What do they expect from you as their teacher?

Within the first thirty minutes of the first class period, you should have made eye contact with every student. Show that you are interested in them and not afraid to be their teacher. One former Los Angeles gang member told us that he always admired the teachers who were not fearful of him and his friends. These teachers treated him as a person instead of a criminal, and today he wants to pay back those who helped him. In addition, his wife just had a baby and he wants his child to be in a safe school environment. He has changed his former habits and is a contributing society member who respects other people. Happy beginning to what could have easily been a wasted life!

Will these suggestions prevent all discipline problems or acts of violence in a classroom? No. However, you have made significant strides when you have students who care about you and know that you care about them. We surveyed thirty-eight teenagers who are in a juvenile correctional institution because of major offenses including aggravated assaults, burglary, robbery, and auto theft. When we asked them what teachers did, and did not do, which affected their lives, students characterized their most respected teachers as nice, helpful with their problems, and listeners. Whereas one stated these teachers "would listen to problems and share their interests," another commented that the teacher was "nice, interested in them and would help them with their problems."

We also asked if they had ever victimized a teacher, and if so why and how. Of the nineteen who had been involved in these assaults, several stated that the teachers either cursed them, "shouted at me," or "started saying stuff about my problems in school in front of the class." Three students mentioned that their victims touched them. As Glenn and other authorities have noted, touching an angry individual can often lead to disastrous outcomes (Glenn, 1990).

In addition, we interviewed several teachers both at this facility and at others. One teacher, who had been a former Bandito gang member, felt that he had earned the students' respect because he knew his vocational trade and could teach these students lifelong work skills. His desire is to eventually become a school principal, and he is currently enrolled in a certification program. All the teachers revealed that you cannot be too soft on these students or nonassertive, but you cannot be aggressive either. Rather than starting confrontations or getting in power struggles, they recommended that you remain calm and in control of yourself and the situation. Cursing back at a student who is yelling at you simply escalates the problem and loses respect for you as a teacher in front of the other students. You are the professional and an adult, so act accordingly. Chapter 9 examines how to handle severe discipline problems.

Crisis Management

Secondary teachers have a major safety concern in working with students, that is, their own safety. One of the authors was teaching a graduate course that dealt with discipline, and one of the teachers taking the class shared an incident that certainly increased that concern. The teacher taught in a middle school just outside Wichita, Kansas. He was retired military and had recently become a teacher. While conducting his class, he heard what sounded like firecrackers exploding in the hall. When he walked into the hall to investigate, he saw a young man standing over the principal with a gun. The principal was on the floor bleeding. The young man turned toward the teacher and pointed the gun directly at him. Everyone in class was hanging on to every word. The class, almost as one, said, "What did you do?" The teacher said that he asked the student, "What are you doing, young man?" Probably, according to the teacher, the dumbest thing he could possibly have said. The student, though, pulled the gun down to his side and ran from the building. The biggest problem in attempting to teach about this area is that every circumstance is different and what works once might not the next time. The actions of this teacher should not be copied just because it worked. There are, however, guidelines that will serve the secondary teacher well in times of crisis. Let's examine some of the crises that most teachers dread.

Fighting

According to the National School Safety Center, there are two kinds of fighting: (1) spontaneous (which usually causes injury) and (2) announced (which involves posturing—usually with no injury except with gangs). The center also notes that studies show that females have a higher injury rate because they have no role models and lack rules and rituals for physical aggression, which males have developed. Also, there is a false perception that females cannot really harm anyone because they lack the strength.

Prevention of fighting obviously needs to be addressed. The National School Safety Center has suggested the following:

1. Identify the sources of conflict—interpersonal, neighborhood, family.
2. Explore school and community options to minimize the conflict—get input from as many sources as possible.
3. Train staff in negotiation techniques.
4. Follow up—reinforce positives—be visible.
5. Develop standards and expectations—students must understand consequences.
6. Consider peer programs.

If a situation has escalated to the fight stage in the secondary school, peer pressure is more important than any possible consequence. Students cannot lose face with their peers, especially if they are in a gang. A female gang member was beaten by her "friends" because she didn't respond when another girl accidently bumped her as she was walking in a store. Other gang members said that she was chicken, and they didn't want her to ruin their reputation (Hubbard, 1998).

Some general guidelines to remember when attempting to break up a fight:

1. Use an authoritative voice to tell students to break it up and go to class.
2. Walk to the location of the fight and observe the surrounding area for potential problems.
3. Send someone to get help from either the assistant principal or campus police. School policy often dictates whom to contact.
4. Avoid physically restraining students who are fighting. Recently, a middle school teacher who jumped in between two students found herself in the hospital with broken ribs.
5. Talk to the students in a calm voice. Tell them, "Break it up. Stop right there. Everyone back off. Move away from each other, now!" (Glenn, 1990, p. 21)
6. Document what has occurred by listing the time, location, students' names, descriptions of students if you do not know their names, and a narrative concerning the fight (Glenn, 1990).

One Florida group, composed of a former police officer, an attorney, a university professor, and a certified defense tactics instructor, is conducting seminars on "Self-Defense Tips for Educators." The content includes recognizing interventions of violence, understanding the liability laws, and examining terms such as *reasonable force* (Bolin, Flesch, Funk, & Osborne, 1997). They, along with Wolfgang, have also produced books that depict and describe various self-defense stances (Bolin, Funk, Flesch, & Osborne, 1998; Wolfgang, 1999).

Weapons

Similar guidelines regarding fighting apply in dealing with weapons. A teacher needs to remain calm, at least outwardly, in both voice and body language. While thinking about how to diffuse the situation, negotiate and use polite language. Rather than making sudden movements or acting as a threat, give the assailant options and try requests. Call the individual's name and treat the person with respect. Obviously, every situation is different and every person with a weapon is different. Yet, by using common sense and remembering that the final outcome can be fatal, a teacher can save lives.

As a reader, you might ask whether the authors have ever been confronted with a weapon. The answer is yes. While working on her doctorate, Williams was held at gunpoint by two men who robbed her friend and then shot him. Fortunately, she was not harmed and her friend lived. By quick thinking, Williams was able to flee and call the police. Henson arrived at a nice suburban middle school to supervise a female student teacher. The principal, who was angrily pacing the parking lot, said that just minutes before, as the student teacher arrived, she had been forced back into her car at gunpoint by a would-be rapist with a previous prison record. The attacker demanded that she drive to a wooded area. Instead, she got out of the car, slammed the door as though she was the one with the gun, and walked to her class. The armed assailant fled and was soon apprehended. Henson walked into the student teacher's class and watched her teach a good biology lesson as though nothing unusual had happened.

Fighting or Using Weapons

A study conducted by several Texas A&M researchers (Kingery et al., 1990) "indicates that violence and drug use are prevalent in our nation's rural schools" (p. 22). Participants included 1,004 eighth and tenth grade students from twenty-three rural Texas communities.

78.6 percent believe that they should fight if someone hits them.
42.3 percent could get a handgun if they wanted.
25 percent have carried a weapon to school.

In many states a reasonable force law helps define what an individual may do. According to the Florida statutes, reasonable force may be used when

> a person is justified in the use of force, except deadly force against another when and to the extent that he reasonably believes that such conduct is necessary to defend himself or another against such other's imminent use of unlawful force. However, he is justified in the use of deadly force only if he reasonably believed that such force is necessary to prevent imminent death or great bodily harm to himself or another person or to prevent the imminent commission of a forcible felony. (Justifiable Use of Force Act, 1995)

Crisis Teams

One proactive stance that school personnel can take is to train a crisis management team. This group, often called the emergency or crisis team, can be composed of four or five faculty and administrators who have had in-depth training in diffusing major problems. Fights, weapons, a drunken student or parent on campus, or somebody on drugs who wanders into the school are a few of the situations in which a crisis team would work. Anyone could activate the team by a prearranged signal over the public address system, and the team would immediately converge on the scene. Teachers would have a predetermined plan to monitor the crisis team's classes in an emergency.

ACTIVITY **10.8**

Crisis Situations—What Will I Do?*

How would you handle the following situations? Divide into pairs and tell your partner what you would do. Does your partner agree with your solutions? Did you consider positive solutions or simply send the students to detention? Which situations would call for crisis management team intervention, and which ones should the teacher handle alone?

1. You observe a student carving what you think is a gang symbol on her desk. When you approach the student, she says, "What's it to you, b****!" She then gets up, and you are afraid she might punch you. How do you proceed? (One of the authors was called a b*** during her student teaching semester.)
2. You overhear several students discussing a scheduled fight at the park for later that afternoon. How do you proceed?
3. In an attempt to collect the homework assignment, you ask Ken where his material is. He retorts, "I don't have time to do your *** busy work. If you want it done, do it yourself. I'm taking care of my own business, and making a lot more than some *** teacher." What do you do?
4. You notice that several students have gathered in the back of the room and are passing photos around and chuckling. You position yourself in the room so that you can see the pictures. You realize that several photos depict students dressed in gang clothing and having sex. What is your response?
5. While your students are supposed to be reading their favorite novel, you discover that Greg, who is always dressed in black, is reading *The Satanic Bible*. As you approach him, he quickly hides the book in his backpack. Do you ignore the situation? What about religious freedom?
6. A student, Jesse, arrives in class, removes a folded bandanna from his pocket, and ties it gang-style on his head. You know that the district has a dress code policy against such attire. What do you do?
7. A drunken parent arrives at school to pick up his thirteen-year-old son. How do you prevent the man from driving with the youngster in the car?

*Reprinted by permission of Marsha Harman, Assistant Professor, Sam Houston State University.

Meeting Students' Needs

Number 1: Involve the Student

In some of his presentations, Glasser has a panel of high school students on stage with him. He asks them what percentage of their classmates enjoy school and want to be there. What do you think these students say? When you were in high school, what percentage of your classmates enjoyed school and wanted to be there? The answers generally range from 10 to 25 percent. If only one-fourth of our students want to be at school, that is an indictment of the system, but for our purposes here it says a great deal about gangs and involvement. Glasser then asks the students on the stage if they are part of the small percentage that enjoys school, and generally they are. He then asks why they enjoy school and what causes them to want to be there. Students often mention extracurricular activities such as band, athletics, debate, and so forth. All of the answers involve something that the students feel a part of or something that they believe gives them an identity (Glasser, 1987).

High school principals love to have a winning football or basketball team. Students cause fewer discipline problems if a team is winning big. Students wear the colors and attend pep rallies and games holding their finger in the air shouting, "We're number one!" Almost all students get into the spirit. Why? Because they feel a part of something. Involvement and self-esteem increase. The answer then is simple. Make sure you have a winning athletic team and your problems are solved. Well, maybe not, but it does help to promote school spirit.

What does this illustration tell us? Find out what the students enjoy doing by simply asking them. Spend time talking to students about their goals, interests, and desires. And share information about you. As Wong and Wong (1998) suggest, you might want to make a bulletin board about who you are.

Or perhaps you could design a questionnaire concerning your students' likes and dislikes, and tell them about you. When you get to know students, you become a real person to them. Plus, if you are perceived to be "real," you are far less likely to be victimized. After gathering the information, use it wisely. For instance, you might need to meet with a coach, band director, sponsor, or administrator to make sure that a particular student is allowed to participate in a favorite activity. Or you may begin researching the value of hot rod autos, a topic you never thought would interest you, but three of your students noted that that was their favorite hobby.

Finding Out about Students: To Whom Do You Talk?

One logical person to talk to is the parent because most are concerned and want to help as much as possible. Hubbard (1998) suggests that, when talking to parents, teachers be aware of how they phrase their comments. Instead of saying "Billy's a gang member," you might state that "Billy's being exposed to gang influences, and we need to help him." Remember that Chapter 7 is devoted to getting parental support. Also talk to siblings. Most brothers and sisters know a lot about each other, and many times they are willing to share. Knowing that their brother or sister needs help may entice them to cooperate if they believe that the teacher is sincere. Other teachers and counselors can provide input. Talk to those who have taught or counseled the student, and look for positive insights that you can highlight.

If All Else Fails: Some Alternatives

If you cannot get the students involved, you may need to seek an alternative or outside help.

Counselor

Allow the counselors to pursue other available options. For instance, they typically have contacts with drug abuse and child abuse counselors, sources that are not always known to teachers. However, you need to check with them periodically for progress reports.

Administrators

Principals and assistant principals frequently know of agencies that may be used in certain cases. Make sure you explain that you are seeking help, not for discipline purposes, but to aid the student in leaving the gang or cult influence and in connecting in a positive way.

Peer Mediation

Many schools offer students opportunities to help others through avenues such as peer mediation and conflict resolution. Check your campus to see if these programs are available and refer students to books dealing with adolescent problems, such as *Cracker Jackson* (anxiety and worry) and *A Formal Feeling* (anger). In addition, you may want to read *Restoring Harmony: A Guide for Managing Conflicts in Schools* if you're interested in developing a conflict-resolution program (Lee, Pulvino, & Perrone, 1998).

Community Sources

Adopt-a-School Programs

Schools are involving businesses in an adopt-a-school program. Many of these businesspersons have unique abilities and resources that could be used to help students. Providing incentives, such as college scholarships, has given hope to students who never dreamed they would be given the opportunity.

Community, Police, and Service Agencies

Agencies such as Boy's Clubs, YMCA, YWCA, Girl Scouts, and Boy Scouts plan special activities to nurture at-risk students, those who have the potential for dropping out of school. The Police Activities League (PAL) uses recreational activities to help students get acquainted with officers, and the Technology to Recover Abducted Kids (TRAK) system prints colored flyers to help locate children (Hubbard, 1998). Lion's Club, Rotary Club, and Junior League are only three of the numerous service organizations that frequently initiate projects to help today's youths. Find out about the resources in your area.

Mentoring

School staff and community members can serve as mentors. Meeting with students after school, having them visit a business office, or taking them to dinner at some place besides a fast-food chain restaurant opens a new world for some students. Then visit their home, meet their family, and dine at their favorite place. Mentors can open the lines of communication when they show they are truly interested and care. One author mentors students on the university campus and has seen the advantages firsthand. Several of the relationships have developed into lasting friendships. It does take *time,* but again, for her, the results have been worth it.

Summary

This chapter investigated adolescents in crises with an emphasis on gangs, cults, and violence. Every secondary teacher needs to understand why students join gangs or cults and what educators can do to aid students who need support. We also provided some suggestions regarding what to do when confronted with dangerous situations.

REFERENCES

Bayles, F. (1997, November 7). Street gangs making inroads into business. *USA Today,* p. 3A.

Bolin, S., Flesch, R., Funk, F., & Osborne, W. (1997). *Self-defense tips for educators* [Brochure].

Bolin, S., Funk, F., Flesch, R., & Osborne, W. (1998). *Use of force (reasonable and deadly) for educators, law enforcement, public safety, and security.* Longwood, FL: Gould.

Byars, B. (1985). *Cracker Jackson.* New York: Viking Penguin.

Cassiel. (1990). *Encyclopedia of black magic.* New York: Mallard Press.

Collins, D. (1994, June). *Gangs in schools.* Paper presented to students in Classroom Management, Sam Houston State University, Huntsville, TX.

Cult Awareness Council (n.d.). *Do you know when your teenager is in danger? Warning signs of occult influences.* [Brochure] n.p.

Edwards, P. A., & Young, L. (1992). Beyond parents: Family, community, and school involvement. *Phi Delta Kappan, 74*(1), 72–80.

Glasser, W. (1987, February). *The application of control theory to problems of young people in school and out of school.* Paper presented at the meeting of the Association of Teacher Educators, Houston, TX.

Glenn, J. (1990). Training teachers for troubled times. *School Safety,* 20–21.

Harman, M., & Williams, P. (1998, February). *Juveniles in crisis: Voices of the perpetrators.* Paper presented at the meeting of the Association of Teacher Educators, Dallas, TX.

Hubbard, J. (1998, October). *Gangs in our schools: An educator's guide.* Paper presented to student teachers at Sam Houston State University, Huntsville, TX.

Justifiable Use of Force Act. (1995). Florida State Statutes, 776.012.

Kagan, S., & Kagan, L. (1998, February). *New cooperative learning—A curriculum for teachers and teacher educators.* Paper presented at the meeting of the Association of Teacher Educators, Dallas, TX.

Kingery, P., Merzaee, E., Pruitt, B., & Hurley, R. (1990). Town and country violence. *School Safety,* 22–25.

LaVey, A. (1989). *The satanic bible.* New York: Avon.

Lee, J. L., Pulvino, C. J., Perrone, P. A. (1998). *Restoring harmony: A guide for managing conflicts in schools.* Upper Saddle River, NJ: Prentice-Hall.

Maslow, A. (1943). A theory of human motivation. *Psychological Review, 50*(4), 370–96.

Maslow, A. (1954). *Motivation and personality.* New York: Harper.

Mayor's Anti-Gang Office. (1995). *Street gang terminology/glossary* [Handout]. Houston, TX: Author.

Morales, D. (1997). *Gangs & community response* [Brochure]. Austin, TX: Office of the Attorney General, Research & Legal Support Division.

Oneal, Z. (1982). *A formal feeling.* New York: Viking Press.

Sava, J. G. (1994, February). *A prescription for America.* Presentation given at the meeting of the Association of Teacher Educators, Atlanta, GA.

Thompson, D. (ed.). (1997). *The concise Oxford dictionary* (9th ed.). New York: Oxford University Press.

U.S. Department of Justice, Office of Justice Programs, Bureau of Justice Assistance. (1997). Urban Street Gang Enforcement. *Series BJA Monographs.* Washington, DC: US Government Printing Office.

Walker, W. (Executive Producer). (1998, October 13). *Gangs in Houston* [KHOU TV News Broadcast].

Williams, P. (Producer). (1985). *Teacher of the year: Meliane Christie* [Video]. (Available from Patricia Williams, Professor of Education, Sam Houston State University, Huntsville, TX 77341).

Williams, P., & Harris, C. (1988). Let's sub and trade. *Phi Delta Kappan, 69* (9), 693–694.

Wolfgang, C. (1995). *Solving discipline problems.* (3rd ed.). Boston: Allyn & Bacon.

Wolfgang, C. (1999). *Solving discipline problems* (4th ed.). Boston: Allyn & Bacon.

Wong, H., & Wong, R. (1991). *The first days of school.* Sunnyvale, CA: Author.

Wong, H., & Wong, R. (1998). *The first days of school.* Sunnyvale, CA: Author.

PART FOUR

Special Populations

Today's teachers are held accountable for teaching all students and helping everyone succeed. At an earlier time, students with disabilities were often grouped in a separate classroom. Specially prepared teachers were responsible for helping these students succeed. Now students with disabilities are together (included) in the same classroom with other students. Chapter 11 explains how all teachers can use positive techniques to modify student behavior and promote academic achievement.

As our nation's population becomes more diverse, teachers face conflicts among cultural groups and conflicts among members within groups. Chapter 12 will help teachers address cultural concerns as they relate to classroom management.

11 Students with Special Needs

All students, including those with special needs, can benefit from school activities.

OBJECTIVES

1. Contrast inclusion and mainstreaming.
2. Adapt your classroom management approach to accommodate students with special needs.
3. Analyze three ways to help students with disabilities succeed.

As Al Medrano walked into his first class, he realized that he had never experienced such an emotional high. Oh yes, he felt great about his academic preparation, at least insofar as the content was concerned. Ever since his junior high years, he had known that he wanted to teach English, and he had mastered the literature and grammar components so that he could become an excellent teacher. But, as he stood in the doorway of his first class, his feelings of confidence were shaken.

He immediately felt a slight panic as his eyes focused on a small, slender boy sitting in a wheelchair. The assistant principal, Mr. Downing, had informed Al that his class would include three students with moderate learning disabilities, one student who is wheelchair-bound, and one student with emotional problems. Furthermore, he had told Al that he would be teaching several highly gifted students. Al understood his own emotions well enough to know that before he could ever feel good about himself as a teacher, he would have to reach all his students and help them succeed. First and foremost, he needed to develop a cooperative spirit among these different students. To manage this class effectively he had to discover ways to help each student deal with unique challenges and overcome learning barriers. He wondered if he could manage his class, meet the needs of these exceptional students, and teach the entire class.

Overview

Students with Special Needs

Teachers at the turn of the century face a unique challenge; they must manage classrooms to meet the needs of students with a wide range of abilities and disabilities. Future classrooms will have an unprecedented number of students with special needs. Across the country, there are more than eight million children who have disabilities. Most are in regular classrooms for a large percentage, if not all, of the school day. Teachers must know how to regulate behavior to enable all students to grow both socially and academically.

Special students are those who need extra help, including gifted adolescents. Because they are also different, these students are often misunderstood and sometimes even ostracized. This chapter will introduce strategies teachers can use to help everyone be accepted. As you continue through this chapter, think of ways you can use these strategies in your classes.

A Review of the Past

During the past few decades, educators have been held accountable for ensuring the success of all students. This law makes many teachers uncomfortable. In the past, a strategy called *mainstreaming* was used to educate all learners. Mainstreaming consisted merely of placing students who are educationally challenged in classes with nondisabled peers. The underlying premise was that exposure to others by itself would enable the challenged students to succeed. But educators learned that this premise was false; simply placing students with disabilities into classrooms with nondisabled students did not result in academic gains for the challenged students and did not prepare them to socialize with their classmates.

The next strategy was a federal law known as the Education for All Handicapped Children Act, better known as Public Law 94-142, and later renamed the Individuals with Disabilities Education Act (IDEA). This 1977 law required that each state provide special services for all its handicapped students. All children aged three to nineteen (later extended to twenty-one) were to be served. In essence, this law implied that just mixing students heterogeneously in classes was insufficient. In fact, the Public Law 94-142 authors carefully avoided using the term *mainstreaming* because they believed that educationally challenged students needed more than mere placement in a general classroom.

Public Law 94-142 mandated specific responsibilities to teachers, giving new rights to parents of challenged youngsters. At a minimum, this law guaranteed that all parents of challenged students must be (1) notified that the school administrators plan to place these students in regular classrooms, (2) afforded a free due process hearing before the final decision is made, (3) provided an opportunity to present evidence, (4) offered full access to relevant school records, (5) given the right to confront and cross-examine officials, (6) given the right to seek an independent evaluation, and (7) given the right to have the impartial due process hearing closed or opened to the public. Public Law 94-142 also gave parents the right to have an individual lesson plan (IEP) specifically designed for their child. This law was replaced with Public Law 101-476, which also provides these rights.

Concerned that many teachers felt underprepared to help students with challenges overcome their learning barriers, Morbeck (1980) studied the problem and reported that most teachers need professional development training. Sometimes in-service training has helped (Althoff, 1981; Hurtado-Portillo, 1980; Koci, 1980); sometimes it has not (Baines & Baines, 1994). Being in contact with challenged students has made some teachers feel more comfortable (Marston & Leslie, 1983), although it hasn't been beneficial to others (Baines & Baines, 1994). One variable, increased knowledge about these students and their conditions, was found to improve teachers' attitudes (Pietroski, 1979).

According to IDEA, there are thirteen categories of disabilities:

- *Deaf*—impairment so severe that the child can't receive information through hearing
- *Deaf-blind*—simultaneous hearing and visual impairment
- *Hard of hearing*—less severe than deaf
- *Mentally retarded*—below average general intellectual functioning
- *Multiply disabled*—several simultaneous impairments
- *Orthopedically impaired*—orthopedic impairment caused by a birth defect, disease, or other cause such as cerebral palsy
- *Other health impaired*—chronic or acute health problems including a heart condition, tuberculosis, asthma, and epilepsy
- *Autism*—"a developmental disability that significantly affects verbal and nonverbal communication and social interaction" (Williams, Williams, Henderson, Goodwin, & Schumann, 1998, p. 28)
- *Seriously emotionally disturbed*—"a condition in which a student exhibits one or more of the characteristics over a long period of time and to a marked degree" (Williams, Williams, Henderson, Goodwin, & Schumann, 1998, p. 28). Characteristics include unexplained inability to learn, inability to maintain interpersonal relationships, inappropriate behavior or feelings, general mood of unhappiness, and a tendency to develop physical symptoms of fear.
- *Specific learning disability*—a disorder of the basic psychological processes used in understanding language and mathematical calculations. There is at least one standard deviation discrepancy between the ability and achievement levels. Individuals such as Cher and Nelson Rockefeller were disagnosed as having learning disabilities.
- *Speech impairment*—a communication disorder such as stuttering
- *Visual impairment*—an impairment that makes an individual partially sighted or blind
- *Traumatic brain injury*—an injury "caused by an external force or by an internal occurrence such as stroke or aneurysm" (Williams, Williams, Henderson, Goodwin, & Schumann, 1998, p. 28)

Inclusion

A newer approach to aiding students with disabilities is called inclusion. *Inclusion* is defined as placing learners with special needs in the regular education classroom and providing special services in that environment (Friend & Bursuck, 1996). More specifically, inclusion involves modifying the curriculum.

Disciplining Students with Disabilities

The history of how schools, teachers, and society have dealt with students with disabilities shows a pretty dismal and shameful track record. Prior to the mid-twentieth century, most youths with severe disabilities were locked in rooms by themselves, not for their own benefit, but to protect others. This practice of isolating students with special needs occurred in private homes and in state institutions. These unfortunate individuals often brought shame on their families because many people believed that the deformities were intentional flaws created by God to punish parents. But now that individuals with disabilities not only are sent to school but also are placed in classes with nondisabled students, many teachers are inclined to ignore their misbehavior and perhaps even exclude (excuse) them from assigned class activities. Although exclusion has been considered a legally viable method, excluding students from assigned class activities actually can cause misbehavior to increase (Katsiyannis, 1995).

Understanding Students with Disabilities

According to Jost (1993), the most generally used categories of learning problems include mental retardation, visual and hearing impairments, and environmental, economic, and cultural disadvantages. Learning disabled students account for about half of all the students who receive special assistance (Kolstad, Wilkinson, & Briggs, 1997). Although many students with learning disabilities are gifted (Ray, 1998), teachers often lack the skills necessary to ensure success for these students (Vaughn & Schumm, 1994). If so, the teacher has the responsibility for either learning how to help them overcome their disabilities or referring them to a specialist, such as a diagnostician, for help.

Before deciding whether students should be referred and how to manage the classroom to best help them, teachers need to consider several factors. The length of time the student has had the disability is important because the duration may affect the degree of damage. For instance, a student who is partially sighted may become blind over a period of time. A second important factor is the level of intensity or the degree of seriousness of the disability. A student with a slight hearing impairment may need less assistance than a student who is totally deaf. A third factor is the level of stability. A student whose vision, hearing, or motor control is rapidly deteriorating may need special help to acquire skills that would be much more difficult to attain once the ability is lost.

To enhance your knowledge, work with colleagues. Collaboration and team teaching have proven to be effective methods in planning and teaching lessons for students with learning disabilities (Dougherty, 1994; Friend & Cook, 1993). Perhaps the first and most critical step in preparing to fully manage student behavior is to admit to yourself and others that you are not an expert in special education. This sounds simple, but most teachers find it difficult because the moment you acknowledge your need for greater skills, you must begin exerting efforts to acquire understanding and develop these skills. Frankly, although many teachers acknowledge that these students need special help, they are unwilling to do anything to prepare themselves (Bateman, 1992).

ACTIVITY **11.1**

How Do You Feel? Journal Entry

This chapter states that you may not have had adequate preparation for helping students with special needs succeed but that you will have responsibility for doing just that. It further says that the parents of students with disabilities have certain rights. It will be your responsibility to ensure that these rights are given to your students' parents.

Think about your responsibilities. Are you prepared to meet these expectations? What do you need to know or do to prepare yourself? Write a journal entry.

A Need to Treat Everyone Alike

Granted, it is agreed that students with disabilities require special assistance, which is also required by law. Ironically, in certain ways students with disabilities need to be treated like all other students. For example, Williams (1997) focused her University of Arizona doctoral studies on the impact that inclusion programs have on the perceptions of nondisabled students. She reported, "Teachers need to be consciously aware of giving equal attention to each individual student, and avoid favoritism among students. Without this awareness, this differential treatment could impact performance and motivation for all students" (p. 150).

A Need to Help Students Belong

Classroom disruptions often result from students' feeling that they don't belong and are detached from the class. Students suffer from knowing that they are different and often shunned or even ridiculed. Both boys and girls need to feel that they belong (Gallagher, 1996). Bernal (1998) and Ray (1998) remind us that all students, including the gifted and talented, share the need to belong.

Students' attitudes toward belonging significantly affect their behaviors; furthermore, it is not uncommon for students to feel that they are members of some classes and not others. When students feel that they are a part of a class, their level of motivation rises and, consequently, they make higher grades (Goodenow, 1993).

Ironically, one way that you can help special students feel that they belong is by holding them to the same expectations that you have for others. Granted, they may need additional help, but they are not excused from the day-to-day routines. Because participation and membership are so important, you should provide your special students with opportunities to develop those skills needed for all class routines.

As a teacher, you set an example with your own behavior. One effective strategy for managing behavior is active engagement in academic tasks. Equal and total involvement for all students are prerequisites for academic engagement. Williams (1997) reported that special students need to be involved.

The cooperative learning method works well with special students because the success of each member depends on the entire group. Small groups of four to six members are used.

ACTIVITY **11.2**

Marty, My Hero: A Case Study

Marty is one the most exceptional kids I've known. You might think it impossible for a fourteen-year-old quadriplegic to be a member of a soccer team. Marty's brother and sister played on the local team. Although Marty couldn't move from his wheelchair, he insisted on attending every game. Marty couldn't speak, but he gave his audible approval each time his team scored.

Marty wasn't the only hero on this team. At the end of the season, when letters were awarded (patches with soccer balls), the rest of the team insisted that Marty receive a patch, too, *and* that he cross the stage to receive it just as the other players did. When his name was called, a team member wheeled Marty across the stage and he received his patch and an applause just like the other players.

Marty's parents were heroes, too. They had a son and daughter of their own when they met Marty. The dad was a physical therapist and the mom was a teacher. Marty had no parents. Because they fell in love with Marty, they and their son and daughter unanimously decided to adopt him. They wanted to be with him, but perhaps even more, they wanted him to have an active and stimulating life and they knew they could offer this to him.

Update: During the writing of this book, one of the authors (who was Marty's middle school soccer coach) learned that Marty has graduated from college and is preparing for graduate school.

Questions

As Marty's classroom teacher,

1. What could you do to strengthen his self-concept?
2. How could you encourage support for Marty from his classmates?

ACTIVITY **11.3**

How Do You React? Journal Entry

One way that people inadvertently isolate people with disabilities is by refusing to look at them. The next time you see an individual with a disability, make eye contact and say hello. Write a journal entry about the experience in which you describe the situation and your feelings.

Each group holds discussions and tutors another. For further information about this method, see *Methods and Strategies for Teaching in Secondary and Middle Schools* (Henson, 1996).

Teacher Power

Teachers have several types of power that they can use to shape and control student behavior. These types are not equal in terms of effectiveness or desirability. They include the following types: legitimate, coercive, reward, expert, and referent power.

Legitimate Power

You may think of your classroom as a democracy and, to be sure, there is value in making it as democratic as possible, but you are still ultimately responsible. Because you are held accountable for your class, you have the right to make decisions. In Chapter 1, Savage (1999) was quoted as saying, "Teachers should not think that they have no rights, nor should misbehaving students interfere with their right to teach and the right of others to learn" (p. 204). Savage is referring to legitimate power.

However, before you know it, you can overuse legitimate power. When you do, student respect for you diminishes. Effective classroom managers depend more on other types of power than their position-derived legitimate power.

Coercive Power

Coercive power equals potential or real punishment. Teachers who overuse coercive power become wardens over their students and, in turn, their students become prisoners. Chapter 1 introduced the concept of a learning community, a safe haven where students feel free to make mistakes, a climate where they feel good about themselves as individuals. Coercive power can quickly destroy all possibilities of your classroom becoming a learning community. Remember that the teacher's classroom management goal should be not to suppress undesirable behavior, but to shape students' thinking and feeling so as to diminish negative behaviors. The use of coercive power will work against teachers who advocate self-discipline.

Reward Power

Reward power refers to teachers' power to modify students' behavior through giving rewards. Those programs, usually labeled *behavior modification,* depend on the use of rewards. See Chapter 9 for a thorough explanation of rewards appropriate for secondary students.

Unlike coercive power, which is negative, reward power is positive. In that sense it is much more closely aligned with teachers' goals of having a supportive, nurturing environment in their classrooms. But reward power places the incentive for student behavior in the teacher's hands. Although this type of control discipline is popular today, and many teachers insist that without it they cannot persuade some students to behave, you should understand

---

ACTIVITY **11.4**

Have You Ever?

The overuse of coercive power often backfires. Instead of diminishing unwanted behavior, sometimes it provokes it. Have you ever misbehaved as a way of retaliating to a teacher's or parent's overuse of coercive behavior? Imagine how a wheelchair-bound student might feel toward a teacher who repeatedly warns students to stay in their seats.

ACTIVITY **11.5**
Who Are the Experts?

The ways teachers are perceived have changed through the years. Do you think of all your former teachers as experts? What qualities must a teacher display to earn your respect as an expert?

ACTIVITY **11.6**
Wyndell's Antics: The Gifted Underachiever

Wyndell, a twelfth grade student, has never gotten into any serious trouble. He is bright and creative. According to the school records, his IQ is 135 and he scored in the 95th percentile on his achievement tests. He gets along well with his classmates and has never had a major problem in school. Although he is a gifted underachiever who could care less if he makes a C rather than an A, he has never failed a subject. Yet he often forgets to do homework assignments.

Wyndell has a slightly less than serious attitude toward school. Unlike those education reformers who place academic accountability above everything else, Wyndell sees life as more than scholarship. He gets up each morning with another goal in mind; he wants to enjoy the day. Unfortunately, Ms. Jones, the twelfth grade math teacher, aligns her values with those of the education reformers. She is a good teacher who is dead serious about her subject. Her seriousness leaves little room for foolishness. It is to be expected that light-hearted students who insist on introducing levity into Ms. Jones' classroom are on a collision course.

The ultimate happened. In his good-natured manner, Wyndell made a few editorial comments that he and his classmates found to be rather entertaining. Intimidated by Wyndell's brightness, Ms. Jones warned him that his grade for the six weeks would be lowered a letter, but he continued to joke and the grade was lowered. Again Ms. Jones reminded him, "If you continue to disrupt, I will lower it another letter." Knowing that he had a C average, his response was, "Ms. Jones, you've already lowered my C by two letter grades. How much lower can it go?"

1. What type of power is Ms. Jones using?
2. Can you think of circumstances where this type of power has been effective? Ineffective? If so, why?
3. Is it fair to punish students more because they are bright? Slow? Different?
4. Is it fair for Ms. Jones to lower the academic grade because of conduct? The answer is no. Why not? Teachers must separate academics and behavior. Penalizing students academically for misbehaving is totally unfair because they earn the academic grade through schoolwork. Have you ever had teachers who mixed the two?
5. Ray (1998) said that the accomplishment of gifted students depends on their teachers' ability to recognize, accept, and promote their brightness. Have you witnessed teachers who cleverly deal with exceptionally bright students? How did these teachers deal with gifted students?

that ultimately it does not reach that goal of self-discipline. Intrinsic motivation, wanting to do the task and feeling good about it, is much more powerful than extrinsic rewards, such as free candy or pencils.

ACTIVITY **11.7**

Resolving Conflicts

Select a partner. Pretend that the two of you are students. Role-play the following scenarios and decide how to resolve the conflict. One student has a disability; the other does not. You must agree on how to handle the situations.

1. In science, your teacher divided you in pairs to complete the lab exercises. You, a student without a disability, are paired with Delores, a student who is slightly mentally retarded. You feel this is unfair because she might affect your grade.
2. Your algebra teacher has asked you to be Josh's buddy and leave class each day a little early to carry his books. Josh had a terrible auto accident and his arms were amputated. You feel terrible about Josh's accident, but you want to walk your "best friend" to class and not have to worry about Josh.
3. In history class, you discover that Ann is receiving a modified test and has a B+ average. She is required to complete only part of the test because her IEP states that she has a learning disability and needs modified tests. You are infuriated because you made a D– on the last test. How can it be fair that she's passing and you are barely scraping by in history?
4. Coach always has the students run laps before beginning the day's game. All the students except John dress out and run laps. John supposedly has a heart condition, at least that's the rumor, so he isn't required to do everything that you must do. You wonder if John is simply avoiding physical activities because he's grossly overweight.

How would you as a teacher help your students work together and develop an understanding of disabilities? Is role-playing an effective tool? Would you teach your students the art of conflict resolution?

Expert Power

Expert power is power that comes from holding special knowledge. Expert power is a prerequisite for high school teachers who want to earn student respect. Teachers who are perceived as experts garner cooperation.

Referent Power

Referent power is the power teachers earn through the way they treat students. These teachers demonstrate a high degree of caring and want students to develop the skills needed to succeed in life. They understand that teachers must show respect for students first if they expect students to show respect for them.

Referent power is especially effective in classrooms that have students of varying academic abilities. Because special students are often rejected outside the classroom, use of referent power to demonstrate concern for and commitment to these students is essential.

As you reflect on these types of powers, notice that teachers who hold the last two types (expert and referent) must have earned them. Such teachers view classroom management as essential because it is necessary to reach the academic goals of the class. They see the ultimate goal of school, and the role of the teacher, not as getting through the day but as helping students participate in and prepare for life.

Conflict Resolution

As problems develop (and you can be sure they will), one strategy you can use is conflict resolution. Because this strategy is addressed later in this text, it will receive only a cursory introduction in this chapter. Conflict resolution is being used extensively throughout the country in intervention classes. Sautter (1995) reported that more than two thousand schools have conflict resolution programs.

Conflict resolution involves discussing the problem and sometimes even role-playing the behavior of individuals in authentic situations. It is based on the theory that conflict is natural. Unlike traditional classroom teachers' efforts to suppress disagreements, this program teaches students that it is permissible to have conflicts. The important goal is to cope with conflict in acceptable ways. Providing opportunities for misbehaving students to discuss and perhaps even "act out" their frustrations can also help all students acknowledge and discuss their emotions (Wheeler, 1994).

Summary

Twenty-first-century teachers face a unique challenge; they must meet the needs of *all* students, including students with unusual talents and students with a wide range of disabilities. Successful management of inclusive classes does not require you to be an expert in special education; however, it does demand your ability to manage all students.

An effective classroom management approach in inclusive classes is to recognize your own limits of expertise in special education and to learn more about helping special students by soliciting the cooperation of the entire class. Recent research shows that when all students work together, they soon learn to think of everyone as classmates rather than focusing on particular disabilities.

The teacher's behavior serves as a role model. Teachers have a responsibility to shape the classroom atmosphere so that all students feel that they belong. You can do this by examining your different types of power and judiciously selecting and using the appropriate ones. These powers include legitimate, coercive, reward, expert, and referent power.

Effective managers of classrooms put more energy into preventing problems than they put into becoming expert problem solvers. Yet, at times all teachers need skills to defuse volatile situations. Conflict resolution skills include discussing problems and role-playing problem situations, giving students opportunities to act out their frustrations.

REFERENCES

Althoff, R. H. (1981). The effects of an inservice training procedure on the attitudes of regular education teachers toward mainstreaming of handicapped students. Unpublished doctoral dissertation, Wayne State University.

Baines, L., & Baines, C. (1994). Mainstreaming: One school's reality. *Phi Delta Kappan, 76*(1), 39–40, 57–64.

Bateman, B. (1992). Learning disabilities: The changing landscape. *Journal of Learning Disabilities, 25,* 28–36.

Bernal, E. M. (1998). Could gifted English-language learners save gifted and talented programs in an age of reform and inclusion? *Tempo, 18*(1), 11–14.

Dougherty, J. W. (1994). Inclusion and teaming: It's a natural collaboration. *Schools in the Middle, 3*(4), 7–8.

Friend, M., & Bursuck, W. D. (1996). *Including students with special needs: A practical guide for classroom teachers.* Boston: Allyn & Bacon.

Friend, M., & Cook, L. (1993). Inclusion. *Instructor, 103*(4), 53–56.

Gallagher, S. L. (1996). *Adolescents' perceived sense of belonging.* Unpublished master's thesis, Fort Hayes, State University, Kansas.

Goodenow, C. (1993). Classroom belonging among early adolescent students: Relationships to motivation and achievement. *Journal of Early Adolescence, 13,* 21–23.

Henson, K. T. (1996). *Methods and strategies for teaching in secondary and middle schools* (3rd. ed.). New York: Longman.

Hurtado-Portillo, J. L. (1980). Effects of an inservice program on the attitudes of regular classroom teachers toward mainstreaming mildly handicapped students. Unpublished doctoral dissertation, University of North Carolina at Chapel Hill.

Jost, K. (1993). Learning disabilities. *Congressional Quarterly Researcher, 3,* 1083–1103.

Katsiyannis, A. (1995). Disciplining students with disabilities: What principals should know. *NASSP Bulletin, 79*(575), 92–96.

Koci, J. I. L. (1980). A study of the needs of regular classroom teachers in implementing Public Law 94-142. Unpublished doctoral dissertation, University of Houston.

Kolstad, R., Wilkinson, M. M., & Briggs, L. D. (1997). Inclusion programs for learning disabled students in middle schools. *Education, 117*(3), 419–425.

Marston, R., & Leslie, D. (1983). Teacher perceptions from mainstreamed versus nonmainstreamed teaching environments. *Physical Educator, 40,* 8–15.

Morbeck, J. U. (1980). In-service education needs of senior high school regular classroom teachers relative to mainstreaming learning disabled students. Unpublished doctoral dissertation, University of Idaho.

Pietroski, M. S. (1979). An analysis of background variables associated with classroom teachers' attitudes toward mainstreaming. Unpublished doctoral dissertation, Boston University.

Ray, J. (1998). Fast forward and rewind: Strategies for gifted students with learning disabilities. *Tempo, 18*(1), 21–22, 38.

Sautter, R. C. (1996). Who are today's city kids? *Education Digest, 61* (Feb.), 4–7.

Savage, T. V. (1999). *Developing self-control through classroom management and discipline* (2nd ed.). Boston: Allyn & Bacon.

Vaughn, S., & Schumm, J. S. (1994). Middle school teachers' planning for students with learning disabilities. *Remedial and Special Education, 15,* 152–161.

Wheeler, E. (1994). Peer conflicts in the classroom. *ERIC Digest,* EDO-PS-94-13.

Williams, L. J. (1997). *Membership in inclusive classrooms: Middle school students' perceptions.* Ph.D. Dissertation, The University of Arizona.

Williams, P., Williams, R., Henderson, D. Goodwin, A., & Schumann, H. (1998). *Responsibilities of the professional educator* (5th ed.). Dubuque, IA: Kendall/Hunt.

12 Cultural Differences

Students of diverse ethnic backgrounds can help open up new lines of communication that benefit everyone.

OBJECTIVES

1. Describe the impact that grouping has had on ethnic and cultural minority students.
2. Analyze how understanding learning styles helps students in multicultural classes meet their academic needs.

Laura Hayes and Lin Callahan were enjoying team teaching their integrated eleventh grade social studies and English class. They were introducing a new six-week unit on Chaucer's *Canterbury Tales.* The word had spread that the "Miller's Tale" was a little spicy, so the motivational level was high. Laura and Lin knew that this was a *teachable moment,* a term they had read many times in journals.

As these teachers began introducing the unit, they were interrupted by a student from South Korea, who handed Laura a note that read: "I am Chin Wan. The only English I can speak is 'I am Chin Wan. I am very pleased to meet you.' "

1. How would you react to the moment at hand?
2. What steps could you take to help Chin Wan benefit from this unit?
3. How could you solicit help from the other students?

Overview

A Shift in Demographics

For several decades, the percentage of minority students in the classroom has been growing. Just over one-fourth of the school population is minorities (Drake, 1993). As the 1990s decade comes to a close, it will have brought with it five million immigrants to U.S. schools (Leslie & Glick, 1991). Even though each of the nation's twenty-four largest cities has a minority majority (Drake, 1993), the majority of teachers are Anglo-Americans (Ducette, Sewell, & Shapiro, 1996). Furthermore, a thorough review of the literature found that teachers are not being adequately prepared to meet the needs in multicultural classes (Zeicher, 1993). What does this mean to you as you plan to teach during the twenty-first century? What are your classroom management responsibilities? How can you best plan to prepare for your responsibilities in multicultural classrooms? Earlier in the century, once cultural differences began being stressed in the schools, the goal was to help students of all cultures to become like the mainstream in this country. This approach was known as the melting pot or soup bowl approach to multicultural education. Educational psychologists refer to the process as accommodation (Henson & Eller, 1999).

During the second half of the twentieth century, the soup bowl approach to multicultural education was replaced by a concept called the salad bowl. Rather than having soup that was all blended together, we changed the analogy to a salad, a mixture of ingredients that are blended but still keep their identities. We can still see individual lettuce leaves, tomatoes, and croutons, but they taste better mixed. The soup bowl approach aims at having students of all cultures become like the American mainstream, whereas the goal of the salad bowl approach is to enable students of each culture to retain their identities while adding to society at large.

Banks (1994) says that the only sensible way for schools to respond to the differences in culture and the demographic shifts is to prepare all students to become better citizens:

> Our society has a lot to gain by restructuring institutions in ways that incorporate all citizens. People who now feel disenfranchised will become more effective and productive citizens, new perspectives will be added to the nation's mainstream conditions. (p. 4)

ACTIVITY **12.1**

How Do You Feel? Journal Entry

What are your feelings toward promoting the preservation of the cultural backgrounds of all students? Do you believe this will strengthen or weaken our nation? Will keeping their native cultures inhibit minority students from developing allegiance to the American way of life? Write a journal entry to express your feelings.

In perhaps less eloquent terms, Banks is saying that if we value our nation, then we cannot afford to let any of its youths' talents be lost. To better manage multicultural classes and address students' needs, you must know about the characteristics of the growing population of nonmainstream students.

More Differences within Than among Cultures

As you begin working with members of various cultures, like others, you may have a tendency to stereotype different groups. Once that is done, the next common step is to label all group members according to those stereotypes. But members of minority cultures are different, just as members of any culture are different. Actually, the uniqueness among individuals is so great in any culture that more differences exist within the culture than among cultures. Casanova (1987) said that the differences among cultural groups mask the differences within groups. This joint idea has at least two strong implications for teachers.

First, it is important that teachers avoid stereotyping, especially if it leads to negative labeling. On the contrary, a far better approach is to focus on the positive contributions group members have made to strengthen our nation. Slavin (1994) has said that the best place to begin preparing to teach multicultural classes is to learn about your students' cultures. But learning about other cultures alone is inadequate. Guyton and Fielstein (1991) remind us that, as teachers, our responsibility goes further; we must help shape the attitudes of our students toward other cultures: "Although information is necessary, by itself, it cannot be expected to modify learned attitudes" (p. 207). What do you know about your school's multicultural education program?

A Change in the Curriculum

Effecting student behavior is what classroom management entails. Teachers in multicultural classrooms have an increased need to effect permanent changes in their students' behaviors,

---

ACTIVITY **12.2**

Testing Your Knowledge: Cultures and Colors

According to *Do's and Taboos of Hosting International Visitors,* a book about avoiding blunders and foolish notions, cross-cultural training and intercultural communication is impacting the world. It lists color tips for American hosts. Can you answer the following questions?

a. Shamrock green is the national color of Ireland, but in Northen Ireland the national color is _____.
b. In Brazil and Mexico, the color _____ represents death.
c. In England, _____ cats are considered lucky.
d. In Asia, _____ symbolizes youth and exuberance.
e. In Egypt, _____ is the national color and should not be used for packaging.

Answers

a. orange   c. black   e. green
b. purple   d. green

What colors symbolize your cultural heritage?

ACTIVITY **12.3**

How Does Your School Rate?

Rate the quality of your school's multicultural education program on a 1 (not at all) to 5 (exceptional) scale.

1 = Never   2 = Seldom   3 = Sometimes   4 = Often   5 = Always

	1	2	3	4	5
1. Pictures of various ethnic groups appear in the building.					
2. The school calendar notes ethnic holidays.					
3. The school administrators ask individuals from different cultural groups to make presentations to the student body.					
4. The teachers and administrators are given professional development training regarding multicultural issues.					
5. The foods served in the cafeteria reflect the school's diversity.					
6. The school library displays books from authors of diverse cultural and ethnic backgrounds.					
7. The school has a professional educators' library that contains books about multicultural education.					
8. The textbooks mention specific contributions that various ethnic groups and particular individuals have made.					
9. The school has programs to celebrate the holidays that reflect the school population's ethnic and cultural diversity.					
10. The school has a written action plan used to promote multicultural education. Teachers, administrators, parents, students, and community members have input.					

Now, score how your school rates as to the quality of the multicultural education program.

40–50	Exceptional	10–19	Mediocre
30–39	Good	Below 10	Poor
20–29	Average		

What does the score tell you?

---

which requires changing how students feel toward themselves. One approach to improving self-concept is to assign tasks that students can work on together (Manning & Lucking, 1991). The goal of multicultural education is to help all students learn to appreciate and celebrate cultural diversity (McCormick, 1984). Most high school teachers worry that they will not have time to cover the content their students will need to succeed when they advance to the next grade level. Spending time on multicultural concerns may intensify that problem.

Good and Brophy (1997) warn teachers that, "Balancing the curriculum to achieve both academic goals and fair representation of various groups is no easy task" (p. 344). This dilemma may well leave you wondering, "What specifically can I do? I understand that as a teacher I have certain responsibilities." At a minimum, your responsibilities include all the actions seen in the following review of teachers' multicultural education responsibilities.

Multicultural Responsibilities of All Teachers

- Learn all you can about the cultures represented in your classrooms.
- Resist the temptation to form negative stereotypes.
- Include contributions that each group has made to our nation.
- Remember that the range of differences within a culture is greater than the differences between cultures.
- Treat each student as an individual.
- Help students appreciate the contributions that various cultures have made to our world.
- Provide opportunities for students to discuss diversity.
- Help all students develop a good self-concept.
- Adhere to the goal "All can succeed."

As you begin planning for your multicultural classroom, you may wish to follow Boutte and McCormick's (1992) advice:

- *Modeling by Teachers.* If teachers show that they value persons of differing characteristics and backgrounds, students will emulate this attitude.
- *Curricular Inclusion of Multicultural Heritage.* Curriculum should include religious customs, music, art, and literature representing various cultures. For example, not all students celebrate Christmas; some students celebrate Kwanzaa, Hanukkah, or other holidays.
- *Multicultural Literature.* Teachers should use literature that reflects gender diversity for children of differing racial backgrounds and home environments.
- *Multicultural Experiences.* By supplementing the curriculum with colloquial and non-English expressions, the teacher can teach students the value of language diversity.
- *Resource Persons from Different Cultures.* Teachers should take advantage of the varying ethnic and cultural backgrounds within the community. Parents and other community members can share their cultures as noted in Chapter 7.

ACTIVITY 12.4

Preparing a Classroom That Welcomes Diversity

Think of ways to prepare your culturally diverse classroom. Here's a suggestion. Begin by letting students design a bulletin board. The board will provide space for each student to bring one story or current event involving another culture. Shelf space can also be designated for students to bring artifacts from other cultures. Locate items at your home that are from other countries. Do you have Italian leather shoes, a Japanese camera, Mexican coins, or a Swiss watch? Provide opportunities to share these through discussion.

The Role of Expectations

Two major roles of the school are to help all students develop academically and socially (Henson & Eller, 1999). To attempt to separate these two goals would be futile because they are interconnected. How many students have you known who are popular among their peers and yet who are academic failures? Contrary to the old myth that most academically inclined students are social misfits, academic success often facilitates social acceptance and vice versa. Knapp (1995) found that many teachers who teach in urban high schools inadvertently and unknowingly limit the academic achievement of many minority students by setting low expectations for them. The Hispanic Association of Colleges and Universities (n.d.) recommends that, to foster success, teachers analyze three components of their classrooms: climate, oral language development, and academic content. To foster a warm atmosphere, have you welcomed the students and displayed on the bulletin board their autobiographies along with pictures of their family and pets? Did you assign them a buddy who speaks the same language or is sensitive to the student's culture? (Hewlett-Gómez, 1998). Have you learned how to pronounce the students' names and identified which is the family name? Your name is very important to you; it's part of your identity. Students feel the same way.

Learn about the pitfalls. Avoid using a loud voice because you think the student will understand more. One teacher told us that she thought the bilingual student could comprehend more if she spoke loudly. The amazed student asked her, in broken English, why she was shouting. Louder is not better. Do you understand more when someone yells?

Study the body language appropriate in different cultures. Flashing the "OK" sign to a Brazilian, beckoning a Malaysian with a curled index finger, and showing the sole of your shoe to a Pakistani are considered impolite. These simple tips will aid you in developing a good classroom climate.

By using graphic organizers, concrete objects, and detailed pictures and models, you can help bilingual students grasp oral language and academic concepts. When possible, "break down the lesson's text into small chunks for shorter periods of time rather than one long lesson" (Hewlett-Gómez, 1998, p. 55). Also, provide hands-on experiences whenever possible. For instance, students can make picture dictionaries and use picture words and sentence stories to understand key terminology.

The Trump Plan Revisited

Near the middle of the century, a public school administrator named Lloyd Trump designed a curriculum that became known as the Trump Plan. This plan reflected his recognition that

ACTIVITY 12.5

Interpreting Erasmus

Consider the statement made by Erasmus (1989): "Teachers must be able to reach beyond their own world to touch that of their students and help students do the same" (p. 274). What does Erasmus mean by "help students do the same"?

students need time to work alone part of the day. Specifically, the plan called for students to spend 20 percent of their time in small groups and 40 percent in independent study.

The Trump Plan has components that make its use in multicultural classrooms preferable to traditional curricula. For example, setting aside time for students to work alone is important. Good and Brophy (1997) said, "Most students enjoy working independently to gather facts on a problem using the information in simulated situations" (p. 343).

Classroom Projects

Some teachers design classroom projects to strengthen the members' knowledge about other cultures and develop a commitment to diversity. By working together, students learn to tolerate

---

ACTIVITY **12.6**

Multicultural Bingo

To help students better understand differences among cultures, have them play multicultural bingo. Directions: After filling in all the squares that describe yourself, find other classmates who can complete the rest. Try to fill all squares within a fifteen-minute period. The person who fills the most squares wins a prize.

Someone who has attended an Italian festival	Someone who knows the culture that gave us fireworks	Someone who celebrates Hanukkah
Someone who speaks more than one language	Someone who can name three leaders of various countries	Someone who can sing a French song
Someone who can name three musical groups or artists from other countries	FREE SQUARE! Write your name and cultural identity in this space.	Someone who has visited another country
Someone who has attended a Juneteenth celebration	Someone who can name 5 of the 7 Wonders of the World	Someone who likes Chinese food
Someone who celebrates St. Patrick's Day	Someone who can name 5 Native American tribes	Someone who can tell you which countries border Morocco

differences between the other cultures and their own. Houck and Maxon (1997) suggest that projects such as neighborhood safety can cause students to care about people. Examples include working with the elderly at nursing homes and building homes with Habitat for Humanity. Such projects also communicate your own caring for others (Cummins & Sayers, 1995).

As you plan classroom projects, involve students in choosing the topics to pursue. When topics are selected, you should ensure that goals are immediately chosen so students will be committed to the project (Vars, 1997).

Accountability

All contemporary teachers face a paradox; they must make their multicultural classrooms a successful arena for all students, yet, they must ensure that students perform well on standardized tests. Vars (1997) stated, "Most of America's teachers today are anxious, if not paranoid, about preparing their students for state proficiency exams and other externally-imposed assessments" (p. 44).

Throughout the country, teachers are feeling an increased need to prepare students to score well on standardized tests. In some states, the pressure is ever constant, so much so that virtually every minute is spent preparing students for exams. For example, in Kentucky each school establishes a performance baseline or benchmark. Each year schools are expected to exceed the performance level set the previous year.

When schools exceed their baselines by wide margins, rewards are given. But when a school scores significantly lower than the previous year, the school can be declared to be in crisis. A distinguished educator is then sent to help the faltering school. If the low scores continue, the administrators can be fired, and the school management can be delegated to the state department of education.

The school in which you will teach may or may not have such a strong penalty/reward system, but you can be sure that your state, district, and school will stress the importance of students scoring well on standardized tests. You must prepare students to do well on these tests; however, this cannot be an excuse for forgetting your classroom's multicultural needs. Perhaps the most effective way to meet both the accountability mandates and the multicultural needs is through a personalized approach.

Personalizing Your Teaching

What is meant by personalizing teaching? How can you personalize when you are assigned a large class? These are good questions. Personalizing begins on the inside, with what you believe and how you feel. Glatthorn (1993) commented,

> The place to start is with yourself—your sense of your own ethnicity, your own biases about ethnic minorities, and your own perspective about the kind of society in which you wish to live. This self-awareness will help you understand your own attitudes and should also facilitate your empathizing with minority students.
>
> There are several ways, of course, for developing this self-awareness. One process that has been found effective is to consider the issues posed below, in the sequence presented here.
>
> Consider your present feelings and attitudes about ethnic groups other than your own. Which ethnic group do you most respect? About which ethnic group do you seem to have the strongest negative feelings? What factors have influenced these biases? What ethnic stereotypes do you find yourself accepting?

ACTIVITY **12.7**

Examine Your Feelings: Journal Entry

Use the think-write-discuss process in examining these issues; reflect on the questions posed; write responses in your journal to discern your positions; and share those responses you feel ready to disclose to others.

Begin by reflecting about your own ethnicity. With which ethnic group do you identify? What is the cultural significance of your name? Which people and institutions were most influential in shaping your own ethnic identity?

Now reflect about your own ethnic identity and the way it relates to the dominant culture. If you are a member of the majority, have you benefited from that membership? Have you ever felt yourself discriminated against? What stereotypes do others hold about your ethnic group? In what ways are your culturally rooted beliefs and values consistent or inconsistent with those of your family?

Next consider your own behavior as it relates to other ethnic groups. Do you interact socially with members of minority groups? Do you ever tell jokes about members of other ethnic groups—or do you listen to such jokes without remonstrating? Have you ever let ethnic stereotypes influence your decisions and actions?

Finally, briefly describe a couple of ways in which you wish to change your attitudes and behavior about members of other ethnic groups. Tell how you might achieve each change. (pp. 385–386)

Vary Your Teaching Styles

Any approach you use in your multicultural classroom is unlikely to meet the learning needs of all students. As stated earlier, the range of learning style preference is greater within than among cultural groups; yet, some learning style differences do exist between students from different cultures (Dunn & Griggs, 1995). Because of this cumulative effect, you can expect the learning styles to be more diversified in those classes that are especially diverse.

As a teacher, your role is not to find a style that meets all students' needs. Although admirable, such a colossal undertaking would probably be impossible. Rather, your role is to be aware of different learning styles and effectively use a variety of teaching strategies to help all students learn to their optimum potential.

Use Small-Group Projects

Students learn to appreciate other cultures when they have positive multicultural experiences both in work and play. Your role is to provide multicultural group assignments and supervise the group activities, but only to the extent that they work together harmoniously. If you wish to have competition, most of the time the competition should be *among* groups and not *within* a group.

Use Individual Projects

Individual projects can be used to meet the learning needs of different cultures. Furthermore, individual projects can be designed to prompt students to examine their attitudes toward both

---

ACTIVITY **12.8**

Preparing a Multicultural Lesson Plan

Divide your class into groups of three to five students. Have each group pair with another group. Both pairs write a multicultural lesson plan for their counterpart group to critique. Include objectives, activities, evaluation methods, and resources in the plan.

---

their own cultures and others. This introspective pursuit can be extended further by requiring students to keep a written record of their thoughts.

Use Technology

Computers offer opportunities to individualize (Magney, 1990). At Blair High School in Pasadena, California, 312 multicultural students found Quick Time and PageMaker to be helpful tools to use to create "multimedia footnotes" in their English class. These students are among the two million children in this country who need bilingual education.

What Can I Do?

Most beginning teachers feel less than competent as they face their future. Knowing that much improvement is needed in our society to enable members of various ethnic groups to work together, the classroom seems like a perfect place to begin. But the question is *how?* Where do I start? Dawson (1974) offers the following suggestions to improve the climate in your multicultural classrooms.

1. Do use the same scientific approach to gain background information on multicultural groups that you would use to tackle a course in science, mathematics, or any subject area in which you might be deficient.
2. Do engage in systematic study of the disciplines that provide insight into the cultural heritage, political struggle, contributions, and present-day problems of minority groups.
3. Do try to develop sincere, personal relationships with minorities. You can't teach strangers. Don't give up because one minority person rejects your efforts. All groups have sincere individuals who welcome honest, warm relationships with members of another race. Seek out those who will accept or at least tolerate you.
4. Do recognize that there are often more differences within one group than between two groups. If we recognize diversity among races, we must also recognize diversity within groups.
5. Do remember that there are many ways to gain insight into a group. Visit their churches, homes, communities; read widely and listen to various segments of the group.
6. Do remember that no one approach and no one answer will help you meet the educational needs of all children in a multicultural society.
7. Do select instructional materials that are accurate and free from stereotypes.
8. Do remember that there is a positive relationship between teacher expectation and academic progress.

ACTIVITY **12.9**

Building a Multicultural Library

Visit your library or favorite bookstore and make a list of books you can use to enrich your multicultural classroom. Choose books that provide insight into cultures or exhibit incidences in which members of various cultures have been successful working together. Use a standard referencing system such as APA or the *Chicago Manual of Style* to record your materials so that you can submit a purchase request to your school administrators when you begin teaching.

9. Do provide an opportunity for minority students and students from the mainstream to interact in a positive intellectual setting on a continuous basis.
10. Do use a variety of materials, especially those that utilize positive, real-life experiences.
11. Do provide some structure and direction to children who have unstructured lives, primarily children of the poor.
12. Do expose all students to a wide variety of literature as a part of your cultural sensitivity program.
13. Do remember that even though ethnic groups often share many common problems, their needs are diverse.
14. Do utilize the rich resources within your own classroom among various cultural groups.
15. Do remember that human understanding is a lifetime endeavor. You must continue to study and provide meaningful experiences for your students.
16. Do remember to be honest with yourself. If you can't adjust to children from multicultural homes, get out of the classroom. (pp. 53–54)

Further Introspection

Have you acquired behaviors that will work against your efforts to meet your students' multicultural needs? For example, do you have feelings that will cause members of certain cultural groups to resent you? Some individuals who wish most to make things right among many cultures seem to draw resentment from members of other cultures. Do you have habits that will create rejection from students of other cultures? Examine the following list of don'ts for teachers in multicultural classrooms and see if any of these items apply to you (Dawson, 1974).

1. Don't rely on textbooks, teacher's guides, and brief essays to become informed about minorities. Research and resources will be needed.
2. Don't use ignorance as an excuse for not having any insight into the problems and cultures of African Americans, Chicanos, Native Americans, Puerto Ricans, Asian Americans, and other minorities.
3. Don't rely on the "expert" judgement of one minority person for the answer to all complicated racial and social problems. For example, African Americans, Mexicans, Indians, and Puerto Ricans have various political views.
4. Don't be fooled by popular slogans and propaganda intended to raise the national consciousness of an oppressed people.
5. Don't get the "save the world concept." Most minorities have their own savior.

6. Don't be afraid to learn from those who are more familiar with the mores and cultures than you.
7. Don't assume that you have the answers for solving the other person's problems. It is almost impossible for an outsider to be an expert on the culture of another group.
8. Don't assume that all minority group students are culturally deprived.
9. Don't develop a fatalistic attitude about the progress of minority students.
10. Don't resegregate students through tracking and ability grouping gimmicks.
11. Don't give up when minority students seem to hate school.
12. Don't assume that minorities are the only students who should have multicultural instructional materials. Students . . . can be culturally deprived in their lack of knowledge and understanding of other people and of their own heritage.
13. Don't ask parents and students personal questions in the name of research. Why should they divulge their suffering?
14. Don't get hung up on grade designations when sharing literature that provides insight into the cultural heritage of a people.
15. Don't try to be cool by using the vernacular of a particular racial group.
16. Don't make minority students feel ashamed of their language, dress, or traditions. (pp. 214–215)

You may wish to go beyond your own introspection to gather information about your potential strengths and weaknesses for teaching in multicultural classrooms. For example, you may wish to share the preceding list with a friend who will give you a rating on each of these behaviors or who will check any quality that applies to you.

Teachers' Responses to Multicultural Demands

In the past, teachers have expressed reluctance to make changes needed to serve students in multicultural classrooms. Perrone (1998) reported the following comments that teachers have made when asked to implement multicultural strategies:

- My students don't know how to read primary documents. I can't afford the time it would take to teach them how to do it successfully.
- My students are not used to writing in math class. It would be disruptive.
- My students expect me to be an authority. It would be very difficult to move so much responsibility for the content to them.
- I am expected to *cover* (a particular subject matter). If I followed the teaching for understanding format, I would only be able to cover part of it. I don't think I can do this.
- I could do one or two short units around the framework, but that would be the limit.
- I have tried using performances before students actually do something. They take a lot of time and the quality is mixed.
- The students are comfortable having a textbook and knowing precisely what they are to do. The teaching for understanding process keeps things too uncertain. There are too many interpretations, too many diverse activities, not enough closure.
- This would be easier if my class met for a longer time each day. Forty-two minutes doesn't leave much time to do interpretive work, organize complex projects, and engage in active learning.
- Our system wants students to have a lot of information about American history. I can't meet that responsibility and also do the kind of in-depth study the teaching for understanding framework demands.
- Where will I get all the materials needed for teaching for understanding?

ACTIVITY **12.10**

Cultural Mapping

Draw a map that depicts your cultural heritage. Use the model shown here. Then have your students draw their own maps and place them on the bulletin board.

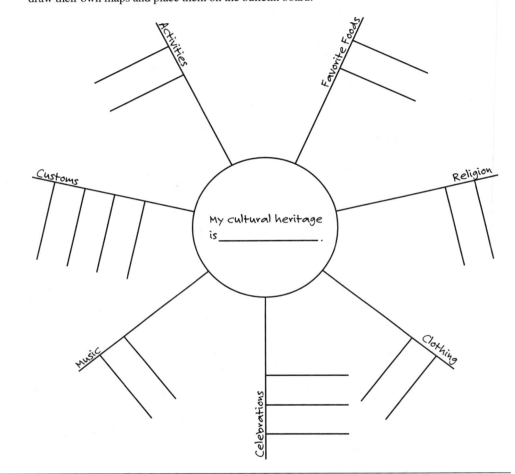

- How can I be the only teacher doing this?
- I have one hundred forty students each day to deal with. Teaching for understanding requires me to organize many new materials, keep track of a wider range of activities, and get students more involved in writing and presenting. I can't read carefully what students are beginning to produce.
- I have been a successful teacher doing what I have been doing. I haven't used large numbers of primary documents before. I don't really know how to use cooperative groups very well. Inquiry makes me feel less competent. I don't want to risk failure. (p. 306)

These concerns have merit and should not be viewed as mere excuses, but they also serve as barriers to the direction that teaching is taking for 2000 and beyond. Martin Haberman (1996), University Wisconsin–Milwaukee, has studied multicultural education and, in particular, the preparation of teachers to teach in urban, multicultural settings. He reports on a few states that have supported efforts to make the entire state's teacher preparation programs more urban and more responsive to cultural diversity.

Undergraduate Preservice Program

A thorough undergraduate preservice program for preparing urban teachers is offered by Alverno College (Diez & Murrell, 1991). The emphasis is on the integration of knowledge and action. This program is not simply another required course in multicultural education but a "total development of the prospective candidate" (p. 6). The Alverno program emphasizes students' ability to perform. By "ability to perform," the Alverno faculty means "an integration of knowledge, professional skill, and professional predispositions that define what a practitioner knows and is able to do" (p. 7). The program has other notable features, including its emphasis on future teachers working with parents and professionals, reconceptualized fieldwork and student teaching, and a thoroughly individualized assessment program. This holistic approach, in effect, led to the development of a knowledge base for urban teacher education.

As you progress through your teacher education program, you can improve your preparation to teach multicultural classes by assessing your own progress. Every course should provide you opportunities to develop specific competencies that will prepare you to deal with diversity in your future classrooms.

Postbaccalaureate Program

Memphis State University offers a program for DeWitt Wallace–Reader's Digest Fellows. This program involves interns actually performing the role of teachers, with the aid of mentors, while they complete required course work (Chance, 1993). As you progress through your program, look for teachers you respect. Solicit their suggestions and advice. Ask them about multicultural lessons that work well in their classes. Good teachers continue growing throughout their careers, using the colleagues they respect most as mentors and role models.

Career Ladder for Teacher Aides Program

The Career Ladder for Teacher Aides program (Haberman, 1996) is distinctive because it requires participants to demonstrate the ability to:

1. orchestrate a learning environment
2. possess a strong belief in students' abilities to learn
3. assume another person's perspective
4. function within the purpose and intent of public education
5. show a high regard for the opinions, experiences, and responsibilities of others
6. have knowledge of the support structures available to protect teachers' rights
7. remain receptive to discovering and gathering useful resources
8. expand others' awareness of the world
9. build a positive support system for youth

    10. remain accepting of the thoughts and suggestions of others
    11. accurately appraise their own strengths and weaknesses (p. 758)

An examination of these programs suggests that there are many ways students can develop skills needed to manage urban classrooms. Paramount among these strategies are spelling out the skills needed to manage multicultural classrooms and assessing your progress at various intervals.

Summary

Major changes in demographics demand that teachers of the twenty-first century have special skills and understandings if they are to survive and succeed in multicultural classrooms. Notable among these are the rapid increase in minority youths and the lack of a parallel increase in minority teachers. For instance, according to the 1995 U.S. Bureau of the Census report, "Hispanic-Americans account for 10.2 percent of the population. This represents a growth rate of nearly 85 percent since 1980." Yet, "4.2 percent of all teachers at the elementary and secondary school level are Hispanic while 12 percent of the public school student population is Hispanic" (Hispanic Association of Colleges and Universities, n.d.). Successful management of multicultural classrooms requires a better understanding of all cultures represented and a willingness to alter curriculum to celebrate the contributions of various groups.

A personal approach seems to be particularly needed in multicultural classrooms. To avoid stereotyping, remember that there are more differences among members within each culture than there are among cultures. Attitudes are as important as content. As a teacher, you will have the responsibility of changing your own perceptions plus molding the views of your students. The ultimate goal is to help students recognize the contributions of each culture and to not only accept but also to appreciate diversity in our society.

Students in multicultural classes need opportunities to gather data on their own and to work together cooperatively. While moving your students ahead in the multicultural dimension, you must also ensure that they are progressing academically. That is to say, efforts to teach students to work with members of other cultures must not diminish the rigor of course content.

REFERENCES

Axtell, R. E. (1990). *Do's and taboos of hosting international visitors* (2nd ed.). New York: Wiley.

Banks, J. (1994). *An introduction to multicultural education.* Boston: Allyn & Bacon.

Boutte, G. S., & McCormick, C. (1992). Authentic multicultural activities. *Childhood Education, 3,* 140–144.

Casanova, U. (1987). Ethnic and cultural differences. In V. Richardson-Koehler (ed.), *Educators' handbook: A research perspective* (pp. 370–393). White Plains, NY: Longman.

Chance, L. H. (1993). *Pathways to teaching program.* Memphis, TN: School of Education, Memphis State University.

Cummins, J., & Sayers, D. (1995). *Brave new schools.* New York: St. Martin's Press.

Dawson, M. E. (Ed.). 1974. *Are there unwelcome guests in your classroom?* Washington, DC: Association for Childhood Educational International.

Diez, M. R., & Murrell, P. J. (1991). *Assessing abilities in expert teaching practice in diverse classrooms.* Paper presented at the fourth annual conference on racial and ethnic relations in American higher education, Washington, DC.

Drake, D. D. (1993). Student diversity: Implications for the classroom. *The Clearing House, 3,* 264–266.

Ducette, J. P., Sewell, T. E., & Shapiro, J. P. (1996). Diversity in education: Problems and possibilities. In F. B. Murray (ed.), *The teacher educator's handbook: Building a knowledge base for the preparation of teachers* (pp. 323–380). San Francisco: Jossey-Bass.

Dunn, R., & Griggs, S. A. (1995). *Multiculturalism and learning style: Teaching and counseling adolescents.* Westport, CT: Greenwood Publishers.

Erasmus, C. C. (1989). Ways with stories: Listening to the stories aboriginal people tell. *Language Arts, 66*(3), 267–275.

Gardner, H., Perkins, D., & Perrone, V. (1993). *Annual report of the Spencer Foundation.* Cambridge, MA: Harvard Graduate School of Education.

Glatthorn, A. A. (1993). *Learning twice: An introduction to the methods of teaching.* New York: HarperCollins.

Good, T. L., & Brophy, J. E. (1997). *Looking in classrooms* (7th ed.). New York: Longman.

Guyton, J. M., & Fielstein, L. L. (1991). A classroom activity to increase student awareness of racial prejudice. *The Clearing House, 64*(3), 207–209.

Haberman, M. (1996). Selecting and preparing culturally competent teachers for urban schools. In J. Sikula, T. Buttery, & E. Guyton (eds.), *Handbook of research on education* (2nd ed.) (pp. 747–761). New York: Macmillan.

Henson, K. T., & Eller, B. F. (1999). *Educational psychology for effective teaching.* Belmont, CA: Wadsworth.

Hewlett-Gómez, M. (1998). Suggested communication activities. In P. Williams, R. Williams, D. Henderson, A. Goodwin, & H. Schumann (eds.), *Responsibilities of the professional educator* (5th ed.). Dubuque, IA: Kendall/Hunt.

Hispanic Association of Colleges and Universities. (n.d.). *Facts on Hispanic higher education* [Brochure].

Houck, J. W., & Maxon, S. (1997). The role of teachers and the schools in assisting children who live with violence. *Education, 117*(4), 522–529.

Knapp, M. (1995). *Teaching for meaning in high-poverty classrooms.* New York: Teachers College Press.

Knauth, S. M. (1993). *Teachers for Chicago: First year evaluation report.* Chicago: Golden Apple Foundation.

Leslie, C., & Glick, D. (1991). Classroom of Babel. *Newsweek, 2,* 56–57.

Magney, J. (1990). Game-based teaching. *The Education Digest, 60*(5), 54–57.

Manning, M. L., & Lucking, R. (1991). The what, why, and how of cooperative learning. *The Clearing House, 64*(3), 152–156.

McCormick, T. E. (1984). Multiculturalism: Some principles and issues. *Theory into Practice, 23,* 93–97.

Perrone, V. (1998). How can we prepare new teachers? In M. J. Miske (ed.), *Teaching for understanding: Linking research with practice.* San Francisco: Jossey-Bass.

Slavin, R. E. (1994). *Educational psychology: Theory and practice* (4th ed.). Boston: Allyn & Bacon.

Vars, G. F. (1997). Student concerns and standards too. *Middle School Journal, 28*(4), 44–49.

Zeicher, K. (1993). *Educating teachers for cultural diversity.* East Lansing, MI: National Center for Research on Teacher Learning.

PART FIVE

A Problem-Solving Model
and the Development
of a Philosophy

An old expression says that we must know where we are going before we can get there. Such is the case with classroom management. If we are to manage our classrooms well, we must have a plan that tells how we expect to get "there" (to the well-managed classroom). This final section will ask you, as a teacher, to reflect upon your beliefs about teaching and to develop a written plan for managing your classroom. This section will also suggest the use of action research as a problem-solving tool to answer difficult questions about your classroom, alter your teaching strategies, and adapt your teaching to your students' needs. Classroom procedures, rules, and consequences of behavior are discussed.

13 A Model for Solving Discipline Problems

Good organization will help you implement fair disciplinary strategies.

OBJECTIVES

1. Distinguish among preventive, supportive, and corrective discipline, and identify at least three management practices that support each.
2. Examine your personal theories and beliefs of practice regarding classroom management.
3. Create an action research agenda that will help you solve classroom management problems.
4. Develop a comprehensive management plan.

Overview

On September 1, Ann Nelson, neophyte geometry teacher, is ready. Class roster, grade book, textbook, and this week's lesson plans in hand, she walks into her classroom and exclaims, "This year will be exceptional. I'm prepared." She's completed her certification requirements, learned about all students' needs in multicultural classes, met with her mentor teacher, and feels confident. During the past month, she even called each student's parents about the geometry class and invited them to visit. What else does she need? Without a workable classroom management plan, Ann's students will not know what behavior is expected in her class. What could be a great year might be a disaster. This chapter explains how to write a plan.

Early approaches to classroom discipline were primarily punitive in nature. In fact, one of the first school buildings in the United States was equipped with a whipping post (Manning, 1959), and in those "good old days" many devices and techniques were used to inflict punishment and even physical pain. As Purkey (1985) points out, fear played a major role in the discipline process with students receiving terrifying warnings from home, school, and even the pulpit about what happens to disobedient children. Although, as Purkey notes, vestiges of the punitive system (e.g., corporal punishment) still exist, contemporary discipline systems generally agree that positive approaches to discipline work best (Cangelosi, 1993; Charles, 1996; Combs, 1985; Curwin & Mendler, 1998; Dreikurs & Grey, 1968; Glasser, 1985b).

"Children are not for hitting!" is a bumper sticker popular in Wichita, Kansas. Today's management systems are mainly developed as preventive systems under the theory that as the old cliché says, "An ounce of prevention is worth a pound of cure." Most contemporary systems also emphasize that classroom management is an ongoing and positive activity undertaken by all skilled teachers. Discipline and misbehavior management are discussed as temporary actions needed occasionally by teachers as they work with students to help them achieve self-discipline (Charles, 1996; Curwin & Mendler, 1998).

Developing a Personalized Discipline Plan

Charles (1992, 1996) divides teachers' discipline management into three types: preventive, supportive, and corrective. Preventive discipline consists of the actions that teachers take to make their classrooms interesting enough so that students are engaged in constructive activity rather than misbehaving. Charles (1996) summarizes preventive approaches to discipline and suggests four basic steps that teachers can take to prevent misbehavior.

Preventive Discipline

1. *Make your class as worthwhile and enjoyable as you can.* Keep the students' need for fun, belonging, freedom, power, and dignity in mind as you plan your instruction. When learning activities have transferability to everyday events in life, students understand the relevancy

Used by permission of Jimmy Dunne, Founder, People Opposed to Paddling Students, Inc.

ACTIVITY **13.1**

What's in a Word: Reflections

In a small group, ask participants to close their eyes and think for a moment as you read the following to them. "What is the first thing that comes to mind as you think of these concepts: freedom, fun, power?" Ask the group to share with others the first thought that came to mind with each term. How often did school and classes come to mind? (In the classes where we have done this activity, few pre-service teachers connected these words with school.)

---

of the material. If you've not studied his ideas, you might wish to see Glasser's (1985a) book on this subject.

2. *Take charge of your classroom in an assertive fashion.* The teacher is the classroom leader who works with students to maintain a positive learning environment. That does not mean teachers are dictators, but they can remind students that they are part of the learning community, and everyone has certain behavioral obligations.

3. *Work with your students to adopt a workable set of rules.* As mentioned in Chapter 9, rules should be few in number (five to seven), stated positively, thoroughly discussed, and posted as a reminder of the students' responsibilities. Most secondary teachers also involve the class in formulating and adopting rules because students are then much more likely to live by them.

4. *Emphasize good manners and living by the golden rule.* Nothing is more powerful than polite language in building respect. You might wish to review the section on polite forms of language in Chapter 4, Communication Strategies. Emphasize that students are expected to be polite to one another and that sarcasm and cruel comments are unacceptable. Of course, you will also live by these expectations; let them know that you plan to do so. You will want to work hard to keep your criticism of student behavior on a positive note. Corrective feedback implies (a) honesty about the quality or appropriateness of the student work, (b) suggestions for improvement, and (c) support for effort that has not yet produced positive achievement. Statements such as "You act like a group of third graders," or "You're a bunch of losers" are inappropriate and unprofessional.

Supportive Discipline

Supportive discipline assumes that misbehavior usually begins in small, unintentional ways. Think of your classroom realistically. As a secondary teacher you probably have thirty or more students together for about fifty minutes every day with thousands of interactions between students. It is, therefore, unrealistic to assume that minor incidents or squabbles between students will not occur. Charles (1996) suggests eight strategies to employ as forms of supportive discipline. The teacher assists and guides students who have trouble while enforcing the behavioral expectations established. A range of activities can be used to remind students of their obligations. These activities assume that you are alert to the behavior of your students and are monitoring both their verbal and nonverbal actions.

1. *Send signals to students whose behavior is beginning to need some support to keep it from becoming unacceptable.* Nonverbal behaviors such as eye contact, head shakes, hand signals, and frowns can communicate with the student whose behavior is not consistent with class norms. These nonverbal cues should be your first supportive actions. Turn to the person next to you and give the "teacher look." How did you know this body language when no one taught it to you? It is taught by thousands of teachers each day. Students know the meaning.

2. *Use your physical presence (proximity) if the signals are ineffective or the student continues to ignore them.* Moving purposefully down the aisle to stand near the offending student sends a clear message. See the section on nonverbal communication in Chapter 4 for other ideas.

3. *Show students that you are interested in their work.* As students' minds wander, move to the student who seems elsewhere and ask questions about the work or comment in a positive fashion. Sometimes offering a challenge is highly effective. "If you can answer five more questions in the next ten minutes you'll have your homework for tomorrow completed."

4. *Offer help with difficult work.* Using the Jones (1987) Praise, Prompt, and Leave (PPL) Model, offer assistance with a problem the student is experiencing. If the student is having unusual trouble, explain and demonstrate the task a second time. Can you make it more interesting? More exciting? Is it too difficult for the student? These are decisions you'll need to consider as you move around the room assisting with the assigned tasks.

5. *Use humor if the lessons have become too repetitive or tiring.* Humor will provide a lift or respite from more serious tasks with which the student is engaged. A momentary break is all that is necessary to change the tenor of the day's activity. There is, however, danger associated with the use of humor to break the tension. The student may interpret the humor as a signal that you are not serious about the task. Humor can easily turn to horseplay, which distracts other students from their task; this can be avoided if you continue to routinely use the PPL Model, thereby turning the focus of your class monitoring to an offer of help where needed.

6. *Remove seductive objects that may be diverting the students' attention from the task at hand.* Students will often bring objects to class; such objects are likely to vary from radios to dangerous items such as knives. Students often begin to play with them without thought to the distraction or the possible danger they cause. As a teacher you have every right to confiscate dangerous items and contact the appropriate administrator immediately. If the object is likely to create a dangerous situation, you must follow school policy and report what items you saw and how you handled any incident. For nonthreatening but distracting items ask the student to please give you the object and return it at the end of the period or day. If only one student has an object, move to the student and make the request in a quiet, one-on-one communication. The quieter the confrontation, the better.

7. *Reinforce good behavior at appropriate times.* When the students are actively engaged in their tasks, nods, smiles, and simple "thanks" are appropriate reinforcers. Oral reinforcers should be directed to the entire class if most students are engaged in the assigned tasks or are working quietly. Public praise or reinforcements may embarrass some secondary school students. Individualized, privately transmitted praise will be appreciated.

8. *Request good behavior and expect it of your students.* If students misbehave, it is appropriate to remind them of their responsibilities to the total class. I-messages, discussed in more detail in Chapter 4, will be useful in these situations. When students are working on tasks under trying conditions, do not hesitate to tell students that you understand their situation. "I know the team got home late last night, and you are sleepy this morning. Give just five more minutes to this assignment, and you'll be able to finish it."

Corrective Discipline

Despite your best efforts, there will be times when misbehavior occurs, and you will be confronted with a situation that requires corrective action. Corrective discipline is utilized when students violate the rules and the teacher must redirect student actions to positive learning activities or when attempts at preventive and supportive discipline have failed. It should be applied expeditiously to be successful. Corrective techniques "should be neither intimidating nor harshly punitive, but instead only what is necessary to stop the misbehavior and redirect it positively" (Charles, 1992, p. 161). Authorities suggest several useful strategies for correcting misbehavior.

1. *Insist on two basic rights in the classroom*—your right to teach without unnecessary disruptions and the students' right to be able to learn. Teach these twin ideals to your class at the beginning of the year and reassert them when misbehavior occurs.

2. *Misbehavior should be stopped at once.* If the misbehavior is a gross violation of rules or is a safety issue, attend to it immediately. It is important, however, to think carefully about the nature of the behavior. For example, has the student been notified that this behavior will not be permitted in class? Often minor, first-time rule infractions are the result of the student's lack of understanding. In such instances you will have a fundamental management decision to make. Should you ignore the student's actions or confront the student about it? Sometimes it is more appropriate to ignore minor misbehavior and discuss it privately with the student at a later time. Safety, however, must be addressed immediately. Incidents such as students poking each other with pencils or tripping others as they walk up the aisles cannot be ignored.

3. *Invoke consequences that are logically tied to the misbehavior.* Assuming you have followed our advice in Chapter 5 and have thoroughly discussed the classroom rules and their consequences, your students should understand that when they choose to misbehave, they have also chosen the consequences that follow. If possible, do not let yourself get upset or show irritation. Apply the consequences in a matter-of-fact manner. As you speak with the student, mention the rule violated and the automatic consequence.

4. *Always follow through.* There is no action in which teachers or parents can engage that will create more problems than inconsistent follow-through in rule and procedure enforcement. Every time you fail to follow through, it will take three to five incidents in which you follow your plan to convince them that you really mean what you say. Don't let the students talk you out of enforcing the consequences they have formulated and you have clearly transmitted. If you do, they'll test you again.

5. *Be constructive in working with misbehaving students; redirect their activity to positive action.* After students have returned to constructive work, talk with them privately about ways their needs can be met while the class's rules are being followed. Let them know you want them to learn as much as possible, but you must also ensure that the other students have an opportunity to learn too.

Jones and Jones (1995) have provided tips for teachers who find themselves confronting inappropriate or disruptive behavior, something that happens to all teachers. Although somewhat similar to Charles's suggestions, the techniques suggested by Jones and Jones are nevertheless sufficiently different to make them worthy of consideration.

- *Deal in the present.* Students are very much present oriented. Sometimes it is important to postpone talking with a student to a more convenient or less disruptive time, or perhaps to a time when the conversation can be private. Generally, however, it is better to converse privately with the offending student as close to the incident as possible. A quiet, stern warning is often sufficient to solve the problem.
- *Talk to the student rather than to someone else.* Adults often want to talk to a parent or colleagues about a student's misbehavior. The underlying assumption is that students aren't capable of handling the information that their actions are inappropriate. Jones and Jones (1995) suggest otherwise and argue that students are very adept at reading adults' nonverbal behavior and often know something is wrong even if nothing has been said to them. Give direct feedback to students.
- *Speak courteously.* Teachers serve as models for students, and the use of polite forms of language (e.g., "please," "thank you," and "excuse me") is imperative. Nothing does more to create positive interactions between teachers and students and to indicate to students that they are respected by the teacher.
- *Make eye contact with the student and be aware of nonverbal messages.* Again, Jones and Jones (1995) note that students are very adept at "reading" the nonverbal cues teachers are sending. The communication between you and your students will be enhanced if your nonverbal cues are congruent with your verbal messages. As Jones and Jones point out, "If you are talking to a student but looking over the student's shoulder, the student will find it difficult to believe that you feel positive about her or him and are sincerely concerned. Similarly, when we shout that we are not angry with a class, the students will be more likely to listen to the tone of voice than to the words" (p. 80).
- *Take responsibility for your statements by using I-messages.* It is hard to overstate the value of carefully phrased I-messages. Often, Jones and Jones (1995) argue, the offending students are deficient in social cognition skills. They simply aren't as capable as their peers in understanding and appreciating others' viewpoints. They may not, for example, understand reasons that a teacher is upset by their seemingly rude behavior of talking when the teacher expects them to listen. The pronoun *you* is usually accusatory in nature and teachers' sentences or directions that begin with *you* are often viewed as demeaning. If you aren't familiar with I-messages, consult the section on use of I-messages in Chapter 4.
- *Make statements and ask what and how questions.* When used initially in a case of disruptive behavior, questions can get the teacher back into the you-message. Statements make it much easier to use I-messages. Some questions misdirect students from taking responsibility for their behavior and create defensiveness. If a question is used, it may be immediately followed by an I-message. "What are you doing?" If the student says, "I was just talking to Jerry," the teacher should then follow with, "When you are talking while someone else is reporting to the class, it is difficult to focus on the report, and

I find this distracting." Resist the temptation to follow with a why question such as, "Why are you doing that?" Such questions as "Why are you talking?" "Why are you chewing gum?" and "Why are you late to class?" evoke excuses and do not solve the problem. Use *how* and *what* questions for behavior and *why* questions for academic discussions.

The Charles (1992, 1996) model and the Jones and Jones (1995) tips are useful to both beginning and experienced teachers. By thinking about classroom management as falling into three types, experienced teachers can reflect on the classroom management habits they have formed since their first teaching year. Careful reflection, along with a desire to improve instruction, is at the heart of good teaching. On the other hand, beginning teachers have a practical model to emulate as they begin developing their classroom management plan and style.

Action Research

As we suggested earlier, action research has become a significant tool to assist teachers with two specific activities that enable them to become better teachers: reflection and problem solving. In their book, *The Reflective Roles of the Classroom Teacher,* McIntyre and O'Hair (1996) suggest using action research to solve classroom problems: "Action research involves a form of reflective self-analysis developed by teachers to improve teaching practices" (p. 256). Furthermore, action research enables teachers to better understand their abilities and attitudes about learning and teaching. Such critical self-analysis is an essential tool for teachers to improve their practice. Relationships with parents, students, peers, and administrators, the classroom environment, teaching practices, and classroom management are factors amenable to action research.

According to McIntyre and O'Hair (1996), the underlying purpose of action research is to put teachers in charge of their profession and its improvement. The process empowers teachers to decide what they wish to fine-tune or change substantially in their own classrooms. Action research is equally useful to both experienced and beginning teachers. For beginning teachers, it helps them get beyond reactive self-absorption practices and the daily struggle to survive, so common to beginning teachers, and enables them to focus on proactive student-centered practices, which enhances their instructional skills and practices. As McIntyre and O'Hair state, "Teachers who use action research discover that the process allows them to answer difficult questions, alter their teaching strategies, and adapt to the specialized needs of their students" (p. 256). Many protocols exist from which to choose (McIntyre & O'Hair, 1996; Hubbard & Power, 1993; Hopkins, 1994; Cochran-Smith & Lytle, 1993). The framework suggested by McIntyre and O'Hair is presented in Figure 13.1.

Define your personal theories and beliefs of practice. What do you think is important? All teachers develop a set of interrelated personal theories and beliefs through their observations and experiences. How do students learn? What helps students become motivated? What do students like in a teacher? These questions represent but a few beliefs that shape teacher actions in the classroom. These personal theories serve as guides to action but are often quite difficult for a teacher to articulate. It is, however, important that teachers become aware of their own theories of practice and articulate them. You, as a teacher, should be able to respond to the questions: "What do I believe is important in my teaching practices? Why?"

FIGURE 13.1   Action Research Framework

1. Define your personal theories and beliefs of practice. What do you think is important?
2. Define your problem or area of self-improvement. What is the question?
3. Collect data that define the parameters of the problem.
4. Establish realistic criteria.
5. List potential alternatives to present practice.
6. Evaluate the alternatives based upon the criteria previously established.
7. Select what appears to be the best alternative and implement it.
8. Evaluate both the success of the alternative and the implementation process. How well is the alternative you selected working? Would it be better to try a different alternative?

Adapted from D. J. McIntyre and M. J. O'Hair, *The Reflective Roles of the Classroom Teacher* (Belmont, CA: Wadsworth, 1996) p. 257.

ACTIVITY **13.2**

Personal Theories and Beliefs

Divide into small groups with five or fewer members. Ask each person to list characteristics of a favorite teacher. Compare your lists. Are they similar, or do they differ? Can you account for the similarities or differences that you find? What does your list suggest about the characteristics you think are important in a teacher? Do you emulate those characteristics in your classroom?

Define your problem or area of self-improvement. What is the question? Action research was designed to help teachers evaluate, alter, reevaluate, and make judgments about their classroom practices. Focusing on a problem in the teacher's classroom is fundamental to the action research process. Some typical questions asked in action research are as follows:

1. How can I get my fifth-period students to take their seats without reminding them?
2. What procedures encourage classroom discussion in a middle school social studies class?
3. Which nonverbal management cues decrease off-task behavior in a high school physical education class?
4. How do students' interpersonal skills change as a result of learning conflict resolution strategies?
5. What will enhance listening and comprehension skills in a high school music theory class?

To keep the research process open to continual discovery, the framing of the research question is crucial. Hubbard and Power (1993) suggest the following.

Frame the question in an open-ended manner so that possibilities that the researcher hasn't thought of may emerge. First, rule out questions that can be answered yes or no. Second, frame questions to elicit descriptions and observations. Key words are often *why, how,* and *what.* How, why, and what questions leave the teacher-researcher free to describe both the pro-

ACTIVITY **13.3**

My Philosophy of Classroom Management

To aid you in forming your philosophy of classroom management, complete the following statements.

I believe that classroom management is _____

_____

_____

I believe that teaching is _____

_____

_____

I believe that students are _____

_____

_____

I believe that teachers are _____

_____

_____

I believe that discipline is _____

_____

_____

_____

cess and changes that occur. Third, focus questions on classroom or school practices that intrigue you. Fourth, build in sufficient time for your observations to take shape and for the nature of the question to shift. Feel free to change the question as new data are collected. Fifth, understand that research is a process that uses logical analysis as a critical tool in refining ideas, which often began in a different place as a metaphor, an analogy, or a hunch. Do not be afraid of hunches or your intuition. To identify your action research question, Hubbard and Power (1993) recommend these steps.

1. Keep a journal for at least a week in which you reflect upon what you've been observing (related to your management concern) in your classroom. If you have no class of your own, try to visit another teacher's classroom.
2. Brainstorm a list of the management issues you worry about in your classroom. What does your journal suggest?
3. Be specific in your concerns (your questions can be broadened later).
4. After you've narrowed your concern, write down your question. Consider it a first draft.
5. When you are ready to focus your question more precisely, try to reframe it as a "why," "what," or "how" question.
6. Give yourself time and permission to modify your question as you continue your investigation. (pp. 7–8)

Collect data that will define the problem's parameters. Consider only solutions that are workable. Remember the principal who tried to suspend 1,200 of her 1,800 students—an

A C T I V I T Y **13.4**

Choosing an Action Research Project

Look at the list of possible action research questions on page 232 and think of a classroom management question that you might develop into an action research project. Share your question with a partner and ask for feedback. Does the question make sense? How would you gather data?

unworkable solution. Gather information from others related to your projected problem or question. Library and Internet searches are appropriate resources to use to analyze your management problem from the perspective of others. Identify additional sources if you can.

Establish realistic criteria. Criteria are guidelines, boundaries, or standards by which we judge information. Try to establish a set of criteria you'll consider as you develop the analysis of your management problem. For example, how much time will you be able to devote to possible practices? Will the data you collect be amenable to solutions you can live with? Will your possible solutions conform to school or district policies? Will they be beneficial for your students? Will they enhance the school's goals and objectives?

List alternatives to the present practice. Brainstorm alternatives to your present practice with your mentor or a colleague. Two minds almost always envision more possibilities than one. Study the notes in your journal. Do they suggest ideas?

Evaluate the alternatives based on the criteria. This step will help you avoid selecting alternatives that are unrealistic or unworkable. Eliminate alternatives that do not fit the criteria you established. Prioritize your list and keep your mind open to other alternatives in case your first choice doesn't work well.

Select the best alternative and implement it. Develop a plan and discuss it with a colleague or peer who understands your classroom and school. If you have a mentor, that person can give you objective feedback.

Evaluate the alternative and the implementation process. How well is the alternative you selected working? Collect data on the alternative. You may want to ask a colleague or mentor to be an independent observer. It is also very useful to write in a journal frequently. If you have trouble doing so, consider using an audio or videotape recording so that you can study your classroom activity more thoroughly when you have time. Above all else, establish a procedure to gather data. If you discover your first alternative isn't working, try the second. Also, consider whether your process or your implementation did not work well. If you've followed our advice, you should come to a conclusion about the alternative that helped solve your classroom management problem.

Creating Your Personal Management Plan

Charles (1996) encourages teachers to develop a personal classroom management plan. We suggest that you develop a written plan before school begins next year, using the format outlined in Figure 13.2. The model may well solidify your ideas about classroom manage-

FIGURE 13.2   My Classroom Management Plan

Your Name

Objectives:
What do I want my students to do?
What kind of classroom do I need to be successful?
What kind of behaviors do I expect my students to exhibit?
What kind of behaviors do I dislike my students to exhibit?
What rules will I insist upon for my classroom?
What expectations should my students have for me to follow?

Activities:
How will I teach my plan? Write a lesson plan that includes activities to involve students. Decide
    what visuals you will use and whether you will give a test on your rules and consequences.
How will I involve the students? Parents?
Will it be *our* class as opposed to *my* class?
How will I promote student ownership?
Will I send the management plan home for parents to read and sign?
Will I contact parents? How often? For what reasons?
Will parents be asked to serve as volunteers? Speakers?
What rewards and consequences will I use?
Should students receive rewards?
Who will decide what the consequences will be?
What happens if a student breaks a rule for the first time? Fifth time?

Evaluation:
How will I evaluate the plan? Is it working?
Will I videotape my classroom?
Will I provide a suggestion box for students?
Will I ask another teacher to watch me teach and critique me?
When will I evaluate? Periodically?

Resources:
What books and classroom management models will I use as I formulate my plan?

---

ment. For example, do you have needs, likes, and dislikes that you "expect" the students to know intuitively? Are the students supposed to know that you must give them permission to leave their seats for any reason? A written plan helps ensure (a) that you have carefully examined your classroom management procedures, (b) that you won't forget parts of the plan as you let students know your behavioral expectations, and (c) that students understand the minimum expectations.

Reread the questions listed under the personal management plan (Figure 13.2) and carefully respond to each in writing. You will then have a realistic plan that will help you establish behavioral parameters for your classroom. What kinds of behavior do you expect your students to exhibit? Do you want them to cease talking when the bell rings? Is it OK if they talk to each other so long as it is nondisruptive? Think of your plan as notes to remind

ACTIVITY **13.5**

Formulating Classroom Rules

Plan a class meeting to discuss rules and procedures for your classes. Have the students sit in a circle to discuss their ideas? What ground rules will you establish for this class meeting? What procedure will you use to determine whether a suggested rule becomes a class rule? Once you and the class have agreed upon a set of rules, what will you do? Should the students also discuss consequences?

yourself of rules, expectations, and consequences that must be shared with your students. Therefore, be honest. Which student behaviors do you want to see, and which behaviors are you trying to avoid? Aim for a balance between behaviors you'd call positive and those you'd rather not see in your classroom. Write positive statements about student behaviors. For example, say "Be on time" rather than "don't be tardy."

Second, what rules will you want for your classroom? As a secondary teacher, you may establish different rules for different classes based on the class's maturity. For example, will your rules be equally useful with high school seniors as with ninth graders? The problem with establishing different rules for different classes is that it's difficult to remember which rules apply to which class—a practice that can be very confusing. A single set of rules, generalized enough to be applicable in all classes but specific enough to have meaning, will probably serve you best. For instance, "Be respectful" is too broad. Each student could define respect differently.

Inviting students to help formulate the classroom rules is also recommended. As noted, students who help formulate the rules will have more ownership and are more likely to adhere to them. Many teachers desire to have students participate in rule setting and yet prefer to develop a single set of rules. To do so, organize a brainstorming session in which both you and the students suggest rules. During each period, have a class secretary write the ideas and then you can develop a common set of rules and present them to your classes the following day. That way, students participate in formulating the rules, and you have a common set to apply to all classes. Be sure, however, that any rule on the final list not suggested the first day in a particular class is discussed with that class. It can be simply mentioned that other classes thought it was important and that you are inviting responses.

Remember that, as a member of this learning community, you can suggest rules too. If you explain the reason for it, your students will usually accept it as a reasonable addition to the list. Seldom, however, do teachers need to suggest rules if they honestly turn to their students for help in formulating them. By the time students reach the secondary level, they know the behavioral expectations. Although we do not recommend this procedure, some teachers create a list of rules, without student input, and carefully explain the meaning and intent of each rule as well as the reasoning behind it. We believe this method has inherent problems because the students do not have ownership. It becomes *my* class, not *our* class.

The genuineness of student-formulated rules troubles some educators (Watson as cited in Kohn, 1996). They argue that when teachers ask students to help formulate classroom rules, the students often engage in a sort of "guess what's in the teacher's rule book" game and are seldom committed to the rules they suggest. But make no mistake, these experts are not saying that students may do whatever they like in a class. On the contrary, they argue that the process of discussing the rules and formulating them is where real learning takes place. The rules themselves are secondary in importance to the process of rule formulation. They believe that students know and want to follow guidelines that are reasonable and fair to all.

Consequences

Will you have a set of positive consequences to be applied when students are working productively on class activities or when they are exhibiting the behavior that you encourage? If so, identify some positive consequences that might be applied. On the other hand, do you want a set of negative consequences to apply when students are not abiding by the rules? If so, think of logical consequences for instances when students violate one of the class rules. For example, what kind of logical consequence might be applied if a student tears spiral notebook paper out and shreds the sides on the floor? Are students responsible for keeping the area around their desks neat and clean? Do they know about their responsibilities? Or is it simply expected behavior for secondary students?

Third, what preventive measures can you utilize to encourage students to continue positive behaviors? How can you send signals to them that their actions are consistent with the class expectations? How can you encourage them to continue positive behavior and not lapse into misbehavior? What supportive measures can you use if the students are drifting toward undesirable behaviors? If rule violations or other forms of misbehavior emerge in your class, what options do you have to get students back on track? Applying the least disruptive corrective measures first is best. Go to more severe measures only if your first attempts fail.

Fourth, what else can you do to maintain a positive classroom climate? Are there other actions you can take to ensure that your classroom has a positive climate? The answer is: "Yes, there are!" The most important steps you can take to maintain a positive classroom climate are to show students that you care and create activities that are appropriate, interesting, and relevant to your students' lives. In other words, make your class so valuable and the time so precious that your students won't have time to misbehave. Look at the planning model in Figure 13.2 again. What else can you do to maintain a positive classroom climate? A sample student teacher's classroom management plan is found in Figure 13.3.

Summary

In this chapter we have asked you to think in a proactive manner about the classroom you want. Charles's idea of three types of discipline is discussed along with the notion of using action research strategies to solve classroom management problems. We have also suggested a model to use in designing your plan.

FIGURE 13.3   Sample Classroom Management Plan

Introduction

My plan stems from my personal philosophy concerning how to manage a classroom effectively so that all students can learn to their optimum abilities. I will use several classroom management models, such as Dreikurs's Social Discipline and Glasser's Control Theory, to explain my ideas. I am not an advocate of behavior modification either, but I feel some of the rewards (reinforcements) can have a useful purpose for some situations. I will consult Wolfgang's (1998) text to understand the different concepts.

I do not believe in giving students a list of rules at the onset of the school year. I feel this inhibits students more than it helps the classroom environment. I believe that the teacher should trust a student from the first day of class until a student acts in a way that causes the teacher to impose restrictions. Instead of displaying posters with lists of don'ts, I want to present posters with lists of do's.

The most important thing I can do for positive classroom management is to set a good example (modeling). I know that how I behave will set the model for how the students are expected to behave.

Objectives

1. I want my students to treat the teacher, other students, and property with respect. Respect for the teacher and students means no name calling or other verbal, physical, or emotional abuse. Respect for others includes not interrupting a current speaker in a class discussion. Respect for property means the student will refrain from defacing the books, desks, or any other part of the classroom.
2. I want my students to feel free to help each other during seatwork assignments. They will be allowed to get out of their seats to help or seek help. Permission from me is not necessary. A violation of this objective would be if the student were not using this privilege to work but to visit.
3. I want my students to feel free to go to the resource shelves in my room for help during in-class assignments. Permission from me is not necessary.
4. I want my students to feel free to enter class discussion without having to raise their hands. Everyone should be able to join in the discussion. The only restriction to this objective is that the student will refrain from speaking until the current speaker is finished. (A violation of this objective would cause me to review Objective 1 with the offending student.)
5. Students will be required to have projects and homework turned in on the due dates. A syllabus will be distributed to the class at the beginning of each semester.

Activities

I will teach my plan by using different types of media. Visual learners will benefit from the bulletin boards and posters displaying the class expectations. These posters will be made by students after the first classroom meeting regarding class expectations. I will speak to the class the first day about class expectations and verbally remind them of rules or homework assignments. Learners will also benefit from having a copy of the semester schedule handout (syllabus) in which I list the course description, assignments and due dates, and test days.

I will let the students decide on class expectations they feel are necessary through the use of the class meeting. We will use the problem-solving approach. This will allow the students to feel ownership in their class regulations (group process model).

The class will hold bimonthly class meetings to discuss new ideas or current problems. During these classroom meetings, students will arrange the chairs in a circle. Therefore, they will be able to communicate better than in rows (group process model).

At the beginning of the school year, I will send parent volunteer forms home with the students. *Any* parent willing to help the class may do so. Help will include being guest speakers, pro-

FIGURE 13.3 Continued

viding special resources for the class, or helping with class projects and activities (Dreikurs's Social Discipline model).

I will strongly suggest that each student's parent(s) attend a personal, face-to-face conference with me each semester. I will inform the parents of this request during my first phone call to them before school begins. I will have at least two personal meetings per student per year. These meetings are to keep parents up-to-date concerning their child's progress and behavior. These meetings are not just for discussing negatives, but for discussing all aspects of the student. I will always begin and end these conferences by making a positive comment about their child. I will stress the importance of parental involvement. I will also keep communication open with *all* parents by making monthly phone calls to them.

I will teach the class the three ego states of Transactional Analysis so they will be able to identify and improve their communications with me and their peers. I will accomplish this by providing reading material geared to their level and videos showing examples and characteristics of each state. I will also conduct role-playing with the students and have them act out various situations involving all three ego states (Harris's Transactional Analysis model).

The class will participate in weekly what-if discussions and simulations to promote social awareness. We will do weekly exercises promoting personal growth using activities such as the "I-Urge Telegram," "What's in Your Wallet?," "I Am the Jury," "Your Personal Coat of Arms," and the "Know Me" handout.

I will not be giving material rewards for positive behavior. Instead, I will give students awards such as extra time near the end of the class period to read their favorite comic books or sports magazines. Although there are various opinions about what constitutes reading material, I am a strong believer that as long as students are reading, they are improving their reading abilities. This reward allows students time to read something enjoyable. I feel I will already be providing plenty of instruction with required literature. I plan to keep a Walkman in my desk for this purpose also. Students can listen to their favorite station for the last ten minutes of a class period, with earphones, of course, while they are doing creative writing.

Logical consequences will be used. Depending on the violation, an appropriate logical consequence will be enforced. For example, if a student is causing a disturbance by poking others with a pencil, the pencil will be taken away. The student must then come to my desk to ask for a pencil each time one is required. I will probably do this as a week-long consequence (Dreikurs's Social Discipline and Glasser's Control Theory models).

The students will write contracts at the beginning of the school year listing the goals they want to accomplish. (They will get an idea of what they want to accomplish by looking over the syllabus I will give them the first day.) The students will sign and date the contract and keep monthly updates to track their progress.

Sample Teacher/Student Contract

Name _____ Date _____

I plan to pursue the following personal goals in English II this year:

    1. _____

    2. _____

    3. _____

    4. _____

(continued)

FIGURE 13.3   Continued

I will evaluate my progress every month.

September:

October:

November:

December:

January:

February:

March:

April:

May:

Overall evaluation:

The students will be arranged in small groups or clusters to enhance cooperative learning. This will also promote social awareness.

I will assign school ambassadors to new students in our class and school. These ambassadors will be responsible for helping new students acclimate to our learning community and school environment. This will benefit not only the new student, but also all students, because they are helping others.

I will keep a sociogram to see how students are relating to each other. This will enable me to see if a student is becoming too passive, which student is perceived as a role model by the others, and so on.

Evaluation

I will evaluate the classroom management plan by videotaping and critiquing a lesson every three weeks. I will use the classroom talk activity on pages 60–61. In addition, I will analyze my strengths and weaknesses and record my observations in my journal. I will also use anonymous questionnaires given to the students. For example, types of questions I will ask are: "Did the teacher explain instructions clearly? Did the teacher state the objectives of your lesson every day?" I will send questionnaires home for the students' parents to complete, too (using different questions, such as "What is your opinion of the homework load for this class? Did the teacher provide opportunities for you to be involved with class projects?"). Some of my evaluation will take place during the class meetings as I actively listen to the discussion. By this, I mean I will listen for topics that are brought up by the *students*. I think if a student brings up a subject, I can be assured that other students have the same concerns. I would step in if I wanted further clarification about a problem; that is, I would try to help them extend their answer so I could get a clearer picture. The evaluations will be done daily at first, and I will taper off as the semester progresses. However, I will use questionnaires for both students and parents about once every six weeks.

Also, I will evaluate student contracts with each student at mid-term and at the end of the year to see if goals were met. I will also review the contract with the student if a situation arises that makes it necessary to do so. However, each *student* will track individual progress monthly.

To determine whether my classroom management plan is working, I will ask students to write ideas and place them in the suggestion box. In addition, I'll have another teacher critique me each six weeks by observing for one class period and making notes.

FIGURE 13.3   Continued

Resources

I plan to use the Control Theory model of William Glasser and the Social Discipline model of Rudolf Dreikurs primarily. The Group Process model will also be used heavily in my classroom by enlisting both student and parental input. To a lesser extent, I will use communication techniques from Gordon's Teacher Effectiveness Training and explain the ego states of Harris's Transactional Analysis to the students. Additional texts that I will consult are *Schools without Failure* and *Quality Schools* by William Glasser. Very little behavior modification will be used. However, any that is used will be in line with B. F. Skinner's ideas.

REFERENCES

Cangelosi, J. S. (1993). *Classroom management strategies* (2nd ed.). New York: Longman.

Charles, C. M. (1992). *Building classroom discipline* (4th ed.). White Plains, NY: Longman.

Charles, C. M. (1996). *Building classroom discipline* (5th ed.). White Plains, NY: Longman.

Cochran-Smith, M., & Lytle, S. L. (1993). *Inside/outside: Teacher research and knowledge.* New York: Teachers College Press.

Combs, A. W. (1985). Achieving self-discipline: Some basic principles. *Theory Into Practice, 24*(4), 260–263.

Curwin, R. L., & Mendler, A. N. (1998). *Discipline with dignity.* Alexandria, VA: Association for Supervision and Curriculum Development.

Dreikurs, R., & Grey, L. (1968). *A new approach to discipline: Logical consequences.* New York: Hawthorn Books.

Glasser, W. (1985a). *Control theory in the classroom.* New York: Perennial Press.

Glasser, W. (1985b). Discipline has never been the problem and isn't the problem now. *Theory Into Practice, 24*(4), 241–246.

Hopkins, D. (1994). *A teacher's guide to classroom research.* Bristol, PA: Open University Press.

Hubbard, R. S., & Power, B. M. (1993). *The art of classroom inquiry: A handbook for teacher-researchers.* Portsmouth, NH: Heinemann.

Jones, F. H. (1987). *Positive classroom discipline.* New York: McGraw-Hill.

Jones, V. F., & Jones, L. S. (1995). *Comprehensive classroom management.* Boston: Allyn & Bacon.

Kohn, A. (1996). *Beyond discipline.* Alexandria, VA: Association for Supervision and Curriculum Development.

Manning, J. (1959). DISCIPLINE in the good old days. *Phi Delta Kappan, 41*(3), 94–99.

McIntyre, D. J., & O'Hair, M. J. (1996). *The reflective roles of the classroom teacher.* Belmont, CA: Wadsworth.

Purkey, W. W. (1985). Inviting student self-discipline. *Theory Into Practice, 24*(4), 256–259.

Wolfgang, C. H. (1999). *Solving discipline problems* (4th ed.). Boston: Allyn & Bacon.

NAME INDEX

SUBJECT INDEX